MURDERING
McKINLEY

MURDERING McKINLEY

THE MAKING OF THEODORE

ROOSEVELT'S AMERICA

ERIC RAUCHWAY

👍 HILL AND WANG

A DIVISION OF FARRAR, STRAUS AND GIROUX

NEW YORK

Hill and Wang
A division of Farrar, Straus and Giroux
18 West 18th Street, New York 10011

Printed in the United States of America
Published in 2003 by Hill and Wang
First paperback edition, 2004

The Library of Congress has cataloged the hardcover edition as follows:
Rauchway, Eric.
    Murdering McKinley : the making of Theodore Roosevelt's America /
Eric Rauchway.— 1st ed.
        p.   cm.
    Includes bibliographical references and index.
    ISBN 0-8090-7170-3 (alk. paper)
        1. McKinley, William, 1843–1901—Assassination.   2. Roosevelt,
Theodore, 1858–1919.   3. Roosevelt, Theodore, 1858–1919—Political
and social views.   4. Presidents—United States—Biography.   5. Czolgosz,
Leon F., 1873?–1901.   6. Assassins—United States—Biography.
7. Anarchists—United States—Biography.   8. United States—Politics and
government—1897–1901.   9. United States—Politics and government—
1901–1909.   10. Progressivism (United States politics).   I. Title.

E711.9.R38 2003
973.8´8´092—dc21

                                                    2003040666

Paperback ISBN-13: 978-0-8090-1638-9
Paperback ISBN-10: 0-8090-1638-9

Designed by Jonathan D. Lippincott

www.fsgbooks.com

10

In memory of

Shlomo (Solomon) Kanigl
1877–1930
arrived in the United States 1901

and

Hans Gunther Belitz
1919–2002
arrived in the United States 1925 and again 1932

migrants and Americans

CONTENTS

PREFACE

The meaning of a murderer's madness depends on who makes the diagnosis. Lawyers asserting a client's insanity mean to get him off the hook, because by law a madman cannot be held responsible for his actions. Politicians calling murder an act of madness mean they cannot imagine a motive for such horror—and if they can, they prefer not to discuss it; mad motives can be safely ignored. Doctors finding a murderer mad believe him irresponsible for his actions, but also (in the spirit of scientific inquiry) seek to explain how someone could have grown so alienated from civilization that he became a killer. But in all cases—and especially when confronting political, symbolic violence—we need murder to mean something so we know what to do about it. If we believe mad killers are born, we resolve to identify and stop them. If we believe they are made, we determine to stop the process of their manufacture, even if it means shouldering some share of the blame for their actions. Most often we act on bits of both beliefs, because in our humble uncertainty of the causes of evil, we hope to prevent further hurt any way we can.

Among the presidential assassinations, William McKinley's had the most dangerously political motive. Abraham Lincoln's murderer was waging the Civil War by other means; James Garfield's assassin claimed divine inspiration. Whatever motives may have spurred John F. Kennedy's killer remain murky. The would-be regicides who fired on Andrew Jackson, Theodore Roosevelt, Franklin Roosevelt, Gerald Ford, and Ronald Reagan suffered from varying degrees of delusion and ambition for attention. Only Harry Truman's attackers had similarly clear political motives—but their cause (Puerto Rican independence) had few supporters. By contrast, McKinley's assassin said plainly that he shot the President of the United States because he hated the politics of state-supported capitalism that the President and his party represented, and in so doing he echoed hosts of critics in the United States and around the world. Because industrial civilization extended its influence over the globe, because it made millionaires of a few men and poor toilers of a multitude of others, because it turned traditional farming and hunting into primitive and untenable occupations, because it uprooted and made wanderers out of peasant families who had for generations lived off the same land—and because the United States was the richest and most powerful industrial country, the center of civilization and the capital of capital—he wanted to strike at the American leader to prove the nation vulnerable, and to shatter its illusions of safety. He knew what he was doing, and he knew he would die if he succeeded. His reasoning was cruel, even inhuman; but however bereft of sympathy and decency his motive was, it did not lack logic. Nor was he mistaken as to its consequences. Killing the President did terrify the leaders of the country. They began treating the immigrant working classes differently. They tried the assassin, executed him, dropped him in a grave, and poured sulfuric acid over his body, but they could not forget the brutal lesson he had taught. Neither could they admit that a low criminal had accomplished so much, and so from the start they insisted he was insane, and his action an accident of a callous fate.

Their fear was greater because the killer identified himself as an anarchist, a member of a shadowy international network who shared abstract theories about an earthly utopia displacing modern society, and who also shared concrete advice on how to make weapons to wage war against any society that stood in utopia's way. Ever since the anarchists' 1881 meeting in Paris praised the murder of the Russian tsar, Alexander II, the threat of terrorist violence hung over the citizens of the Western world. Nobody knew when a bomb or a gunshot might burst from a crowd.

The anarchist murder of William McKinley in September 1901 forced American opinion makers to confront a terrible problem. As society became more urban and more complex, and individuals had less control over their own fates, people grew surer that the only way to keep a populace sane and healthy was to keep the social environment sane and healthy—to have good schools, clean streets, green parks. Social movements to create and sustain all of these benefits grew to fruition during the Roosevelt presidency in the years following the assassination, giving shape to the liberal political ideology Americans came to call progressivism. At the same time, the more emphasis they placed on environmental influence—on nurture, rather than on innate moral character—the closer Americans came to the anarchist critique of modern society, in which a sick environment developed sick inhabitants. And as far as Americans of that era would go—as far as Theodore Roosevelt would lead them—they could not go that far. McKinley's specter loomed over and limited the very progressive movement to which the President's unhappy end had given so bloody a birth.

Traditionally, historians see McKinley's death as finally making way for political modernization, a terrible but effective way of clearing the decks. Students of American history take guilty pleasure in McKinley's end: at the dawn of the twentieth century in the United States, all forces sloshed aimlessly at a grim doldrums. The Spanish-American War was the only excitement in a presidential Administration dourly concentrated upon that perennial bore of old American politics, the tariff. At the center of this dull debate over exclusion and reciprocity was the substantial, respectable figure of the godly McKinley himself, who could not even be bothered to leave his front porch to run for president against William Jennings Bryan. Suddenly a wild-eyed anarchist bearing an unpronounceable name chockablock with consonants looms out of a crowd and strikes McKinley down. Theodore Roosevelt takes the helm and off shoots the ship of state in five directions at once, leaving the nineteenth century far astern, and it is not till 1921 that Harding Republicans can begin to restore normalcy (and, not incidentally, the importance of the tariff with it). In a sense, therefore, William McKinley had two killers: the man who shot him and destroyed his body, and the man who succeeded him and erased his legacy. This book tells the story of how both earned their historical roles—anarchist assassin, progressive President—through an act people preferred to regard as mad.

The law does not require a prosecutor to prove motive in a murder trial, because unlike corpus delicti and the cause of death, motive is not an element of the crime. But as any prosecutor will tell you, a jury always requires what the law does not: a reason for killing. Thus the prosecution puts tremendous energy into accumulating evidence for motive. So does the defense, in an effort to disprove the prosecution's theory of motive. And in a sensational case like a presidential murder, the press, the politicians, and other professional opinion-shapers try to explain motivation as well.

In the pages that follow, I present the evidence supporting both the prosecution's theory and the defense's theory of motive. The district attorney sought to prove that the weak-minded defendant sanely and unforgivably succumbed to the temptations of radicalism out of anger at his social position. The court-appointed defense argued that a man made mad by social conditions acted out of delusion and deserved mercy. And though at trial the jury had to decide between these explanations, many ordinary Americans tended afterward to hold elements of both theories. Indeed, their ability to believe bits of both shaped Theodore Roosevelt's response to the assassination and social policy generally.

Theodore Roosevelt plays a central part in the story of his predecessor's assassination. Of all the early interpreters, he did the most to make the murder meaningful to Americans. When he argued strenuously that the assassin was a sane anarchist who threatened social order, the progressive President played on his constituents' legitimate fears so that they would support him in his efforts to stamp out radical dissent. When he argued with equal energy that the assassin was a man made mad by society, Roosevelt played on his constituents' legitimate hopes so that they would support him in his efforts to render American industrialism more humane. That he made both arguments points to what I regard as the essential fact of his personality: Theodore Roosevelt acutely understood that stories were a means to political ends. He was, as his friend Rudyard Kipling remarked, a master "spinner"—someone who made his career by controlling stories.[1] Contrary to biographers and historians who describe Roosevelt as a boyish, romantic, immature, or impulsive creature, I present him here as I find him in the moment of his ascent to power: a man energetically and conscientiously struggling to control the stories told about him among his peers and in the press. If by presenting a canny and manipulative Roosevelt I contradict the tales told by his admirers and detractors alike, I am only corroborating the opinions of his contemporaries—not only Kipling, but the reporters who regularly covered him, and also the politicians, like Booker T. Washington, who assessed him as a role model: "What he did was not a matter of impulse, but of carefully matured plans," Washington wrote. Roosevelt himself agreed: "[Observers who] think me indiscreet and overimpulsive," he wrote, "cannot understand what it is that makes me act."[2]

This portrait of the means and meaning of Theodore Roosevelt's ascent to power sharpens our understanding of the Progressive Era over which he presided. The elements that gave the United States its peculiar industrial politics were all present in the episode that made Roosevelt President: the murder of William McKinley pressed Americans to give voice and clarity to their opinions of a working class that was largely immigrant in its composition, to the place of race in a developing democracy, to the position of the government with respect to social ills. Most important, the question of whether McKinley's assassin was a sane radical or a deranged victim of society hinged on key assumptions about human nature in the age of industry. The notion that he was sane and responsible appealed to those keen to discipline the unruly elements of society and keep the tools of mischief—including, not least, citizenship and the ballot—away from them. The idea that the cruelties of global industry made a madman of someone ground by the teeth of modern machinery appealed to those hoping to improve living conditions and nurture society's wounded to health.

Neither presumption alone, but both in conflict together, characterized the period. These incompatible interpretations warred inces-

santly, obscuring the story of the solitary, murderous man—and his
presumably solitary motive—whose action gave impetus and meaning
to the reform movement that ensued, led by a President who set the
course of twentieth-century politics. By returning to this critical man
at this critical moment at the start of the twentieth century, I show
how progressivism got its start in a story that yielded easily to no single meaning. If we can thus make some sense of this crime, we may
also make sense of the Progressive Era and the President who began it.

As for a final theory on the assassin's motives, historians all have
their opinions, and I do, too, though I will save mine for later in the
book. But I try to present both sides fairly so that you can reach an independent judgment. In so doing I try also to eliminate the most sensational, gossipy hearsay on both sides of the story—or, at least, to
indicate its unreliability. Even so, the pages that follow necessarily
include accounts of murder, torture, and electrocution, as well as the
casual racist language common to American speech of that period.
Historians have a broader definition than attorneys of material evidence, so we need to consider these unpleasant data, too, as elements
of the historical crime.

MURDERING
McKINLEY

1

A WEEK AT THE FAIR

At or about four o'clock in the afternoon of September 6, 1901, President William McKinley arrived in an open carriage outside the Temple of Music at the Pan-American Exposition in Buffalo, New York. He walked inside and to the head of a receiving line, where he began shaking the hands of Exposition visitors. His handlers expected him to remain only a short while, and about ten minutes later, one of them pulled out his pocket watch and made a show of looking at the time, signaling the Secret Service that the appearance was coming to an end. Just then, the man next in line stepped forward and raised his right hand. Instead of opening it to meet McKinley's grasp, he revealed that it was covered in a clean white bandage. Underneath the bandage he held an Iver Johnson .32-caliber pistol, which he fired twice into the President, hitting him in the chest and stomach.

McKinley straightened up, staggered from one potted plant to another, and collapsed, blood seeping into his pale shirt. Secret Service agents and other bystanders tackled the shooter. A fairgoer grabbed him by the throat and tried to choke him. Through this mayhem the assailant insisted stubbornly, "I done my duty," while the President implored his avengers to have mercy, crying, "Be easy with him, boys."[1]

In the instant before he was shot, William McKinley stood at the peak of his power. In November 1900 he had won reelection by a strong majority, carrying 52 percent of the popular vote against the same opponent he had trounced in 1896, the oratorical marvel William Jennings Bryan. Now, six months into his second term, in this late, lazy summer of the first year of the twentieth century, it looked as though the McKinley Administration would continue peaceably unbroken for another four years, going on as it had begun, a government devoted to prosperity and standing firm against demands that it become an engine for social betterment.

THE PRESIDENT

In 1896, McKinley had presented himself to the voters as the embodiment of conservatism, and he looked the part. His stern, square features, topped by the level lintel of a dark brow, had all the expression of a closed door. He was known to turn on the charm principally when trying to tell someone, graciously but firmly, no. He wore a carnation in his lapel, and when he wanted to turn a petitioner away, he would pluck it from his coat as his granite face cleaved into a smile, and hand over the flower as consolation.

His steadfastness made him a comforting President in an age of crisis. The early 1890s brought economic depression to the United States, and in the crash of 1893 great fortunes melted within weeks. Armies of the unemployed straggled across the roads between towns whose factory chimneys rose mute and unsmoking into the kind of clear sky that, in the age of coal-fueled industry, only bad times could bring. The U.S. Treasury, depleted of gold, shamefacedly had to sell bonds at rates advantageous to J. P. Morgan and the other barons of Wall Street. In reply to this terrible trouble there arose from the debt-pinched farmers and unemployed workers of the country a cry of protest, demanding relief: that the government should coin silver, and inflate the currency; that the government should tax incomes, rather than imports; that the means of electing U.S. senators should change so that the people could wrest control of their leaders away from the vote-buying millionaires. This howl raised Bryan to the candidacy of the combined Democratic and Populist Parties in 1896. From the plat-

William McKinley in 1900, presiding over prosperity and empire, and preparing to confirm his ascendancy by defeating William Jennings Bryan a second time. (Library of Congress)

form of farmers and laborers, Bryan thundered against the conservative economic policies of the government, railing that to keep the
currency on the gold standard would be to "crucify mankind upon a
cross of gold."[2]

Seeking to thwart this protest, the Republicans wanted a candidate
who could dam the tide of revolution. McKinley, an experienced congressman and governor of Ohio, was their man. The businessmen of
America—who over their morning coffee read with increasing alarm
each day's report of riots, strikes, and proposed new schemes of taxation—paid for his campaign, which he organized around the theme of
immobility. Nothing would budge—not the monetary policy, not the
fiscal policy, not the taxation schedule. Indeed, not even the candidate: for the duration of the campaign, McKinley himself would not
move. Instead of following Bryan through the heartland, McKinley
stayed on his front porch in Canton, Ohio, and let reporters and citizens come to him. And he promised them that even though he would
not change the policies of the government, prosperity would return to
the nation.

The voters chose McKinley in November of 1896. In March of
1897 he took office, and then as if by magic his promises came true.
Factories opened their gates, workers returned to the mills, and once
more smoke poured cheerfully from the chimneys into sooty American skies. Though the recovery owed more to an incidental increase
in the world's supply of gold than to the policies of William McKinley,
the President received the credit.

And even when, the following summer, the President led the nation into one of its greatest changes ever, he invoked a comfortably
Christian justification so as to preserve a sense of safe familiarity. For it
was under McKinley that, in 1898, the United States stopped being a
mere continental republic and became an international colonial empire. After a short war with Spain, sparked by conflict in Cuba, the
U.S. Army and Navy occupied the former Spanish possessions of
Cuba, Puerto Rico, and the distant Philippine Islands, across the Pacific, off the China coast. The President had not wanted colonies, and
wished fervently that his generals and admirals could have left the
islands in peace—but to do that meant letting some rapacious Euro-

pean power (probably Germany) take and despoil them. Yet William McKinley did not want to make himself the first emperor of a free people, so in the troubled hours after the war ended he petitioned God for guidance, praying on his knees in the nighttime White House for divine advice. And the Lord complied, as the President testified: "And one night late it came to me this way—I don't know how it was, but it came . . . There was nothing left for us to do but to take them all, and educate the Filipinos, and uplift and civilize and Christianize them, and by God's grace do the very best we could by them as our fellowmen for whom Christ also died. And then I went to bed, and went to sleep, and slept soundly."[3]

The presence and approval of God let the President rest peacefully, and his fellow citizens shared in the soundness of his slumber. When he ran for election again, he found it even easier to present himself as the picture of calm stillness; his new running mate, Theodore Roosevelt, had more than enough energy for both of them. And though Bryan returned in the election season to trouble the people with visions of the problems that empire would bring, McKinley defeated him a second time.

So it was that the President found himself in 1901 at the Pan-American Exposition, celebrating the mighty United States he had helped to build. The Exposition paid tribute to the international reach of American power, glorying in its links throughout the hemisphere and across the seas. Its buildings fit loosely into a Spanish mission style, assimilated and Americanized, coated liberally with gilt-edged European baroque decorations. Throughout the grounds stood evidence of power, both figurative and literal; drawing current from the hydroelectric plant at Niagara Falls, the new electrical circuits of the fair gave the Exposition a glow unknown before, culminating in the Tower of Light that the Edison Company had put up not far from the Temple of Music, which housed the Exposition's largest reception space.

On September 5, the President spoke in an open-air pavilion to a crowd eager to hear him rhapsodize on the theme of what lay before the modern nation: a greater fleet of ships to ply the seas with the commerce of empire; a trans-Isthmian canal through the center of the

Americas that would give those ships free passage from ocean to ocean; and a trans-Pacific undersea cable that would carry to the further shore of the western sea the most precious American cargo of all: information, ideas, and culture. On a stage decked with bunting, leaning lightly on the rail before him, holding a single small sheet of notepaper in his left hand, McKinley painted this picture of global glory to come while promising that, even so, the familiar America would not change. Specifically, though Bryan and his supporters might clamor for a federal income tax, McKinley reaffirmed his faith in that hoary standby, the tariff, which shielded American industry from overseas competition (albeit at the expense of the American consumer).[4] The crowd, which included a slight listening man with a gun in his pocket, heard from McKinley what it had come to expect: a confidently stated platform of conservative policies meant to aid the growth of American economic might. That evening the President towered benevolently over his constituents, and the next afternoon he lay in the dust, felled by twin bullets fired from that still, slight listening man's gun.

The report of gunshots drifted out of the Temple of Music and over the crowd waiting to see the President. Men in stiff collars and bowler hats, women in bonnets, boys in straw boaters, and girls in fine dresses jostled each other in front of the Temple, anxiously pressing forward to find out what had happened behind its scarlet façade. At the front of the tightly packed throng, helmeted Exposition guards scurried back and forth, keeping would-be vigilantes at bay. Above and behind the crowd, a cameraman of the Thomas A. Edison Company cranked away, recording the scene on film.

Today, at a century's distance, we can still watch. In a darkened, silent room we can see the flickering images of onlookers, most with no hope of getting through the mass of their fellows, standing horrified and still. Faces in the crowd, turned one-quarter profile to the camera, reveal little of thoughts or emotions. Here and there, someone somehow aware of being filmed glances back at the panning camera. One man, thoroughly respectable in his pince-nez, bowler, and brush mustache, turns idly, catches sight of the camera, looks directly into the lens—and suddenly smiles before turning away.[5]

In our time we know too well the emotions that rippled through that crowd. We know how it feels to believe that not only news but history has just happened. We know how an icon of an epoch can crumple. We can imagine reacting almost any way at all—except, perhaps, smiling. Whether it was a reflex to the camera lens, bloodlust, political cynicism, or nerves, that smile—that overwhelmingly inappropriate, incomprehensible smile—had a meaning that remains inaccessible to us now. The strange smile shares two important characteristics with the assassination itself: we know that it happened, and that it was the product of a mind now closed to us. And for us, a troubled century later, the smile matters as much as the murder. Because it, along with the millions of other reactions to the killing, gave the assassination a meaning that the killer alone was powerless to provide. Those meanings of the McKinley assassination, to Americans then and now, tell us how we make sense—or fail to make sense—of the madness that history visits upon us.

THE PRESIDENT-TO-BE

The assault on McKinley dropped an uncertain mantle on the shoulders of the Vice President, who could not know and would not hope that he would soon become President. The assailant had accomplished the astounding: he reduced Theodore Roosevelt, however briefly, to dithering inactivity. Suddenly irresolute and unable to see his way forward, Roosevelt felt strangely like an ordinary, helpless citizen.

Despite his low opinion of the vice presidency, Roosevelt could not have aimed more unerringly for the office if he meant to. He had become inescapably popular during the Spanish-American War of 1898, resigning his post as Assistant Secretary of the Navy to lead a cavalry group of Rough Riders in Cuba. As a Manhattanite who could credibly don a cowboy hat, he proved irresistible to reporters, who found in turn that the amateur naturalist, historian, and full-time politician could endlessly produce quotable copy. Moreover, with his flashing spectacles and clacking, oversized teeth, his brushy mustache and ready grin, he presented an image already so near to caricature that he endeared himself to cartoonists. The Republican Party dared not leave idle a politician so beloved of the press. Yet Roosevelt kept making trouble; except during election season, when he remained scrupulously loyal, he trained a harsh fire on the corruption among his fellow Republicans. There was only one safe place for a party's most popular troublemaker: the visible, and powerless, vice presidency.

Roosevelt's war record made him a choice candidate for governor of New York in 1898, and he won the election that autumn. He immediately became a headache for the state Republican boss, Tom Platt, most significantly by supporting a tax on corporation franchises. As the governor's two-year term wore on through 1900, rumors surfaced that Platt might prevent Roosevelt's renomination. The two men might have had an ugly fight had not the sitting Vice President, Garret Hobart, died. This vacancy on the national ticket gave Platt the upper hand. He could withhold renomination from Roosevelt by making him an offer he could not refuse. The Rough Rider would ascend from the governorship to serve party and country gloriously and impotently at the President's right hand. When Platt put this case to him, Roosevelt realized he had been outmaneuvered, and he glumly accepted the job. When McKinley won reelection, Platt and his fellow party stalwarts believed they had finally neutered Roosevelt. On the eve of the inauguration, Platt told his friends he was "going to Washington to see Theodore Roosevelt take the veil."[6]

The vice presidency was every bit as dull as Roosevelt feared. The constitutional limits on him were bad enough. The Vice President was, on paper, a "functionless official," as Roosevelt wrote, "who possesses so little real power," that, regrettably, "his political weight . . . is almost nil."[7] But the attentions of the press made his situation even worse. McKinley was, as one reporter complained, habitually "silent," and a terrible chore to a press that wanted ballyhoo.[8] Roosevelt presented no such obstacle to coverage. But if the Vice President spent too much time in the headlines, he risked, as Roosevelt feared, making the President "jealous."[9] Roosevelt found himself the recipient of McKinley's smiles, which icily signified his increasing irrelevance. He recognized this, and wrote grimly, "I have really much less influence with the President now that I am Vice-President than I had even when I was governor."[10] He found himself spending more and more time out of Washington altogether, and on the fateful September 6, 1901, was visiting the Vermont Fish and Game Club when he received the telegram calling him to Buffalo.

Even as the electric wire sought out Roosevelt and jolted him from his insignificance, an electric ambulance whisked President McKinley away from the Temple of Music, heading for the Exposition's emergency hospital. A Secret Service agent named George Foster rode with the President. On the way, McKinley felt about inside his shirt and closed his fingers on something that did not belong there. "I believe that is a bullet," he told Foster.[11] Upon the ambulance's arrival at the hospital, the President yielded the bullet to Foster, and Foster yielded the President into the care of a gynecologist, Dr. Matthew Mann, who was the only remotely qualified doctor immediately available. Mann discovered that one bullet had grazed the sternum and bounced off, to be collected by the President himself, but that the other had entered the abdomen. Assisted by two other surgeons, Mann cut open the President's belly. Despite the Exposition's generally superior wiring, lighting in the operating area was inadequate, and Mann had at first to work under the glare of a mirror angled to catch the sun, before an electric light could be brought in. Mann repaired the internal wounds he found, but searched in vain for the other bullet. X-ray equipment was being displayed at the fair, but doctors did not use it in McKinley's case.[12] In the end Mann cleaned and sutured the abdomen, leaving the second bullet behind. Hoping for the best, aides moved the President to his temporary official residence, the home of the Exposition's president, John G. Milburn. A police detail surrounded the house and roped off the streets for a block in each direction, allowing no vehicles to approach. A detachment of soldiers from the 14th U.S. infantry augmented the police guard.[13]

Roosevelt arrived at his wounded chief's side amid these emergency fortifications. He received the doctors' report of "entire confidence" in the President's swift recovery.[14] Thereupon the Vice President once more found himself with nothing to do but fidget. The case lay in the hands of fate. But even with nothing to do, Roosevelt had plenty to say. The next day, McKinley woke alert and rested, uninterested in his would-be assassin and curious to know what the papers had made of his speech.[15] With the President recovering so nicely, Roosevelt fumed that "the scoundrel who attempted the assassination" might serve only seven years in prison for his attempted murder, a "crime against this Republic and against free government all over the world." And the President's apparent return to health did more than let his assailant off the hook: it obliged Roosevelt to send messages meant to quiet "the boom" that had prematurely started among his supporters, some of whom had already announced their confidence in his impending presidency.[16]

By September 9 the ghastly episode seemed well behind them all, and Roosevelt prepared to bounce out of Buffalo again, bent on a stint of mountaineering in upstate New York. But first, he fired off a letter to his friend, Senator Henry Cabot Lodge of Massachusetts, airing the anger that had built up in him over the course of these three uncertain days. He excoriated the "Judas-like dog" who had shot the President, and declared that the would-be assassin had fired "not on power, not on wealth," but upon a man innocent of association with the plutocracy: "McKinley is a man hardly even of moderate means. He is about as well off say as a division superintendent of the New York Central Railroad." No, Roosevelt figured, the only possibility was that the assailant—whom he would never call by name—was "so crazy a fool" as to wreak vengeance for imagined ills upon a guiltless man.[17]

Whatever he said, Roosevelt believed otherwise in his heart. His defense of McKinley was literally true—the President had never been rich, and indeed, during his days as governor of Ohio had suffered a nasty scrape with debt.[18] But there was money behind and around him, notably in the person of his chief fund-raiser, adviser, and campaign manager, Mark Hanna. While McKinley fought for the Union in the Civil War, Hanna minded his own business back in Cleveland, where he put his money wisely into steel and oil. McKinley came out of the war an honorable major; Hanna came out of it a rich man. Hanna went into politics to protect his fortune from inflationists and income-taxers, and he took McKinley with him. He organized McKinley's 1896 presidential campaign and raised the money for this Ohio-based bid from the new-money businessmen of the Middle West.

Although Roosevelt, as a loyal Republican, went along with the party and backed McKinley in 1896, he did not like the smell of the men behind the new President. "The victorious Republicans have taken to feasting themselves, and especially Mark Hanna, and I have been at several Capuan entertainments," he wrote his sister after the victory in November. The festivities looked to him like the "gloomiest anticipations" of what moneymen would do to the country, and he looked without cheer on "our gold-ridden, capitalist-bestridden, usurer-mastered future." Even after getting to know Hanna better, and serving as McKinley's Assistant Secretary of the Navy, Roosevelt believed the Administration to be plagued by "the craven fear and brutal selfishness of the mere money-getters," which "have combined to prevent us from doing our duty."[19]

Despite his belief that President McKinley represented the tyranny of money over principle, on the morrow of the assassination attempt Roosevelt stood firmly for the prosecution's theory of the crime, denouncing the misplaced anger that struck down a devoted public servant. In his letter to Lodge he blamed as many of the usual suspects as he could, in his rage, recall. He noted with certitude the madness of the assailant himself, but then proceeded to explain that someone so fragile of mind must surely suffer from the bad influences that dominated the culture in which he dwelled: the newspaper magnate William Randolph Hearst, "who for whatever purposes appeals to and inflames evil human passion"; the liberal Democratic governor of Illinois, John P. Altgeld, who had pardoned the anarchists accused of a terrorist attack at Haymarket Square and who refused to call out troops to quell the strikes against the Pullman Company in 1894; and likewise "every soft fool who extends a maudlin sympathy to criminals," including the novelists William Dean Howells and Leo Tolstoy.[20]

Just three days after the shooting, and well before McKinley's assailant became his assassin, Roosevelt first expressed what would become the popular explanation of the tragedy. A madman had shot the

President—a weak-minded madman, preyed upon by delusions he found in the press, delusions given shape by the liberal writers of the day. It went without saying there was no justification for his act, but even beyond that, there was no conceivable rational explanation for it, not even one that deserved refutation. Imagining comprehensible motives behind such an act meant giving it more legitimacy than it deserved—and, as Roosevelt knew, it also meant suggesting one's own complicity. For Roosevelt, like so many Americans of good sense and good education, believed the working people of the country possessed by a "genuine fanaticism"—a wrong-headed one, to be sure, but no less genuine for that; he believed American laborers honestly "feel the eternal and inevitable injustice of life."[21] While even Mark Hanna was ridiculing the prospect of violent revolt, Roosevelt took it seriously, and its specter haunted him.[22] By calling it madness he might, barely, keep it at bay.

THE ANARCHIST

Even as the Vice President was making out a case for the assailant's insanity, the Buffalo district attorney, Thomas Penney, was trying to prevent the shooter from making such a case in his defense. Two precedents loomed over him: the assassination twenty years before of President James Garfield by the decidedly eccentric—though perhaps not quite insane—Charles Guiteau, and the British case of Daniel M'Naghten, who in 1843 had murdered Edward Drummond, the private secretary to British prime minister Robert Peel, mistaking Drummond for Peel himself.

Guiteau's case mattered more in terms of popular perception, for many Americans yet living remembered how he had blurted out unsolicited and often irrelevant testimony at his trial, how he believed himself the chosen instrument of a theologically peculiar God, and how generally strange the man seemed. Even his motive was strange, and never wholly persuasive: Guiteau apparently believed that by murdering Garfield he could deliver the Republican Party into the hands of its conservative Stalwart wing, which he believed owed him some sort of federal appointment for his small service to them in the 1880 elections. The presiding judge admonished him for his "lawless babble,"[23] but the doctors called to testify in his case tended to insist on his sanity, and therefore his legal responsibility for the crime. He was hanged, though not without some controversy.

M'Naghten's case, though less publicly known on the American side of the Atlantic, mattered more in court. For it was the case of the similarly eccentric murderer M'Naghten, acquitted on the grounds of madness, who inspired the judicial definition of legal insanity that underlay most American law in the matter. Public outrage greeted M'Naghten's acquittal. Queen Victoria herself believed the decision would allow a garden-variety English eccentric to take her life with impunity. Impelled by such indignation, Parliament called a panel of judges before it to demand an explanation. In reply, the judges argued that so far as the law had an interest in insanity, a defendant could plead his madness as a defense if he could establish that at the time of committing a crime he was "labouring under such a defect of reason, from disease of the mind, as not to know the nature and quality of the act he was doing: or, if he did know it, that he did not know he was doing what was wrong." Almost immediately after the Queen's Bench spoke, American jurists began adopting the M'Naghten test in their insanity-related decisions, and it had entered the boilerplate language of New York State judges by the middle of the nineteenth century. It became abbreviated as the ability to know right from wrong.[24]

Happily for the district attorney, McKinley's assailant appeared to have no evident interest in establishing his insanity. The instant after the would-be killer fired his second shot, the Secret Service and other bystanders swarmed all over him, grabbing his arms and legs and turning him away from the President—but he twisted back, trying to see the consequences of his actions. Secret Service agent George Foster straightened him up and tried to search him, but his determination to see the success of his assault was so great that he dared to crane his neck while being searched to watch the President bleed. This thoroughness so enraged Foster that he "smashed him right in the jaw," knocking him to the floor and opening a cut in his right cheek.[25]

Foster had good reason to feel not only angry, but guilty. In the seconds before the shooting, he had looked the assailant in the eye and dismissed him, focusing instead on "a dark complexioned man with a black moustache" in another part of the line, whose "general appearance" aroused Foster's suspicions. The spare, well-groomed man with the bandage on his hand looked inoffensive, like "a mechanic out for the day to do the Exposition," Foster said; he looked like hundreds of other fairgoers. When the Secret Service agent looked him in the eye, there was no glint of madness, and his pale complexion made him seem inoffensive enough.[26]

After decking the suspect, Foster left with the President in the Exposition ambulance. Detective sergeant James Vallely of the New York City police department, detailed to the Exposition as captain of its detective bureau, took custody of the prisoner. Vallely was a forcible cop, quick to violence when he thought it appropriate, but he had at least a dutiful sense of his suspects' rights and even, perhaps, a sense of decency.[27] He escorted the assailant to a cell in Buffalo police headquarters, let him sit down on the narrow bed, and then sank onto the cot next to his prisoner—a slim man, weighing about 140 pounds at a height of five foot seven or so. The detective took a couple of cigars from his coat, lit both, and gave one to the prisoner. Then, sitting comfortably as possible in a jail cell, smoking companionably with a criminal caught red-handed in the most dastardly of acts, Vallely asked, for the first time, the man's name.

"Fred C. Nieman," he said. Vallely had him spell out "N-i-e-m-a-n." It was "Polish German," the man explained. If it was, it meant "nobody." He told Vallely he was twenty-eight years old, and gave him his address, on Broadway, in Buffalo.

"Why did you shoot the President?" Vallely asked.

"I only done my duty," Nieman said.

"Why?" Vallely persisted. Nieman looked him in the eye, but said nothing. Vallely saw a young man's smooth face, with fair hair parted on the left and falling over his forehead, framing blue eyes and small, even features. Apart from the cut that Foster's punch had opened on his right cheek, there was nothing distinctive about his face, save a small, almost unnoticeable scar. Foster had been right: Nieman could have been any workingman, dressed his best for a brief audience with the President.

"Are you an anarchist?" Vallely asked.

"Yes, sir," Nieman said. And the policeman asked no more; he had found out as much as he needed to know. The details could wait for the district attorney.[28]

To most Americans at the turn of the century, anarchism meant the politics of terrorism and violence. New Yorkers like Vallely associated it with the city's notorious publisher and activist Johann Most, whose 1885 pamphlet *The Science of Revolutionary Warfare: A Handbook on the Use and Production of Nitroglycerine, Dynamite, Gun Cotton, Mercury Fulminate, Bombs, Fuses, Poisons, etc., etc.* was as practical and chilling as it sounded.[29] The New York Court of Appeals had found in an 1891 case against Most that simply to identify oneself as an anarchist, in front of a listening public, was a misdemeanor crime, for breaching the peace.[30] During the two decades since the anarchist movement first announced its enthusiasm for terrorism, its practical and philosophical teachings had borne bloody fruit. Within the previous ten years, the Spanish prime minister Cánovas del Castillo, the French president Sadi Carnot, the Hapsburg empress Elizabeth, and the Italian king Umberto I had all been assassinated by anarchists. Anarchist bombers François-Claudius Ravachol and Emile Henry killed dozens of Parisians in terror bombings throughout the 1890s, and in the United States the deaths of seven policemen in the 1886 bombing at Haymarket Square in Chicago had been laid at the door of the anarchist movement.

Implicit in this brutal violence committed randomly or by surprise was Emile Henry's expressed belief: *"Il n'y a pas d'innocents."*[31] And also implicit in the practical anarchist philosophy was the independence of terrorists and assassins. There was no coordinating committee, no chain of command. There was only a network of allies, contacts, publications; a shared, and increasing, body of knowledge about the modern weapons of mass destruction; and a commitment to war on modern civilization, whatever the cost. Alienated by a society that reduced men to faceless drones—to nobodies—the terrorist anarchists determined to dismember, piece by piece, the system that they believed oppressed them.

After the short interview with Vallely in the cell, Nieman did not want to talk further until he had something to eat. The officers brought him a large meal, which he ate entirely. Full and satisfied, he was willing to chat. Police chief William S. Bull obliged him. Nieman was so calm and self-possessed that Bull described him as "haughty." Nieman said he was glad he had killed the President. Bull told him the President had survived the shooting—so far—but that if he died, it would go hard for Nieman. As Bull remembered it, the prisoner shrugged, saying,"People sometimes escape being hung."[32]

Soiled from the scuffle at the fairground, Nieman demanded clean clothes. The police offered to get him some if he paid. The prisoner had about a dollar fifty on him, and gave it over for a clean shirt and handkerchief. He had been playing with his dirty handkerchief, wrapping it repeatedly around his right hand, but when chief Bull asked him to show how he had hidden the pistol with it, he refused to make a demonstration until he got the clean one.[33]

Assistant district attorney Frederick Haller, who had been at the Temple of Music during the attack, rushed to police headquarters and now prepared to conduct a more formal investigation. He had the detainee, "Fred Nobody," moved to a seat at a large table in chief Bull's office. There, several stenographers, policemen, and lawyers gathered to hear his story. None of them represented Nieman. They could hear the sounds of angry citizens in the streets. Police chief Bull ordered a heavy guard placed around police headquarters. Twice that night, groups of would-be lynchers rushed the line, only to be repulsed by Buffalo policemen, who sympathized with them but felt duty-bound to let the law take its course.[34]

District attorney Thomas Penney led the detailed questioning. The prisoner now admitted his name was not Nieman, but Leon F. Czolgosz,* and that he had been born in Detroit, had grown up in Alpena, Michigan, and had worked in various jobs throughout the industrial cities of the Great Lakes states. He had cleaned himself off

*Pronounced "Cholgosh."

since being tackled at the Temple of Music, and he held a fresh white handkerchief to the right side of his face where Foster had punched him. At first, he complained that his eyes hurt, too. But after a while he got into the rhythms of explanation. He did not refuse to answer questions, though he sometimes paused before speaking.[35]

In a clear voice, he recounted the shooting in brief, saying, "After I shot twice they knocked me down and trampled on me. Somebody hit me in the face. I said to the officer that brought me down 'I done my duty.' "[36] He said he had been studying anarchist teachings for seven years, and had attended anarchist meetings and speeches. He specifically mentioned reading Free Society, the newspaper of Chicago anarchist Abe Isaak, and hearing the charismatic Russian-born anarchist Emma Goldman speak. Telegrams went out from Buffalo headquarters to the Chicago police, who arrested Isaak and his family that night, and Goldman within the next couple of days, charging them with conspiracy in the President's shooting.[37]

The record of Czolgosz's statement included only what he said, not what the D.A. asked him.[38] James Quackenbush, a Buffalo lawyer who witnessed the shooting and the interrogation, said later that Czolgosz gave his testimony freely, often volunteering details that went beyond the questions Penney posed. But Czolgosz's explanation of why he had done what he did clearly reflected D.A. Penney's determination to satisfy the terms of the M'Naghten test of a defendant's sanity: "I am an anarchist," the stenographers took down. "I fully understood what I was doing when I shot the President. I realized that I was sacrificing my life. I am willing to take the consequences." The elements of the M'Naghten rules were all there: he knew the nature and quality of the act, and its consequences.[39]

Quackenbush asked Czolgosz if he would provide a signed statement for the press, and the prisoner agreed. He took up a pen to write, but his hand shook so badly that he gave up the effort. Czolgosz asked that a stenographer write it out for him. "I want to say to be published—'I killed President McKinley because I done my duty. I don't believe in one man having so much service and another man having none,' " he dictated, and signed the statement.[40] In so few words, the people of Buffalo and the nation learned what so many already suspected: an anarchist had struck at the chief executive of the republic, meaning to kill him. Not only did he appear sane, his words had the cold logic of anarchist terrorism.

Even so, it was far from certain he would come across as sane in the press. Reporters and politicians had a habit of referring to anarchism as itself a form of lunacy. Its hopes for the future were so utopian, its opinions of the present so radical, its methods for bringing about the millennial society so cruelly callous, it did seem divorced from reality. Only a year before McKinley's shooting, a physician had written in *The North American Review* about what he jokingly, if anxiously, called "the assassination mania." He suggested that the anarchist belief in "abolition of organized government" sounded very much as though it belonged to the annals of "mental pathology."[41] Determined to take care in such an atmosphere, the Buffalo police surgeon Dr. Joseph Fowler advised D.A. Penney to arrange to have Czolgosz's case evaluated by professional alienists.

THE ALIENISTS

Dr. Fowler had been on the grounds at the Exposition and heard the shots that hit the President. He had rushed to the hospital, anticipating the President's arrival, and had assisted in his treatment. Now he had come to police headquarters to examine the gunman, and was determined to see the case through to its finish. He watched Czolgosz devour his dinner, clean himself up, and give his statement to D.A. Penney. In consultation with Penney, Fowler negotiated unrestricted access to Czolgosz for the dual purpose of caring for him and determining his sanity. To that end, he called in two University of Buffalo experts on sanity and crime, Dr. Floyd S. Crego (Professor of Insanity and Brain Diseases) and Dr. James W. Putnam (Professor of Nervous Diseases). The three of them became a prosecution panel devoted to documenting Czolgosz's mental health.[42]

The alienists (as doctors of mental pathology were called in the late nineteenth century) who stepped into the Czolgosz case were seasoned veterans in a long battle waged along a front between medicine and law over the responsibility of mentally addled defendants. The struggle had begun in the eighteenth century, when courts first began tentatively to recognize the special value of expert testimony on the subject of sanity. For centuries, the law no more required the assistance of an expert neurologist to detect a disturbance of mind leading to madness than it required an expert meteorologist to detect a disturbance of the atmosphere leading to rain. People who were not themselves crazy knew a madman when they saw one. Witnesses to wills, swearing to the sound mind of a testator, needed no more experience of mental pathology than they might have gained in the ordinary course of life. A doctor, bearing leeches and plasters, had no more expertise than a layman in seeing soundness of mind.

The emergence of medicine as a scientific profession began a slow, awkward shift in the law. Ordinarily, courts required that a witness have direct experience of an event to testify about it. But as doctors codified the practice of medicine, classifying diseases so that diagnosticians could recognize them even if they had never seen them before, courts began to allow doctors to offer their informed professional opinions about the health of patients they had never seen. And insanity was among the first conditions for which the courts allowed doctors to offer such indirect expert testimony.[43]

Even so, judges remained leery of the special value of this expert testimony. They could not be sure whether it outranked the testimony of nonprofessionals, or whether expert opinion was required to determine sanity. It was not till the late 1880s that New York judges began considering "expert testimony" as a special category worth their attention, and even then they struggled to determine its relation to laypersons' testimony. In one 1888 case, a New York court ruled that a "non-expert witness" could not testify about the mental strength of someone, even if he had spoken directly with him.[44] But in another case in the same year, a well-known expert had his testimony thrown out in favor of the lay witnesses' contrary views.[45]

The appearance in the 1880s of Crego, Putnam, and others-like them as expert witnesses signified a comparatively recent change in the courts' opinions. Even when setting aside expert testimony in one case, the judge recognized the doctor as "a medical expert, whose experience as an expert witness in cases where the mental capacity of persons is at issue is well known to us all."[46] When Crego appeared in a pivotal 1899 case, it was only the second time a New York judge recognized the existence of such a thing as an "insanity expert" in a reported opinion. And in this case, the judge recognized the special authority of experts like Crego, ruling licensed doctors had automatic status to testify as to sanity and that a witness without a medical license needed special proof of ability to testify as an expert.[47]

The trend toward elevating expert opinion above the normal rules of opinion evidence rested on a dubious premise, rendered ever more shaky in the public mind by the prominent trials in which insanity experts played a part. The general notion behind waiving the rules of evidence for expert testimony was, in the words of evidentiary scholar John Wigmore, that "a reliance on the *reported data of fellow-scientists*" allowed the scientific formation of professional opinion.[48] But neither Wigmore nor the case law offered a firm reason why the courts should offer special treatment to a science—like that of insanity—that remained resolutely divided over the conclusions to be drawn from its collective knowledge.

The gains that expert witnesses made in the late nineteenth century depended on preserving the image of scientific opinion unmarred by political controversy. Judges remembered that not many decades before Wigmore, another scholar of evidence had noted skeptically that expert witnesses' "views can be made to correspond with the wishes and interests of the parties who call them."[49] At all costs, expert alienists in 1901 wished to avoid another cleft like the one the Guiteau case drove through the profession in 1881.

In the Guiteau case both prosecution and defense put alienists on the stand, and their testimony revealed a dramatic difference of opinion about the nature of insanity, and indeed of scientific opinion about moral character. The prosecution's experts held that insanity was not significantly hereditary, that personalities were fluid, and that the environmental influence on a developing mind shaped it decisively. The defense, by contrast, held insanity to be hereditary, and therefore not the responsibility of the defendant. Paradoxically, therefore, it was the law-and-order side—the prosecution experts—who identified themselves as classical liberals by discounting heredity in favor of environment.[50] For in an age when the frontier was still wide open, men could choose their environment. Even a misfit could find health and fortune on the frontier, where the challenges of settlement would teach him independence and where evangelical Protestantism flourished, fostering virtue. If a man instead chose surroundings that reinforced his dissolute tendencies—as Guiteau chose a utopian freethinkers' commune—he bore responsibility for the environment's effects on him. In an age of self-made men, a man had to take responsibility for what he made of himself.

In these respects the nation had dramatically changed in the twenty years since the Guiteau trial, and these changes shook the alienists' expert complacency. The frontier had closed, or so the 1890 census said: there was no longer any open place for a misfit to go to improve himself. As economic combinations grew larger—as unions took the public place of individual workingmen, and as corporations took the public place of individual entrepreneurs—Americans no longer felt so free to decide what kind of environment they would live in. And if they could not choose what kind of place they would inhabit, they could not bear responsibility for the influence of environment on their development. Alienists, now sometimes known as psychologists, began to reflect this new social determinism in their work. With the watershed work of William James's 1890 *Principles of Psychology*, doctors began to see the developing mind as the product of innocent interactions between instinct and an unchosen environment.[51]

As environmental determinism expanded, earthly troubles replaced divine action as the source of madness. Doctors began to conclude that all manner of city cares—debt, want, stress, and disease, all unchosen and unavoidable in an urban civilization—caused mental disturbance and insanity.[52] As more and more Americans moved into cities and undertook increasingly industrial occupations, these conditions maddened increasing numbers of a once-free people now helpless to seek better circumstances. Caged under such conditions, few would forbear from violent reaction.

As environment grew ever more important in determining charac-

ter, judges and professional alienists alike grew ever more uneasy about
the implications for legal responsibility. The value of expert testimony
would diminish to nothing if doctors could not distinguish between
the expanding influence of environment as recognized in professional
journals and the narrow concerns of the courts. The Guiteau case had
exposed a profession already badly riven and unscientifically split on
the very definition of insanity. Twenty years later, with the professional position on individual responsibility shifting toward the opinions of Guiteau's defense, the profession's assessment on Czolgosz
divided even more widely.

The prosecution argument—made not only by the district attorney
at trial, but by politicians, newspaper editors, and all sorts of public figures seeking revenge—held that Czolgosz bore legal responsibility for
his actions because he had put himself in the way of the corrupting influences of anarchism. He had allowed himself to be seduced by this
decadent philosophy. Even if he was somehow mentally deficient—
which he had to be, for why else would he shoot the President?—he
made a fatal and responsible choice, whose importance and outcome
(as he himself admitted) he knew, and knew to be wrong.

The defense argument—made not only by the court-appointed
defense at trial, but by public figures who saw Czolgosz as representing
a class of the American downtrodden, deserving public sympathy and
assistance lest they come to desperation—held that Czolgosz could
not possibly bear responsibility for his actions because the powerless-
ness and hopelessness of industrial life had driven him mad. Paid a
poor wage, put routinely out of work by the tycoons to whom McKinley had close ties, despised for his ethnic origins and his Catholic heritage, he had gone insane and focused his delusions on the President.
He could not possibly have chosen a better environment, flung about
as he was by these mighty forces that were reshaping the whole world.
Besides, the defense reasoned, it was far better to conclude that only a
madman would shoot the President than to suppose that a perfectly
sane and responsible person could come to the conclusion that it was
now necessary to wage war on the symbols and leaders of American
government.

Brief though Czolgosz's actual trial would be, these arguments had such resonance and disturbing force that they continued long after his conviction and death. Indeed, it was precisely the recognition that they might resonate and disturb society while the trial continued that spurred the prosecution to such speed in carrying out due process.

The concern to decide quickly and surely was uppermost in the minds of Buffalo lawyers and physicians as they prepared an evaluation of the President's assailant. The business of expert testimony had, in the end, as much to do with reputation as with science. As Buffalo alienist Arthur W. Hurd wrote, Crego was "constantly doing expert work . . . He appears frequently in trials and has a good reputation." Likewise Putnam "has been considered one of our prominent experts in this part of the state for some time."[53] As Hurd suggested, the power of the expert lay in his reputation and public prominence. And the public prominence of alienists had been damaged by the evidently uncertain opinion the profession rendered on Guiteau. Nothing similar would happen here. Buffalo's professionals would be proud, Hurd claimed, to avert "such an unseemly controversy as arose after the death of Guiteau."[54]

Fowler, Crego, and Putnam began their assessment of Czolgosz with the notes from the district attorney's interview of Friday night, in which Czolgosz appeared to have satisfied the M'Naghten test. On Saturday morning, they added to their observations an interview between Czolgosz and a man named Walter Nowak, a printer from Cleveland, who burst into police headquarters begging to confront the prisoner. Chief Bull decided to let him, and led both men into his office, calling in D.A. Penney as well. In their presence, Nowak first identified Czolgosz, saying he had known him in Cleveland, and then launched into a harangue:

> You know me well, Czolgosz, I have always been a friend of yours. Why did you do this? Why did you commit this crime? Why have you committed an act that is going to bring disgrace upon the Polish race? Why have you committed this crime that brings disgrace on your father and mother and entire family?

At first Czolgosz said nothing, just smiled. But at the end of Nowak's spiel, he said, "I don't know whether you have been a particular friend of mine or not."[55]

Under the circumstances, Nowak did not want to argue himself into a closer friendship than was necessary with the anarchist terrorist. Speaking more for the benefit of the listening police than to Czolgosz, he said, "You and I belonged to the same society, attended the meetings together, but it became so radical, the talk was so radical, I gave it up, I couldn't stand it, I wouldn't listen to it." Then, drawing and playing the trump card of political loyalty, Nowak declared, "I am not a Socialist or Anarchist, I am a Republican."

Czolgosz looked at him, raised his hand, and rubbed his fingers together in the universal street gesture for folding money. "Oh yes," he said. "You are a Republican for this . . . For what there is in it."[56]

As far as the police and the doctors were concerned, this interview supported their conviction that Czolgosz was sane, suffering only from an absurd political conviction: that Republicans were in politics for the money.

On Sunday, the interviewers and the assailant rested, and when they returned to their task on Monday, it was amid the news that the President was well on the road to recovery. With the worst of the crisis seemingly past, the alienists' discussion with the prisoner took on more of the character of a game. When the doctors asked why Czolgosz had shot the President, he looked quizzically at them.

"Did I shoot the President?" he asked. The doctors gaped.

For half an hour they pressed him on this point, while he denied knowing anything about any such crime. Fowler looked at his notes and thought "it was all up." As a last tactic, Fowler decided to scold Czolgosz "quite severely," as Fowler recalled, "telling him that he had signed his confession and reminding him that he had made the statements before many witnesses."[57]

Czolgosz dropped his act, and admitted, as he had before, having stalked and shot McKinley. And finally, he added, "I am glad I did it."[58]

The gratified doctors took their notes, compared their opinions, and declared on the basis of these three days' observation,

The most careful questioning failed to discover any hallucinations of sight or hearing. He had received no special command; he did not believe he had been specially chosen to do the deed. He always spoke of his motive for the crime as duty; he always referred to the Anarchists' belief that the killing of rulers was a duty . . . He is not a case of paranoia, because he has not systematized delusions reverting to self, and because he is in exceptionally good condition and has an unbroken record of good health.

He is the product of Anarchy, sane and responsible.[59]

Fowler, Crego, and Putnam tendered this judgment to D.A. Penney, putting the seal on his case against Czolgosz for attempted murder.

After a quiet couple of days, Thursday morning arrived, and with it the news that Charles McBurney, a prominent Manhattan physician called to consult in McKinley's case, was returning to New York, confident of the President's recovery. There was no longer cause to worry about sepsis, or peritonitis. The President could turn on his side comfortably, and admitted of no tenderness in his abdomen. His spirits were up, and his mind was skipping ahead of his recovery to the political events of the moment. Reporters asked McBurney about the bullet left in the President's body. He laughed: where it was, he said, the bullet "couldn't even shorten Methuselah's life by a single day."[60]

Medical hubris never pays. By noon that day, McKinley's pulse sped up, then grew weaker. The President was in shock. Doctors administered digitalis, strychnine, and adrenaline. They plied him with camphor, coffee, and clam broth.[61] His heart began to fail. McBurney arrived in New York City only to hear the news of his patient's sudden turn for the worse, and immediately boarded an outbound train for Buffalo.

Friday afternoon, a week after McKinley was shot, proved a fine day for a hike, and Vice President Roosevelt put off his few official obligations and seized the moment for a swift jaunt up Mount Tahawus. He had come to the summit and started down again when he decided to have lunch by a little lake, clear and blue in the heights of the

Adirondacks. With sandwich in hand he surveyed a most satisfying scene—marred only by the huffing and puffing of a ranger approaching from down the slope, bearing what news the Vice President could sadly guess. The President was dying—he would be dead before the sun rose again—and Theodore Roosevelt would soon be President of the United States.

2

THE LETTER OF THE LAW

THE INQUISITORS

That there are gaps in the official record of Leon F. Czolgosz's arrest and custody is scarcely surprising. Nobody knew just how to treat a presidential assassin. Out of the optimism that makes life bearable, nobody had compiled a handbook on what to do with a presidential killer, in the hope that there might not be another. The alienists had handbooks for diagnosing insanity. The anarchists had handbooks for committing acts of terror. But the district attorney could do only what attorneys generally do: work from accumulated precedent—with the caveat that, in this case, the precedent of the Guiteau trial furnished a greater quantity of lessons on what *not* to do. Do not, the record of Garfield's assassination cautioned, let the definition of insanity come up for debate. Do not let the defendant and the press collude to make a circus of the proceedings. Do not take too much time.

And because of this speed, not to say haste, the gaps in the record fall in such a way as to inspire the suspicious mind. Between the shooting at around 4 p.m. on Friday and the arrival of the D.A. and other lawyers to take Czolgosz's formal statement, some six hours had passed. It was a long time, much longer than it should have taken for detective Vallely's brief reported interview with "Fred C. Nieman," much longer than it should have taken for assistant district attorney

Haller to feed Czolgosz and set up an interview session in police chief
Bull's office. And nobody could say quite what happened in that time.
Some worldly-wise informants would darkly speculate that the police had used the time to give the prisoner "the third degree"—that by
"torture" they had drawn his "so-called confession" out of him.[1] One
alienist believed that older photographs of Czolgosz clearly showed evidence of insane "exaltation," but that he appeared calmer afterwards
because this mad inspiration had been "crushed out by the brutal hand
of the authorities."[2]

Compounding the impression of conspiracy, a missing transcript
went along with the missing time. D.A. Penney arrived at police
headquarters between 10 and 11 p.m. and began talking to Czolgosz
on the record, with stenographers typing up what was said. Penney refused afterward to release this confession. Fowler, Crego, and Putnam
published a version of the confession that included some of Czolgosz's
statements—"all of importance which he said," as Fowler later put
it—but not the questions Penney asked, nor anything purporting to be
the whole of what Czolgosz said.[3] The statements, strung together on
the page, made it look as if Czolgosz had delivered a long explanation
of his actions without any prompting. But he had not; Penney (and
others, including Bull, Haller, and the physicians) had been questioning and prompting him all along. Neither Penney nor Fowler showed
other investigators the full transcript of the interview with Czolgosz.[4]

In the transcribed statements they did show, nobody mentions a
lawyer for Czolgosz. Nobody represented him or offered him advice
(nor did the law then require the police to offer him an attorney). Afterward, a number of witnesses claimed he had refused representation
(although the transcribed statements do not quote him saying so), on
the plausible ground that as an anarchist he did not believe in the legal system. And so he had no legal counsel till the eve of his trial—
which came as swiftly after the President's death as the President's
death had come after the shooting. No sooner did Czolgosz become an
assassin than he became a defendant.

An Englishman by birth, Penney had come to the law unsteeped
in the Bill of Rights. He believed he needed all the speed that was
seemly, and with it such silence as he could produce. He wanted as lit-

tle discussion as possible, telling a later investigator that "any writing or talking on this matter only kept it before the public." It encouraged irresponsible speculation. Under such circumstances, he put forth a frank "plan to suppress all that was possible." The case did not warrant thoughtful or extended discussion of the defendant's sanity or motives. "Czolgosz was sane and an anarchist without question," he said flatly.[5]

And if Czolgosz was an anarchist, Penney and the police would have wanted very much to find out whether he was in league with other anarchists—who might have provided him with more than mere inspiration. Without knowing what they asked Czolgosz, outsiders could not know how vigorously police pursued the question of any connection to anarchist cells or networks. But given their certain enthusiasm for finding such connections if they existed, the disappearance of Czolgosz on the eve of the President's death created another suggestive gap in the official record.

On Friday, September 13, with the President in his final illness, Czolgosz vanished from the jail at police headquarters. With the exception of the officers directly in control of him, nobody knew where he was. Even the alienist Dr. Fowler, who otherwise had unlimited access to him, knew only that the prisoner "had been spirited away somewhere else."[6] Czolgosz reappeared on Monday, when he was arraigned and indicted for first-degree murder.

It emerged later that he had been moved to the women's dungeon of the Erie County Penitentiary. Those inclined to speculation and sensation suggested he had been smuggled away in disguise for the purpose of further interrogation. One prison guard afterward maintained that "he was tortured but did not confess a word" that would "implicate anyone else."[7] The police reported that he had been moved because the jail needed repair, and the only thing approaching a disguise given him was a new hat, as he had lost his own in the scuffle at the Exposition.[8]

D.A. Penney wanted to bring justice swiftly to Leon Czolgosz. The sooner he could put the admitted assassin in his grave, the sooner Buffalo's professionals could put behind them the horror and guilt of the President's murder. The law could restore stability, a sense of order, if only it could explain this anomaly, this anarchist, and expunge him from society. By working quickly, Penney avoided the media circus and professional embarrassment that haunted the Guiteau case. But by muzzling Czolgosz (at first figuratively, and in the end literally), the prosecution raised more questions than it buried.

THE TRANSITION

Even as Penney was working to change Buffalo from a crime scene to a seat of judgment, another shift was taking place. Theodore Roosevelt was taking over the reins of the presidency with as little guidance and as much concern for speed and order as Penney had shown.

The stock market had closed on news of McKinley's death, uncertain what to expect from Roosevelt. The men who had worked with McKinley were just as uncertain, but the cabinet officers did their best to keep a brave face, agreeing to leave Secretary of State John Hay and Secretary of the Treasury Lyman Gage in Washington, while the rest of them went to Buffalo to pay their respects to the old and new Presidents. On Saturday they made their ceremonious way through the cordon of militia and police. Speaking through Secretary of War

Leon Czolgosz shortly after his arrest for shooting President McKinley. (Massachusetts Historical Society)

Elihu Root, the cabinet formally requested Roosevelt to take the oath of office, which he did that afternoon at the house of local attorney Ansley Wilcox, before he could manage to pay his respects to Mrs. McKinley or to the President's casket. On Sunday morning, as was customary with the change of chief executives for any reason, the cabinet tendered their resignations en masse to the new President, who hoped to see his predecessor's earthly remains that afternoon.

In addition to the cabinet officers who had served McKinley, two of his other allies were working their way through the guards that Sunday afternoon to see him one last time. One was Mark Hanna, now a senator from Ohio. The other was Herman Henry (H. H.) Kohlsaat, onetime baked-goods entrepreneur and now newspaper publisher from Chicago.

Kohlsaat was a small, well-groomed man with a sharp eye for quotable anecdotes and a nose for power. He was a businessman first, a Republican second, and a publisher third; he had bought Chicago's only two Democratic newspapers so he could make them Republican papers. He had known McKinley since the beginning of the Ohioan's political career, and now went to Buffalo to cover its sad end. But Kohlsaat by himself could not get through the military cordon around the President, so he phoned Hanna, who had always known how to get to McKinley. Together the two of them skirted the tree-shaded front yard of the Milburns' house, avoiding the conspicuous columned front entrance, and made their way through the kitchen door to the library, where the President's casket lay.

In the public eye, as in Roosevelt's private judgment, Hanna represented the plutocracy—or rather, Hanna was himself the preeminent plutocrat. The newspaper cartoonist Homer Davenport had created a guide to caricaturing Hanna as an ogre of capital, with dollar signs on his suits and, dangling from his fingers, the marionette strings by which he controlled a puppet McKinley. The devastating portrait had so thoroughly suffused the popular imagination that the real, rather mild-mannered, soft-eyed and white-haired Hanna disappointed spectators who had come to gawk at the monster who manipulated the trusts.

When he walked with Kohlsaat into the Milburns' library, Hanna looked less like an inconvenienced puppet master than a bereft lover. He felt toward McKinley, Kohlsaat wrote, like "a big bashful boy toward the girl he loves."[9] Now he sat at the foot of his friend's coffin, head in hands, grieving, as Kohlsaat watched over them both.

The three Republicans had sat together, under very different circumstances, almost ten years before. In the summer of 1892, then-governor McKinley of Ohio was chairing the Republican National Convention, meeting in Minneapolis. In an absurdly hot, newly pine-boarded hall dripping with resin, McKinley narrowly escaped a political gaffe. During the nominating session, the overheated and irritable delegates spontaneously began to vote against the unpopular incumbent President, Benjamin Harrison, and for chairman McKinley instead. However popular, however qualified the chairman, it would run against all sense of party order if he were to preside over a session in which he unhorsed the sitting President. McKinley tried to stop the upset, even disputing his home state's right to vote for him, and only barely averted a colossally awkward breach of protocol. Fleeing the hall, he arrived at his hotel to the clamor of a cheerful crowd, which hoisted him on their shoulders and carried him in his near triumph into the lobby. Wobbling on their hands, he frowned at the indignity of it all, which was magnified as the jostling sent one of his trouser legs creeping up to his knee, laying bare his leg and stocking garter. Struggling to put it back in place, trying to regain his balance, he spotted Kohlsaat in the throng, and asked if they could meet in his room, as McKinley's would surely house yet more troublemakers.

The two escaped to the relative quiet of Kohlsaat's room, where they took off their clothes and lay down to cool off in their underwear. Sweating and sipping ice water, they said nothing as they contemplated the near miss. A knock came at the door. It was a messenger from Hanna, who had guessed his friend's whereabouts. "Tell Mark to come up here," McKinley shouted. Kohlsaat took a sheet from the bed and threw it over a sofa, so that when Hanna arrived in the closeness of the hotel room, he too stripped off and lay in the hot silence. After about fifteen minutes, Hanna said, "My God, William, that was a damned close squeak!"[10] And the three of them began thinking about what they could do with McKinley's popularity in 1896, when they would have free play.

That had been the beginning of McKinley's presidential run, and now, in the autumn of 1901, the three of them sat together at its end. At the foot of the President's casket, Hanna raised his head, folded his arms, and squared his jaw. Anger fought with sadness for the uppermost place in his mind, for his friend's death meant also that a decade's political work lay in ruins, and atop the rubble of his ambition stood the undependable Theodore Roosevelt, who Hanna and Kohlsaat feared would wreck the McKinley legacy of steadfast conservatism.

Supporters of both Roosevelt and McKinley saw the same flood tide of revolution rising in the land; they differed only insofar as McKinley wanted to dam it up, while Roosevelt wanted to ride it. Few substantive differences separated the two Republicans. Both stood strong for the rights of capital- and property-holders. Neither cared for labor unions. Roosevelt disliked the way McKinley's beloved tariff subsidized corporations, but he would never seriously challenge it.

Indeed, when it came to the great clashes between capital and labor, Roosevelt talked a much harder line than McKinley. The merest mention of a strike turning violent brought him swiftly to the topic of shooting his fellow men. "I like to see a mob handled by the regulars, or by good State-Guards, not over-scrupulous about bloodshed," he wrote. "If it comes to shooting we shall shoot to hit. No blank cartridges or firing over the head of anybody." He and his rancher friends from out West would, he believed, enjoy "a chance with rifles at one of the mobs . . . my men shoot well and fear very little."

On the other hand, as long as the unions remained peaceable in asserting their rights—as long as they stayed within the democratic process and did not become a mob—Roosevelt would do what they wanted whenever it seemed at all reasonable. And his version of what was reasonable covered much more territory than McKinley's. As Roosevelt said when he was governor of New York, "If there should be a disaster at the Croton Dam strike, I'd order out the militia in a minute. But I'd sign an employer's liability law, too."[11]

Roosevelt spoke about all the plaintive portions of the American population the same way he spoke about "the negro":

Inasmuch as he is here and can neither be killed nor driven away, the only wise and honorable and Christian thing to do is to treat each black man and each white man strictly on his merits as a man, giving him no more and no less than he shows himself worthy to have.[12]

In Roosevelt's America, troublesome people deserved nothing as much as a good shooting, but as long as shooting was politically unfeasible, he believed everyone might as well have fair and equal treatment.

All this talk unnerved Hanna and the other McKinleyites. These casual comments about killing people when appropriate and acknowledging their rights when unavoidable portended major political changes. As it turned out, Roosevelt would indeed preside over the killing and driving away of one class of insurgents: the Filipino rebels who fought against American rule of their archipelago. But to domestic campaigners for justice, he tended instead to extend the protection of his neutral consideration. Brooding over this possibility, Hanna worried that a President who claimed to know and understand the demands of Populists and workingmen might seriously erode the business basis of the Republican Party.

Roosevelt knew how little the McKinley men cared for him—he had spent enough time on the receiving end of the cabinet's collective cold shoulder—and he knew, too, that Hanna posed the greatest danger to him in this new and uncertain political world. He sent, therefore, for Kohlsaat, asking that he meet him privately later that day. That afternoon, Roosevelt led McKinley's cabinet in a solemn procession beginning at the Milburn house, after which the President's body lay in state at Buffalo's city hall. Then, as the city's people shuffled before McKinley's bier, Roosevelt went quietly back to the Wilcoxes' house with the cabinet.

Kohlsaat arrived at the Wilcoxes' to find the President in one front parlor room and the cabinet in another. Roosevelt had in hand the cabinet's pro forma resignations. With political and economic stability hanging in the balance, the most frightening thing the new President could tell a McKinley loyalist was that he intended to shuffle the cabinet—which was precisely what Roosevelt said he would do.

"I am going to let John Hay go and appoint Elihu Root Secretary of State," he said. He went on to tell Kohlsaat that he would dismiss Treasury Secretary Lyman Gage. "He always gets his back up against the wall, and I can't get around him," he complained.

Among the cabinet, Gage and Hay conspicuously represented the conservative economic policies of Hanna and McKinley. Both Midwesterners—Gage from Indiana, Hay from Ohio—both men sympathized with moneymen and had little interest in labor. In the policy-making circles of Washington, it was an open secret that Hay had anonymously written the antilabor novel *The Bread-winners*. And Gage, as U.S. treasurer, had lobbied hard for the most anti-Populist measure imaginable—the Gold Standard Act of 1900, which tied the dollar legally to the gold currency that Bryan had, in 1896, claimed was crucifying American labor. Roosevelt could not have picked two more tempting targets to threaten.

As the new President might have predicted, Kohlsaat panicked. "You propose to fire [McKinley's] Secretary of State and Secretary of the Treasury!" he sputtered. "[T]he stock exchanges of the country closed when the news came of McKinley's death. To-day's papers report there is great uneasiness as to what will happen when they open to-morrow. Why? Because you are considered a 'bucking bronco' in finance, and now you propose to let Gage out of the Treasury Department, and Heaven only knows whom you will appoint. It will probably cause a panic, and it will be known for all time as the 'Roosevelt panic.' "[13]

The President smiled, and let Kohlsaat talk. He would not, he allowed, fire Gage and Hay after all. When the newspaper publisher left the Wilcox house, Roosevelt went to the parlor door and grinned again at the cabinet members in the parlor. "I have changed my mind. I am going to keep all of you," he said. But he had reminded Kohlsaat, and with him the McKinley wing of the Republican Party, that he could, and just might, fire anyone he pleased. He would go on talking about shooting troublemakers, be they radicals or government officials, for the rest of his career, and nobody quite knew when, or whether, to take him seriously. As it turned out, Hay served as Secretary of State until he died in office in 1905. Gage was gone in four months, but the man who replaced him, Leslie Shaw, was practically his twin, another conservative Midwestern banker who believed in using the Treasury to keep a stable currency. There would be no Roosevelt panic on Shaw's account. What the President could theoretically do—order troops to fire on strikers, or fire cabinet officials at his pleasure—gave him much greater scope than he would in good conscience exercise. But loose talk and the occasional sudden move kept people on their toes.

On Monday morning, McKinley's funeral train left Buffalo. The President, his cabinet, and the press were all on board in a series of special Pullman cars. Kohlsaat sat in one, and as the Erie shore rolled away behind him, Hanna sat down beside him, nursing a furious resentment of the new President. "I told William McKinley it was a mistake to nominate that wild man," he said. "I asked him if he realized what would happen if he should die. Now look, that damned cowboy is President of the United States!"

Emboldened by Roosevelt's apparent reasonableness in reconsidering his cabinet shake-up, Kohlsaat suggested Hanna try meeting with the President privately. He did. When he returned to Kohlsaat's car, he was smiling broadly. "He's a pretty good little cuss, after all!"[14]

In the fearful atmosphere following the assassination, with everyone on edge and uncertain what threat the anarchist terrorists really posed to the American government and economy, Theodore Roosevelt used the first forty-eight hours of his presidency to bully and flatter his closest enemies into submission. It worked: apart from the grieving widow, Ida McKinley, alone at the back of the train with her thoughts and what remained of her husband, the old President's closest friends had all but forgotten to worry about the anarchist threat and were thinking now of Roosevelt's threats and promises.

THE DEFENSE

As the trial drew closer and Leon Czolgosz remained without legal counsel, the Bar Association of Erie County determined to secure for the defendant some manner of decent representation. Czolgosz was indicted on Monday, September 16, with trial set for Monday of the following week. Local attorneys were growing nervous that they might suffer professional censure if they did not somehow acknowledge their duty and undertake the odious task of representing an anarchist before the bar of justice. Twenty years before, the assassin Guiteau, himself an attorney of sorts, had been represented by his brother-in-law and himself, and it had led to endless absurdities of legal protocol. The Erie bar had decided it must act to produce "a dignified trial on a high plane, free from pettifogging." As much to the point, they believed that it would be impossible to put Czolgosz to death if he had no defense. Thus the vengeful and self-protective elements of the bar cooperated to nominate two former judges and state senators, Loran L. Lewis and Robert C. Titus, a Republican and Democrat respectively, to represent the assassin. They were eminent men. Both demurred, and only reluctantly accepted the duty. By this time it was late in the week; the judges had not been able to consult with each other, or to get Czolgosz's cooperation.[15]

By Thursday, in keeping with the vogue for expert testimony, the bar association also sought some alienist as an expert in behalf of the defense to examine Czolgosz. They telegrammed Carlos F. MacDonald, Professor of Mental Diseases and Medical Jurisprudence at Bellevue Hospital Medical College in New York City.

Dr. MacDonald was regarded by pupils and colleagues alike as an ideal teacher, and he had a broad, friendly Scottish face, so it was all the more jarring that he talked a great deal about using the power of the state to kill people, and, moreover, had often done it. Not only had he killed in wartime to save the Union (including fighting in the bloody battles at Antietam and Petersburg), but in peacetime at the state's request he had presided over the first legal execution by electrocution, and since then had become the doctor most identified with the scientific production of death by modern means.[16] As with any chore, there was a craft to the business of wiring up men to kill them, but it was a philosophically troublesome business for even the toughest of minds. The state allowed—indeed, required—Dr. MacDonald not only to know, but also systematically to catalogue in clinical detail the speed and pain of a deliberately caused human death. When this data cropped up in the press, even in the driest of professional journals, it had the whiff of sulfur about it; however modern, however electric, the manufacture of death by industrial means touched some primitive nerve of fear.

Nor did it ease anyone's conscience that the first electrocution had not gone especially well. William Kemmler, a mild-mannered murderer who had killed his girlfriend with an ax for constantly nagging him, became the first miscreant sentenced to electrocution in the summer of 1889. At Auburn State Prison in upstate New York, MacDonald and a colleague, the neurologist Dr. Edward C. Spitzka, authorized the introduction of 1500 volts of alternating current into Kemmler's body for a period of ten seconds—though they had no way of being sure just how much electricity would come in, as the execution room in the basement at Auburn was bereft of ammeters, voltmeters, or other measuring devices. Kemmler was brought into the basement of the prison and strapped into the specially designed chair, where he obligingly arranged himself so as to "be sure that everything was all right," as he told the doctors. When the circuit was closed, his body spasmed for the duration of the electrocution, and when the current was released, it relaxed. Bruises appeared on his face. The skin split on one of his fingers, and from this wound dripped a drop of blood.

"Turn on the current instantly. This man is not dead," Spitzka ordered, whereupon the circuit was again closed, this time for over a minute, just to make sure. Spitzka was horrified. He preferred (so he said) the guillotine to this contraption. But MacDonald remained devoted to the electric chair, working hard from one execution to the next to eliminate the "certain defects of a minor character" which marred the early electrocutions. Observing the blistering of the skin, the effects of saline wettings and of head and back electrodes, he sought progressive improvements. Despite his confident optimism that one day the process of electrocution might be perfected, his was not a cheering presence to a defendant.[17]

But MacDonald had another specialty, namely, as a crusader for a more liberal definition of legal insanity—hence his friendship with Spitzka, the neurologist who had testified most vigorously to Guiteau's insanity at his trial in 1881. Spitzka and MacDonald alike believed the M'Naghten test was intellectually bankrupt. As MacDonald wrote just two years before he became a consultant in the Czolgosz case, "The law . . . holds that the question of responsibility is not to be settled by the mere *existence* of insanity, but by the *degree* or *extent* of its existence." In other words, someone who was merely mad might not be mad enough to get away with murder; one had to be mad enough to be unable to tell the difference between right and wrong. This "so-called legal test," MacDonald railed, "is wholly at variance with nature as interpreted by medical science." As MacDonald saw it, to bear responsibility for his actions a killer not only needed to know right from wrong but also needed "the power to choose the right and avoid the wrong." Responsibility was a matter not only of moral understanding, but of a healthy willpower and an environment that allowed it to operate.

A considerable part of the medical profession agreed with Mac-Donald, and had indeed agreed since the middle of the nineteenth century. But the law did not budge. "The lawmakers of the Empire State . . . with a wisdom superior to nature's . . . have attempted to define the conditions of responsibility in mental disease by declaring in law what shall be, rather than what is," MacDonald wrote. In so doing, they had devised a test "so narrow in spirit and so untenable in reason that every experienced alienist must regard it as artificial, arbitrary, and fraught with danger to humanity and the ends of justice."[18]

MacDonald knew more than anyone exactly what happened to killers when the law caught up with them. He had smelled their skin burn and he had watched the blood vessels in their face burst under the pressure of electric current. And he thought that the law ought to err on the side of caution in sending men to the electric chair.

He was an authority on justice and mercy, and he was also a Manhattan doctor, which earned him automatic resentment for his city sophistication. If the only alienist to speak on Czolgosz's case was a downstate New Yorker, it might (if it was possible) further arouse passions against the accused. MacDonald called in Arthur W. Hurd, the superintendent of the Buffalo State Hospital, to assist him in his examination. Hurd flatly refused MacDonald's request to appear on Czolgosz's behalf, but when the Erie Bar Association asked his help, Hurd consented "as a matter of public duty."[19]

Dr. MacDonald arrived in Buffalo on Friday, September 20, and presented himself to D.A. Penney. Penney was willing to let MacDonald and Hurd examine Czolgosz over the weekend, given that the trial would begin Monday morning. The doctors met with the prisoner both days. He appeared to them much as he had appeared to the prosecution's alienists: "a well nourished, rather good-looking, mild-mannered young man," who described himself as "a laborer by occupation." He had given up Catholicism, could read and write, smoked and drank in moderation only. His father, brother, and married sister were living, and he had no insanity in the family. "He admitted having sexual intercourse with women," MacDonald noted, "but denied masturbation or other unnatural practices." And he showed neither much depression nor exaltation.

In short, he was sane and normal. When asked about why he had shot the President, he said simply, "McKinley was going around the country shouting about prosperity when there was no prosperity for the poor man. I am not afraid to die. We all have to die sometime."

MacDonald figured that Czolgosz's remarks about prosperity might have constituted a delusion "in the broadest sense of that term; that is, it was a false belief, but it was in no sense an insane delusion or a false belief due to disease of the brain. On the contrary, it was a political delusion, so to speak,—a false belief founded on ignorance, faulty education and warped—not diseased—reason and judgment." If he was insane, then so were all "the various groups of anarchists—not to mention other terrorists."[20]

The only aspect of his behavior that either MacDonald or Hurd remarked on as being at all out of the ordinary was his refusal to answer questions about "his connection with the anarchistic bodies,"[21] as Hurd wrote—and that might only mean that he was covering for his friends within the movement. If they had more time, the alienists might have sought evidence of madness in Czolgosz's family tree—but he had said there was none.

On Monday morning, MacDonald and Hurd met Czolgosz's attorneys before the trial began, and tendered their opinion to counsels Lewis and Titus: even by MacDonald's liberal standards, their client was sane and responsible. They could raise no defense either within the scope of the law or the wider boundaries of psychiatric theory. Furthermore, the trial was scheduled to begin within minutes. It looked as though MacDonald would be called upon to practice his primary area of expertise upon Leon Czolgosz.

THE TRIAL

At ten o'clock on Monday morning, September 23, 1901, in the grandly turreted and baroquely decorated City and County Hall on Franklin Square in Buffalo, Czolgosz's trial began, under paired sixteen-ton granite statues of Justice and Commerce. Despite the stately surroundings, it would be a brisk trial. Counsel for the defense would afterward be criticized for their work on behalf of the assassin, but in truth they mounted a daring effort to get their client acquitted on grounds of insanity. It was as much as they could do under the circumstances, and more than district attorney Penney had prepared to overcome.

Even so, the first thing Czolgosz's attorneys did was try to wriggle out of seeming too zealous in their defense of their client. On the morning of September 23, the courtroom came to order, and the court solicited a plea from Leon Czolgosz in the murder of William McKinley. Before he could open his mouth, his counsel were bobbing up from the defense table to request the judge's attention. The white-bearded Lewis and the dark-bearded Titus looked like a photographic negative one of the other, and their matched effort to circumvent their client's plea irritated Judge Truman C. White before the trial was minutes old.

"I think the prisoner was about to speak," he suggested. "Czolgosz, did you understand what the District Attorney said to you?"

"I didn't hear it," Czolgosz said. Judge White asked him to plead in the matter of McKinley's murder. "Guilty," Czolgosz said. It was the last thing he would say in his own trial, and it would be ignored. After this small effort to claim responsibility for his crime, his fate would rest entirely in the hands of others who sought to demonstrate that either anarchy or insanity—but in any case not Leon Czolgosz of his own free will—had killed William McKinley.

"The plea can not be accepted in this Court," White ruled, as the guilty plea could not be allowed in cases where capital punishment was a possibility. "The Clerk will enter a plea of 'not guilty' and we will proceed with the trial."

Now Titus was able to get the court's attention. As it turned out, he wanted it so that he could say, for the record, that he would rather be elsewhere. "If the Court please, it has been thought best by my distinguished associate and myself . . . that something should be said, not in the way of apology, but as a reason why we are here in defense of this defendant," Czolgosz's attorney began.

It was made to appear, to Judge Lewis and myself that it was a duty which we owed alike to our profession, to the public and to the Court that we accept this assignment to see that this defendant, if he is guilty, is convicted only by such evidence as the law of the land requires in a case of this character, and that in the trial of this case the forms of the law shall be observed in every particular.[22]

After Titus tried to explain that he and Lewis were present more or less under duress, and expected themselves to perform a purely formal role, to see that the rules were observed, Judge White indicated his impatience with this foot-dragging.

"I am sure you gentlemen will protect him to the same extent that you would if you were retained for a munificent compensation," he said, and added by way of ending the discussion, "It is my pleasure not only to confirm, but if it should be deemed necessary, appoint and designate you gentlemen to the task which you have set out to perform."

With that, the D.A. commenced the trial, the court drew and swore the jury, and testimony began.[23]

To be sure, it was unbecoming that the defendant's counsel should have sought to excuse themselves from the trial. But they had been asked to represent this low criminal who was fully prepared to admit his guilt, and they had absolutely no case at all, as the trial swiftly showed. There were eyewitnesses to the shooting. The prosecution had the defendant's own statement, in which he indicated sympathy with anarchists, to suggest a motive. And the only reed to which the defense could cling, the possibility of claiming insanity, had just that morning been discounted by MacDonald and Hurd, the experts retained for the defense. There was little they could do, and to their credit, they did every bit of it.

Penney, in proving the material elements of first-degree murder, showed cause of death. He had therefore to put the doctors who had treated McKinley on the stand. The physicians admitted some failures of treatment; for example, they did not use the X-ray equipment to find the fatal bullet, and indeed could not find it even after four hours of searching during autopsy, after which the McKinley family finally prevailed on them not to "injure the corpse any longer."[24]

Lewis tried his best to discredit the physicians. He played upon the general mistrust of medical men, admonishing doctors to speak plainly, and suggesting they might have mishandled antiseptics in the President's case. He tried to get the medical examiner, Dr. Harvey Gaylord, to admit that because he had used antiseptics, he must have suspected the existence of deadly microorganisms—which might themselves have been the cause of death—in the President's body.

"Did I understand you to say that you found cancerous germs?" Lewis asked.

"That I found what, sir?" Gaylord replied in evident incredulity.

"Cancerous germs," Lewis insinuated.

"No sir," Gaylord insisted.[25]

These efforts amounted to little more than desperate feints, as Penney's dogged redirect examination of Gaylord showed.

"What is your conclusion as to the cause of death?" Penney asked.

With medical precision, Gaylord replied, "He died as the result of absorption of this breaking-down material in this area back of the stomach."

"What was the cause of the breaking-down of the material?" Penney continued.

"The cause of the breaking-down of the material was, in the first place, injury to the tissues and was probably further facilitated by the escape of the secretion of the pancreas into this cavity," Gaylord offered, elaborating on the process by which the President's injured body had poisoned itself.

"What was the cause of the injury to the tissues?" Penney asked patiently.

"That I should attribute to the bullet," Gaylord replied, finally detecting the district attorney's drift.

"Well, getting back to primal causes then, the result"—Penney stumbled slightly in running down his conclusion—"or cause of death, rather, was the bullet wound?"

"Was the bullet wound," the doctor recited.

"That is, in plain, ordinary language?"

"That was the specific factor."[26]

However difficult it was for Penney to guide his experts along to a plain English conclusion, he got there, and the defense could do nothing to stop him.

Nor could they cast doubt on the defendant's confession, though they tried. Penney put the policemen Vallely and Bull, and the attorney Quackenbush, on the stand to establish the defendant's behavior after the shooting, and to introduce the brief signed statement Quackenbush had put out to the press. On cross-examination of Quackenbush, Titus tried another hoary courtroom tactic to suggest Czolgosz had behaved in a manner to indicate madness.

"Did he become animated at all in this talk, in his own conversation?"

"No, not—" Quackenbush trailed off.

"His talk was suppressed, all the time?" Titus tried this old debaters' stunt—if not animated and insane, his manner must have been subdued and insane—to produce even a glimmer of hope for his client. But Quackenbush, a lawyer himself, did not take the bait.

"It was not suppressed. I was hesitating about the word 'animated.' It was natural."[27]

And so it went, with the eyewitnesses identifying Czolgosz as the shooter, the doctors showing that the shooting had killed the President, and the defendant's statement indicating, as Penney elicited from Quackenbush on redirect, that Czolgosz's "own individual theorizing" about government, "in connection with . . . the lectures and speakers he had heard" had led him to anarchistic beliefs, and thus a political motive for murdering McKinley.[28] He had the murder weapon, the cause of death, the confession, and the motive. It was an open-and-shut case, and in the course of an afternoon and a morning of testimony, he had opened and shut it. He had left only one small opening, and when the defense rose to present its case, Lewis leapt forward to put his foot in the door.

"If your Honor please," he said, "the defendant has no witnesses that he will call, so that the testimony is closed at the close of the testimony of the People." With a defendant who insisted on professing his guilt at every chance, and an expert panel of alienists who insisted he was sane, there was little point in presenting testimony. All Lewis could do was talk, and the white-haired old politician could talk beautifully.

"This being the first time in over twenty years that I have had occasion to address a jury as counsel in a case, you may imagine that I feel somewhat in a strange position, especially in a case of the importance of this. A great calamity has befallen our nation. The President of the country has been stricken down and dies in our city. It is shown beyond any peradventure of doubt that it was at the defendant's hand that he was stricken down," he told the jury, and then made the only move he could make in his client's defense: "And the only question that can be discussed or considered in this case is the question whether that act was that of a sane person. If it was, then the defendant is guilty of the murder and must suffer the penalty. If it was the act of an insane man, then he is not guilty of murder but should be acquitted of that charge and would then be confined in an insane asylum."[29]

Lewis continued on, telling anecdotes about the importance of defending the dignity of the law, and how even the meanest criminal—even a confessed anarchist—deserved a fair trial. But Penney was already fuming. He could have presented expert testimony to Czolgosz's sanity, but he had fallen prey to his own cleverness. He knew that the psychological experts for the defense believed that Czolgosz was sane and responsible, so he never bothered to prepare a rebuttal for an insanity defense. He did not foresee that Lewis would try to make an insanity plea by rhetoric alone. As Dr. Hurd explained later, Penney knew "the defense was unable to offer evidence of any kind, including insanity." Under these circumstances, "the District Attorney did not feel called upon to introduce his experts." Nor could he now call Hurd or the other alienists nominally standing for the defense without the consent of the accused.[30] Penney could show no expert testimony as to the sanity of the accused, and had simply to sit as Lewis waxed eloquent on the defendant's right to mercy.

"The law presumes this man is innocent of this crime," Lewis piously reminded the jury, then slyly went on to extend the presumption of innocence into a presumption of criminal insanity: "and we start, in investigating this case, with the assumption that for some reason or other he is not responsible for the act which he performed on that day." Now Penney was really worried, enough to make a note for the judge's charge to the jury, to refute this contention. For if the presumption of innocence meant a presumption of irresponsibility, the burden of proof would have fallen on the prosecution to demonstrate the defendant's sanity.

Indeed, Lewis went further in just this direction, arguing that the shooting itself provided a prima facie case for Czolgosz's madness: "Death is a spectre that we all dislike to meet, and here this defendant, without having any animosity against our President, without any motive, so far as we can see, personal motive, we find him going into this building, in the presence of these hundreds of people, and committing an act which, if he was sane, must cause his death. Now, could a man, with sane mind, perform such an act?"[31]

Nor was Lewis finished making his argument for a verdict of not guilty by reason of insanity. He pressed further, to ask the jury if everyone would not be happier if it turned out Czolgosz was insane. "If it can be that you find this defendant was not responsible for this crime . . . you would aid in uplifting a great cloud off from the hearts and minds of the people of this country and of the world." For anarchist terrorism was an international threat, and if an American President was to join the Spanish prime minister, the French president, the Hapsburg empress, and the Italian king in the ranks of those who had fallen victim to its black hand, then the chill of fear would deepen upon the civilized peoples. But if the assassin was mad, then the killing was an incident of fate. "If our beloved President had met with a railroad accident coming here to our city and had been killed, we should all regret very much, we should mourn over the loss of such a just man, but our grief would not compare to the grief that we have now . . . But if you could find that he met his fate by the act of an insane man, it would amount to the same as though he met it accidentally."[32]

With that, Lewis had finished the course of his argument. The old rhetorician concluded with an encomium to his fellow Republican, the fallen President, and sat down. It had proven so brilliant a performance that his colleague Titus decided not to give the speech he had prepared, and let the defense rest.

The district attorney rose to counter Lewis's speech. It was, he conceded, "a remarkable exhibition of feelings." But, he insisted doggedly, the state had proved its case. The defendant had shot the President, who died as a consequence. Moreover, he continued, "We have shown you, by witnesses who have been called to the stand, the admissions of this defendant concerning his premeditation and deliberation, for how long a period he had thought about this awful crime, where he was born and educated and where he got the seeds of this terrible deed in his heart." Indeed, Penney repeated, if there was anything wrong with the defendant at all it was with the seat of his compassion, not of his reason: "anarchistic and socialistic meetings" had "embedded in his diseased heart the seeds of this awful crime." Penney conceded the benefits of a system in which even such a villain should have a trial, but now that he had had one, it was time to address the needs of the heart: "I am convinced, if I never was before, that there is such a thing as a national heart, and that that great national heart is broken and it will take God's own time and God's own way to heal it, such a great calamity has been brought about." And now, to deliver the coup de grâce, he turned on the defendant:

> Brought by what? By this instrument [pointing to defendant] of an awful class of people that have come to our shores, a class of people that must be taught, that should be taught and shall be taught that it is entirely foreign to our laws, to our institutions and to the laws and institutions that evolved such a man as William McKinley that they have no place upon our shores, that if they cannot conform to our laws and our institutions, then they must go hence and keep forever from us; that they will not be permitted to come here, to stay here to educate themselves into the notion that they can take the life of any individual irrespective of consequences.[33]

As himself a member of a class of people only recently arrived on these shores and educated into American law, Penney knew just how Americans talked about immigrants. With a further brief oration on the majesty of the law, he rested.

Judge White then delivered his charge to the jury, covering the elements of murder in the first and second degree, manslaughter, and, finally, legal insanity: "If he was laboring under such a defect of reason as not to know the nature and the quality of the act that he was doing or that it was wrong, it is your duty, Gentlemen of the Jury, to acquit him in this case." White several times used this phrase, direct from the M'Naghten case, as a routine element of the charge, and concluded.

Penney stood to make a request. "I ask your Honor to charge the Jury that the law presumes every individual sane." Suddenly there was confusion.

"Just a moment," White said.

"I ask your Honor to charge the Jury that the law presumes every person sane," Penney repeated.

"The law in this case presumes that the defendant was sane," White said.

But Penney was not satisfied and pressed White to yield him a further advantage. "I ask your Honor to charge the Jury that the burden of overthrowing the presumption of sanity and of showing insanity is upon the person who alleges it."

"The burden of showing insanity is upon the person who alleges it," White said. "Is that all?"

Now Titus was on his feet. "You do not want that charged in that way?"

The New York State Court of Appeals had ruled five years before that to charge a jury that the burden of proof was upon the defendant in an insanity defense "is prejudicial to the defendant and constitutes reversible error."[34] Titus knew this; Penney probably did, too. Penney immediately granted that it be struck out of the record—but he had said it in front of the jury.

White tried finally to set straight the charge by correctly summing up the law in all its nuances. "The burden in the first place, Gentlemen of the Jury, upon that proposition is with the defendant to give some evidence tending to show insanity on his part, or irresponsibility; but in that connection, when evidence of that kind is given, if it is given at all, it is incumbent on the People to rebut or meet it with other evidence and"—here White stumbled—"remove all doubt in your minds—all reasonable doubt in your minds upon the subject."

Upon this slip as to the nature of doubt, Titus was petitioning the bench again. "I did not intend to ask your Honor to charge anything before the counsel got up to request your Honor to charge, but I now ask your Honor to charge that if the Jury are satisfied from all the evidence in the case that at the time of the committing of this assault he was laboring under such a defect of reason as not to know the quality of the act he was doing or not to know the act was wrong, that then he is not responsible and they must acquit him."

White had grown tired of the effort to get the charge right. "I so charge. I intended to make it very plain to the Jury in the first place."[35] At that, the jury were allowed to retire. Nobody expected them to be long. When impaneled they had all announced a prejudice toward the defendant's guilt—though each allowed "his opinion could be removed by reasonable evidence."[36] They returned within twenty-five minutes with a guilty verdict. Sentencing was set for two days hence.

On that Thursday morning, September 26, Judge White permitted Leon Czolgosz to speak briefly: "I would like to say this much; that the crime was committed by no one else but me; no one told me to do it and I never told anybody to do it."[37] White, addressing the prisoner simply as "Czolgosz," sentenced him to death in a month, omitting even a perfunctory request for God's mercy on his soul, and ordered the prisoner removed.

That same day the Edison Company released to the public a series of films showing McKinley's burial in the Westlawn Cemetery at Canton, Ohio. After the funeral train went to Washington and the President lay in state at the Capitol, the train headed for McKinley's hometown. Edison dotted Canton with its cameras, showing the military honor guard parading past the Canton Hardware Company and the cortege entering the cemetery. But Edison was proudest to show the public the face of the principal consequence of Czolgosz's crime: President Theodore Roosevelt, a man far too entertaining and unpredictable ever to have headed the Republican ticket in the normal course of events, brought to the leadership only by an assassination—and who had never before been filmed at such close range. It was the start of Theodore Roosevelt's years at the center of a camera lens. Even though he was a talkative man who knew the power of speech, he would from then on have to struggle to speak for himself, as so much would be said for and about him. Being a celebrity, as Roosevelt undeniably was, meant being a creature of hearsay.[38]

The cameras did not show the widowed Ida McKinley, whose hand the dying William had clutched, asking her to sing with him "Nearer My God to Thee." Mrs. William McKinley had not often appeared on film while her husband was alive, either: some disease or defect in her brain—the product of a complication of childbirth, or so they thought—made her prone to seizures. She would not touch visitors, and kept herself sedated. She would seize in the middle of dinners, and the President would softly drape a napkin over her head, hiding her from the company until the fit passed. As odd as it looked to some ob-servers, there was tenderness and tact in this treatment of the men-tally eccentric Ida, who would now lack such support. Without William there was nobody to speak for her, but everyone was happy enough to speak, and sing, in her behalf.

When Leon Czolgosz came to face his end, under the expert super-vision of Dr. MacDonald at Auburn State Prison, he uttered neither prayer nor imprecation, for his guards hurried him past the witnesses into the electric chair while he was still trying to say his last words. "I shot the President because I thought it would help the working peo-ple, and for the sake of the common people. I am not sorry for my crime," he said as they marched him along. Then they sat him in the chair, and he said, "That is all I have to say." But as they tightened the straps on his head and chin, so that his last sentence was, one witness said, "mumbled rather than spoken," he continued, "I am awfully sorry because I did not see my father."[39] And then he did not speak again for himself, except through the hearsay testimony of witnesses to his life and death. Nor could even his remains bear witness, for after au-topsy they were buried, and then—taking a measure that had been de-veloped and tested specifically to get rid of Czolgosz's remains as quickly as possible—the jailers poured a carboy of sulfuric acid upon the body, dissolving it swiftly into the earth.[40]

3

DESCENT

THE INVESTIGATORS

In the genteel Boston suburb of Brookline, the news of Czolgosz's execution stirred an uncharacteristic flurry of concern that disturbed the sanitarium of the taciturn Dr. Walter Channing. Channing, an eminent alienist who ranked among the psychologists who attributed insanity to a variety of causes—listing "heredity, want, domestic anxiety or affliction, business cares, over education," in his catalogue[1]—returned in November 1901 from a year's stay in Europe to find his hospital a hive of nerves. The young Dr. Lloyd Vernon Briggs, whom Channing employed to oversee his Brookline patients during his vacation, had spent the year increasing the inmates' activity and exercise on the principle that vigor would dispel mind-clouding vapors. The experiment succeeded to a degree, but it also excited the asylum to an unaccustomed pitch of enthusiasm. This buzz of freshly cheerful neurasthenics combined with the newly arrived Czolgosz autopsy report from Auburn State Prison to irritate Channing's even sensibilities, and he looked with alarm and increasing heat at the state of his once-peaceful affairs. With a Yankee economy of motion, he decided on a single course of action that would salve both sources of his trouble: he would send Briggs away on a trip—to gather evidence for his own postmortem of the Czolgosz case.

The autopsy report that so incensed Channing had been leaked ahead of publication, and rumors of its conclusions permeated the psychological profession. At long last it appeared in print in all the major journals of insanity, asserting that Czolgosz belonged exclusively to the courts, and not to the alienists at all. The report affirmed that the state of New York, in the persons of Dr. Carlos MacDonald and Dr. Edward A. Spitzka (the son of MacDonald's friend and colleague Edward C. Spitzka), oversaw the execution of Leon Czolgosz on October 29, 1901, and determined from an examination of his corpse that he bore no physical sign of insanity—no lesions or tumors in the brain, no evidence of syphilis. But the alienists examining Czolgosz had time only to consult his statement, interview him briefly on their own, and search his body for the "stigmata of degeneration"[2] after death. They had not been able, nor perhaps had they been inclined, to take a full family history, nor did they examine the circumstances of his upbringing. They had not therefore looked into either the environmental or the hereditary factors that psychologists agreed could also cause insanity. Channing, who had argued in the Guiteau case— to no avail—that the assassin was mad and therefore irresponsible, believed Czolgosz offered him a fine chance for vindication. With this controversial report before him, Channing assigned Briggs to conduct a fuller investigation of Czolgosz's background, foregrounding what the official inquiry had left out and paying special attention to environmental and familial factors.

Between them, Channing and Briggs represented the two major factions of progressive thought at the turn of the twentieth century, and the difference between their opinions reflected the difference between their family trees. The alienist Dr. Walter Channing was the son of the essayist William Ellery Channing and the great-nephew of the minister William Ellery Channing, founder of Unitarianism. His grandfather had been Dr. Walter Channing before him, and had begun practicing medicine in Boston in 1812, when the republic was just gaining its true independence. Through the luck of getting sons by well-born wives, the family comprised the main line of descent among the Boston Channings, born leaders of church and community.

They belonged to a little group of well-off Boston families who had created the city's great public institutions—and yet, despite making them for the public, believed deep down that they owned them. As one minister said in a eulogy for the elder Dr. Channing, these good families bore proud responsibility for the city's "good institutions, institutions of education, of religion . . . its beautiful common, its public library, its churches and schools, its hospitals and charities." They regarded these institutions rather as they might regard a familial trust, a bequest begot of their liberal Christianity, intended for the use of their fellow men yet still within their control.[3] And the younger Dr. Channing's sanitarium in Brookline was also such an institution, as was the Boston State Hospital, on whose board he was pleased to serve. People of Walter Channing's class looked after the ill and the indigent, whose misfortune it was their birthright to allay.

Channing's class of Bostonians occasionally opened its ranks to talented, like-minded, and ambitious members of society, and kept their eyes out for meritorious up-and-comers. So Channing had taken on an ambitious, but chronically unlucky, case in Lloyd Vernon Briggs. Channing gave Briggs work as a physician and tutor to his sons. Like Channing, Briggs came from a family fond of namesakes— he was the son of Lloyd Briggs and would one day be the father of Lloyd Briggs—but his interest in continuing the family name and heritage was born of aspiration, whereas Channing's was born of tradition. Channing was by birth what Briggs desperately hoped to become through effort.

Briggs's father, Lloyd Briggs, Sr., of the small seacoast town of Scituate, Massachusetts, trained as an engineer and worked in the Charlestown Navy Yard. Having married for love rather than money, he switched careers so he could make a better salary as a bank teller in Boston. He had made some headway in this line of work when sickness struck his children and he had to move out of town for their health. Despite this move, the Briggses' eldest child, Hattie, died of consumption in 1879, and when the youngest, Lloyd, Jr., came down with a bloody cough the following year, the family swiftly sentenced him to a healthful exile as a shipmate on a Pacific-bound ship. They could not afford to pay his way, and so at the age of sixteen he became a middle-class jack-of-all-talents, trying his hand at whatever would help him earn his keep.

In seeking healthier air, the younger Briggs found a dangerous life on the American frontier. Having studied some medicine aboard the ship, he became a circuit-riding smallpox fighter in Hawaii, traveling with a police escort to forcibly vaccinate the native population, immunizing them (whether they wanted it or not) from the disease the Europeans had brought. Returning to the mainland, he witnessed the last phases of the Apache wars in Arizona, and observed how "the Indian method of waging war in these mountain fastnesses made it difficult to suppress them by civilized military tactics"—and so the white men had adopted uncivilized tactics, and "outdid the savages in cruelty and treachery."[4] He worked a pecan farm in Georgia and labored with American blacks. He did business with the entirety of the American ethnic spectrum in New Orleans and San Antonio: the Sicilians and the Jews, the Spanish and the Indians—"every race of the earth . . . except perhaps the original Oceanicans," he wrote.[5] And he had treated them all and seen one or another of them casually murdered more than once.[6]

Briggs observed and wrote home about a vigorous, often violent, expanding civilization that was happy to assimilate people who would aid its growth, and completely careless of those who would not. And he saw, too, how life on the edges of America changed life at its center, noting how even staid old Boston had filled with immigrants from the South Pacific, southern and eastern Europe, and the Southern states, darkening the complexions of its streets, enriching its marketplaces, and sometimes making the city more dangerous. Mankind in motion carried with it ideas, diseases, species—and he had seen snakes and microbes and crime transplanted the world over. Briggs knew the specific details of the America that Theodore Roosevelt spoke about in general principles—it was no longer a slow-moving farming republic, half of it given over to the rigid caste system of African slavery. It had become a humming, busy home to a mix of migrants on the make, who in their hasty zeal would overrun you if you did not keep pace or get out of the way. By the time Briggs took up a residency with Channing on Boylston Street in Brookline, he had seen America at its borders and its center, and knew what kinds of peoples teemed throughout it.

With such different experiences behind them, the two men thought differently about American society. When Channing, heir to a family tradition of Boston civic virtue, thought about helping the poor, the sick, the people who had the bad luck to be born somehow (or even just somewhere) different from him, he thought in terms of making them comfortable in their circumstances—not so much of changing those circumstances. By contrast, Briggs, who had worked hand-to-mouth since the age of sixteen, saw the immigrant poor, the sick and the mad, the hustlers and the hooligans simply as other climbers who started lower on the ladder than he, and needed only enough help so they could gain an equal footing. Channing sympathized with the disadvantaged; Briggs empathized with them.

Both of them believed that Americans who had money and education should help those who did not. Dedication to this principle made them progressives, and pitted them against the conservatives who opposed government regulation and social reformism. But they differed on the question of ultimate social equality. Channing never expected the poor to rise, the immigrant to attain the respectability of the Boston-born, or the truly sick ever to heal—whereas Briggs did. But for the time being, like progressives in both the Democratic and Republican Parties, they shared the impulse to help, somehow, those who otherwise received no help at all.

The great talent of Theodore Roosevelt as a progressive leader lay in his ability to argue both sides of this progressive debate. Roosevelt also was the namesake of his father, Theodore Roosevelt, descended from a long, rich line of Dutch Calvinist New Yorkers, and he believed himself obliged by virtue of his social position to do something for those less fortunate than he. But for his own reasons, he had in his youth given up some of his comforts, and he sought the firsthand experience of American hardship, working ranches in the West and doing battle as a soldier in 1898. He did know, even if in only a small way, what it was like to struggle. He had both sympathy and empathy for the trodden-upon. Like the Channings, he pitied the lesser classes while holding them slightly in contempt—hence his enthusiasm for the imaginary possibility of doing away with them altogether. But like the Briggses, he knew what it was like to work hard and to fear that he might not get what he wanted out of life. It took both aspects of his character to make him an effective progressive Republican, just as it took both Channing and Briggs to make a case that would persuade progressive psychologists as to Leon Czolgosz's insanity.

The defining factor that divided these types of progressives was race. Americans at the turn of the century did not use the idea of race simply to differentiate white from black, but to denote national difference as well—to them, the French were a different race from the English, who in turn differed from the Germans, and so forth. The American race (for those who, like Roosevelt, believed in one) was an amalgam of European strains, beset from the beginning by its sin of African slavery. The presence of blacks from the beginning of American history did not, for Roosevelt, make them part of this American race; the blood barrier that historically separated black from white defined an all but ineradicable imagined racial difference. But he held out the possibility that other European peoples might successfully become part of an American race, if they took part in the American experience—settling the West, civilizing nature, and building a new democracy. Other Americans, like Channing, were not so sure, and looked on people like Czolgosz as altogether and irrevocably foreign.

The Polish diphthongs of Czolgosz's name helped Americans identify him, usually with relief, as utterly alien. In the week after McKinley's murder, a Buffalo citizen named Chauncey Weatherwax wrote the *Evening News* that "we are pleased to know the Assassin is not an American."[7] Such opinions were not limited to New Yorkers with comically English names. The *Journal of the American Medical Association* described the shooter as "a man . . . who, thank God, bears a name that can not be mistaken for that of an American."[8] Even decades after the murder, a historian could blithely remark that "Americans had difficulty pronouncing Leon Czolgosz's name." To be sure, some Americans did, but not those thousands who, like Czolgosz, belonged to families from eastern Europe.[9]

Born a citizen in Michigan, Czolgosz was an American. Under the Constitution, he was eligible to be elected president, whereas, for example, an immigrant like Buffalo D.A. Thomas Penney was not. What made him seem un-American was the indelible taint of race in the sound of his name. And his alienation from American society, as well as his consequential action, helped cement a change in public language about national origin and race. Afterward, and throughout the earlier decades of the twentieth century, the violent, politically active immigrant joined and to an extent displaced the violent, politically active African-American as the foremost racial threat to American society.

Under Roosevelt, the Republicans would begin to awaken to this change. Sometimes they would act as if they believed immigrants suffered from nature and other times as if they suffered from nurture, but they were constantly and increasingly concerned with the place of immigrant workers in the expanding American order, and correspondingly eager to ignore the fate of African-Americans. Through one of the gaps in the record of Czolgosz's trial gleams a vivid illustration of this critical shift in their attentions.

THE NEGRO WHO SAVED McKINLEY

A white man kills a white man, and white men arrest, try, and execute him: and yet, despite the evident absence of race as a factor in McKinley's murder, it runs throughout the story. Again, it comes to a question of what does not appear in the official record. Like all the compelling evidence for and against Czolgosz's madness, it lies just underneath a rough spot in the straight story.

In his testimony at trial, Secret Service agent George Foster was embarrassed to admit that while guarding the President from the fairgoers he had passed over Czolgosz to focus on "a dark complexioned man with a black moustache." As he told Titus during cross-examination, seeing a "colored man" made him suspicious. "Why?" Titus asked. "I didn't like his general appearance," the agent replied. So while the white, good-looking murderer advanced on the President, Foster was motioning to his colleague to keep an eye on the darker man—whom, he said, he lost track of afterward. "I never saw no colored man in the whole fracas," he told Titus.

Foster's testimony contradicted the Secret Service's initial state-

"A dark complexioned man with a black moustache"— James Parker, the hero who saved the President, in a portrait published in the *Savannah Tribune.*

ments to the press and eyewitness testimony to the shooting. Far from posing a threat to the President, the black man had saved him from a third bullet. During the week that McKinley clung to life and seemed to improve, the suspicious swarthy man with a mustache enjoyed a hero's acclaim for his actions: "brave Jim Parker" was the "colored defender" who saved the President's life.[10]

The day after the shooting, Secret Service agent Samuel Ireland released to the press his version of events. Agent Ireland, who had been standing just in front of the President and next to agent Foster before the shooting, issued an extensive statement to reporters explaining the moment-by-moment details of the assault. Just as the President's handlers were making ready to bring the event to a close, the organist in the Temple of Music had halted in playing a program of J. S. Bach. Two shots rang out from a gun held by a youthful, inoffensive-looking assassin. And, Ireland said, immediately "the big negro standing just in back of him, and who would have been next to take the President's hand, struck the young man in the neck with one hand and with the other reached for the revolver." Parker's blow knocked Czolgosz onto the floor, but did not stun him: the assailant spun around and "tried to discharge the revolver, but before he could get it pointed at the President it was knocked from his hand by the negro."[11]

James B. "Big Jim" Parker became an instant hero. Excited bystanders told reporters how swiftly and bravely the big man acted. "He hit the murderer a smash in the nose and he went down," one said.[12] Parker himself related his story to reporters, modestly at first, and then with increasing pleasure in the attention. In the days after the attack, crowds of citizens and visitors gathered in clots in Buffalo's public spaces. In an era before radio, people hungry for information jammed the streets in front of telegraph and newspaper offices and in the city's open squares, seeking news of the investigation and a chance to share their emotions and experiences. Wherever Parker went, they recognized him and pressed him for his story. Caught by a group in the street four days after the episode, he told how he had hit the assassin and tackled him, bearing him to the floor with the weight of his body—with, indeed, the very waistcoat he was now wearing. Onlookers begged for a piece of the historic vest. When he gave one, but balked at giving more, someone offered twenty-five cents for a piece, which he sold. A richer bidder offered a dollar for a button, and Parker sold it, too. No sooner had he auctioned off the heroic garment than he was fending off bids for his shoes, with which he had kicked the killer. A reporter for the *Washington Evening Star*, who observed this episode, remarked that though Parker stood six foot six, "if Parker had been twenty feet tall with a waistcoat reaching from his chin to his toes, with buttons on it every inch of the way, the supply would not have been sufficient to the demand."[13] In the tense uncertainty that followed the assassination attempt, Parker gave Americans what they needed—a hero who could think and act while others stood paralyzed.

And in all the attention, neither Parker nor the press could let Americans forget his race. When a woman admirer begged him for a lock of his hair, "Parker laughed and said he could not give her a lock, but he might be willing to spare a kink."[14] He was not merely a hero, but (as the *Washington Bee*, an African-American newspaper, reported) heir to "the line of black heroes" stretching from Simon the Cyrenian, who bore the cross at Calvary, to the buffalo soldiers of the Spanish-American War.[15] However little he shared with the Africans of the first century, Jim Parker shared a great common experience with African-Americans of his generation: born and bred in the South, he moved to a harder job in the North to escape the violence and race-hatred of the newly segregated states.

The Parkers, "respectable" slave parents, gave birth to their son James in about 1856. Jim Parker knew slavery only in his childhood. After emancipation, he attended schools that the federal Freedmen's Bureau established in the postwar South as part of Reconstruction, the abortive effort to rebuild the seceded states and eradicate the stain of slavery. For twelve years after the war's end, the U.S. Army remained stationed in Southern states, charged with keeping order. In the late 1860s and early 1870s, under orders from President Grant, U.S. soldiers stamped out the Ku Klux Klan, which would not return until the 1910s. They watched over polling places and, as best they could, enforced the citizenship and voting-rights provisions of the new Fourteenth and Fifteenth Constitutional Amendments and the Civil Rights Acts of 1866 and 1875. And they stood as guarantors of the new black citizens' rights to attend school, mingle in public, and take part in the civic life of their country. As a consequence, during those dozen years, the blacks of the South could vote and hold office—a right that African-Americans would all but lose after the U.S. government gave up reconstructing the South, after which the army withdrew, leaving white Southerners to their own devices. Jim Parker grew up a citizen in this occupied South, partly sheltered by the law and the U.S. Army from his white neighbors.

He benefited directly from Reconstruction after leaving school, too. In the nineteenth century, the federal government could influence local life most easily by dispensing post office jobs. Republican Presidents seeking to give hope and a living to their African-American constituents in the South freely gave postmasterships to black partisans, who in turn hired the members of their community they most trusted. It was a time-honored method of building local loyalty to a national party. It had worked for the Democrats throughout the earlier part of the century; now it was the Republicans' turn to try.

Jim Parker, a sound Georgia Republican, took a job as a letter carrier in Atlanta. And true to pattern for Southern blacks during Reconstruction, the postal service opened the door to regular politics for Parker: he was elected constable of Savannah a few years later. As a lawman in the South, he stood on the militarized lines between blacks and whites, Republicans and Democrats. As constable of the Fourth Militia District, he stood for civil order in a tense region of the country still at war with itself, occupied by an invading force from within. As a powerful black man in government uniform, he stood as a powerful symbol: a "lion hearted, big fisted Savannah man," he represented the full loyalty of blacks to the Union; "The Negro is always 'in it,' " his hometown newspaper, the *Savannah Tribune*, trumpeted after Parker downed Czolgosz. "The life of our chief magistrate was saved by a Negro. No other class of citizens is more loyal to this country than the Negro."[16]

And yet, despite his loyalty, despite his strength and success, despite the reelection of McKinley in 1900 and the continued federal ascendance of the Republican Party, Parker dropped his constabulary, left his uniform and his hometown behind, and moved north to Buffalo in 1901 to work in the service trade—which was how he came to the Exposition. That summer the former lawman had found work as a waiter in the Plaza Restaurant in the fairgrounds. He took the afternoon off to shake McKinley's hand, and would have had shortly to return to the routine of waiting tables for the clientele of the Pan-American Exposition. As to why he should have left a respected job in government for a position in menial service, the press recorded only a curt mention of "offensive partisanship."[17] The partisanship of turn-of-the-century Georgia—and, indeed, the rest of the South—was a simple matter of whites wresting from blacks what little political power and dignity they had gained during Reconstruction. Jim Parker's actions in Buffalo made him a singular man, but in other respects he was a statistic: one of over 180,000 African-Americans who left Georgia and the other South Atlantic states in the 1890s, one of almost 91,000 who had settled in New York and the mid-Atlantic region in the same period. From the end of Reconstruction through the First World War, over half a million blacks would leave those states

for points north and west, like Jim Parker leaving behind their home-
towns for uncertain futures in low-paying jobs. But they made their
decisions in the light of cold logic. They wanted to stay out of another
grimmer statistical column: the growing number of blacks lynched in
the slow-burning race war of the late-nineteenth-century South. According to the numbers kept by the Tuskegee Institute, a black man
was lynched in America (mainly, though not exclusively, in the states
of the former Confederacy) on average once every three days. Black
men who posed a challenge to the notion of Negro inferiority—big,
strong black men used to freedom, who came of age in an era after
slavery, who appeared out of place—were the most likely targets of
mob hanging, burning, and mutilation. No wonder, then, that Jim
Parker put down his pride with his badge and uniform and went north
to put on a servant's livery. Better by far to serve, even if it meant
standing and waiting tables, than to swing.

REPUBLICANS, RACE, AND REGION

The Tuskegee reports on lynching comprised only part of that institution's influence in the 1890s and early 1900s. The Institute's director,
Booker T. Washington, became a prominent black figure in 1895 owing to his speech at another exposition—this one in Atlanta—and in
the six years since he had become an indispensable resource to the Republican Party. By the time of McKinley's murder in 1901 he had risen
to such eminence that he was the first and only person Theodore Roosevelt wrote to on the day he took the oath of office. "I must see you
as soon as possible," the new President said.[18] Just a month later, Roosevelt's dinner with Washington at the White House wiped the Czolgosz death watch out of the nation's headlines. Southern newspapers
like the Memphis *Commercial Appeal* believed by inviting a black man
to dine at the Executive Mansion the President had committed "a
blunder that is worse than a crime." Roosevelt expressed sadness
and—he said—surprise at the reaction. But as Booker T. Washington
himself noted, Roosevelt had planned a political strategy for the

South many years before the McKinley assassination, and nothing about the peculiar region would have surprised him. And in the 1890s, with populist anger inflaming its depression-wracked farmers and with whites waging a partisan and race war against blacks, the South in general and Georgia in particular had become increasingly important to Republican presidential hopefuls.

Georgia preyed on Mark Hanna's mind as he contemplated the math of making McKinley President in 1896. When Hanna announced his retirement from business in 1895, he declared the Ohio winters too severe for his constitution, and leased a vacation house in Thomasville, Georgia, for five years—just long enough to last him through the next two presidential elections. And on his first seasonal sojourn in Thomasville he was joined by his friend Governor McKinley, also suddenly drawn to the healthful airs of Georgia.

The men basked in the sun parlor of the once-quiet cottage, receiving a stream of visitors whom Hanna had invited by twos and threes, booking a solid schedule of Southern hospitality. The latewinter sun gently lit their high foreheads, whose genial expressions betrayed no anxious cunning. But Hanna and McKinley knew that much depended on this vacation. They were campaigning as hard as they decently could for the Southern vote in the party's upcoming presidential nominating convention. When their friend and coplotter H. H. Kohlsaat visited the Thomasville headquarters, he was impressed with the effect of McKinley's winning manner on the Southern visitors, recalling, "I think, without exception, they were delighted with the governor, and pledged him their support in 1896, and most of them kept that pledge."[19] McKinley earned his warm winter, walking away from Thomasville with the Southern delegations in his pocket. Try though they might, his challengers could not shake his hold on the South at the convention.

As the journalist Herbert Croly wrote afterward about the sunroom campaign, "No color line was drawn. Negroes as well as white men were introduced to the amiable Mr. McKinley."[20] But it was not the black visitors who should have surprised anyone. Black Southerners had been loyal Republicans for a generation. It was the whites who were a novelty, and their fresh interest in the Republican Party would threaten to reshape the racial canvas and regional calculus of electoral politics.

The Republican stronghold of the Northeast and Middle West stood fast through most of the late nineteenth century. There the American people had settled in their densest thousands, there they lived along rivers, there they trafficked in the raw and finished materials of new industry, and there they opposed slavery and all that went with it—including its voracious consumption of land for plantation agriculture rather than settlement, a habit that had left the South comparatively underpopulated. This distribution of the citizenry meant the Northern states of the East and West could win the electoral college for a President without a single Southern vote, and when a sectional issue—slavery—divided North from South, this was precisely what happened. Abraham Lincoln became President without a single Southern state's electoral support, and so the Civil War came. The Republican Party preserved this reliable political pattern in the decades that followed, carrying the Northeast and Middle West against the traditionally Democratic South.

Yet the Republicans had a loyal, though dwindling, Southern constituency: African-Americans still clinging hopefully to the party of Lincoln and emancipation. Come the November elections they could do little for Republicans; legal disfranchisement and the terror tactics of segregation rendered them so small a proportion of Southern voters that they could never, by themselves, carry a Southern state for a presidential candidate. After the advent of disfranchisement techniques, Southern black turnout in general elections dropped from Reconstruction-era highs of 85 percent to the single digits. But in the presidential primary season, Southern blacks stood a chance of attracting the courtly attentions of Republican statesmen, who needed to woo delegations for the party's nominating convention. So every four years, hopeful Republicans would spend part of the humid spring and summer canvassing blacks in enemy states below the Mason-Dixon line, piously condemning Jim Crow and lynching and dispensing federal jobs with an open hand to loyal black Republicans of the South. To nurture their nomination hopes, they had to woo the party faithful by twisting the noses of Southern whites (who would never vote for a Republican President anyway) and so keep the sectional resentment of the Civil War smoldering.

But during that winter of 1895, McKinley and Hanna discovered an anger among conservative Southern whites at the populist radicals who controlled the state's Democratic Party and had won the Georgia legislature, making laws that favored the poor and disfranchised of the state, regulating and taxing business, and even establishing a college for the education of blacks. White businessmen of Georgia wanted the support of a party that would oppose such regulation and taxation—a party like the Republican Party—as long as it would also allow them to preserve white supremacy.

McKinley listened to the so-called lily-white Republicans with the avidity that only a candidate for the presidency could muster for such minor sectional machinations. The lily-whites were yet so few they could not sway an election, but they might increase in number. And the possibility of preserving white supremacy without offending loyal black Republicans suddenly seemed possible after Booker T. Washington's speech at Atlanta in 1895. As head of the Tuskegee Institute, Washington had lobbied Congress for the money to support an exposition in the South, arguing it could showcase the possibility of good feeling between the races. When the Atlanta Exposition planners decided a separate Negro Building at the fair should demonstrate the progress made by blacks since Reconstruction, they turned to Washington to deliver a speech at its opening. As a white Alabama farmer said to him, "I am afraid you have got yourself into a tight place"—to address "the Northern whites, the Southern whites, and the Negroes all together" while offending none posed no small challenge. Washington met it by proposing what became known as the Atlanta Compromise—that whites should support blacks in their struggle for economic independence as they learned trade and industry, and in return blacks would not challenge the political or social order of Jim Crow: "In all things that are purely social we can be as separate as the fingers, yet one as the hand in all things essential to mutual progress."[21]

In casting Southern blacks as social conservatives, Washington pointed his finger at the true racial threat: "those of foreign birth and strange tongue and habits." Immigrants coming into the country posed the greatest threat to blacks wishing to move from their traditional rural occupations into modern industry. By embracing a compromise between whites and blacks, Washington wanted to slam the door on any other race's inclusion in the America that was to come. "In the future, in our humble way, we shall stand by you with a devotion that no foreigner can approach."[22]

The racial compromise Washington offered at Atlanta provided a formula Southern whites could use in the 1896 campaign and after as they waged a battle for McKinley. J. F. Hanson, a white textile manufacturer of Macon, Georgia, argued that "the Negro is not a socialist, he is not an anarchist, he is not an enemy of property, or capital, or money"—unlike, Hanson believed, "the forces for whom the Democratic platform speaks." Thomas Ivory, the chairman of the Republican State Committee of McKinley Clubs of Georgia, argued that in seeking the free coinage of silver, the Democrats represented not only an economic but a racial threat far beyond that posed by Southern blacks. "To us, who pin our faith to gold it is a consolation to know that our allies are the white races of the world. The mongrel races alone have silver for a standard," he warned—to adopt silver would mean joining the miscegenated peoples of the earth, while standing with loyal Southern blacks for gold and Republicanism meant continuing racial segregation.[23]

The invention of a Republican black-and-white coalition standing for conservatism against a combined economic and social threat posed by mongrel races could not, in the end, stand against the routine corruption of Southern electoral politics—but it came close. In the "solemn farce" that was the Georgia vote count of 1896, Bryan beat McKinley 94,672 to 60,091—the closest a Republican would ever come to winning the Peach State between Reconstruction and the civil rights era. McKinley had done especially well in Atlanta, where he took over 40 percent of the vote.[24]

The overall pattern of the 1896 election underscored McKinley's determination to win some piece of the South. For though the Republicans handily carried the electoral vote with their customary wins in the densely settled states, Bryan had carried more states outright than McKinley, and owned a broad swath through the country's heartland, taking the South, the mountain and prairie West, and Washington state, as well as garnering one elector from California's split delegation. The map stood as a warning to McKinley that he had to regain either the South or the West, and, encouraged by the cooperative racial conservatism of Booker T. Washington and the growing economic conservatism of white Southern businessmen, he looked fondly on the possibility of winning in Dixie.

But the black-white coalition of Southerners, strong against Bryan and foreign radicalism in electoral battle, could not easily survive the strains imposed by success. McKinley soon found himself embroiled in the partisan squabbles that Big Jim Parker had found so offensive. Loyal blacks suited conservative whites as fellow voters, but when McKinley followed tradition and appointed blacks to postmasterships, he met the usual racist protest from his erstwhile white supporters, and the Southern conservatives fell to bitter sniping at the President's behaving like a Republican. The Atlanta Journal sniffily editorialized, "He has not befriended the black man by this unwise policy and he has lost the confidence and respect of a large majority of the whites."[25]

The splendid little war of 1898 provided McKinley with one last, golden chance to press his suit for the white South as ardently as he could. For the first time in fifty years, Southern and Northern whites had borne arms against a common enemy, and the President seized the moment for reconciliation. In December 1898, he returned to Atlanta to address the state legislature. The President of the United States and veteran of the Union army wore a gray badge in his lapel to signal sympathy for the old Confederacy. He left the climax of his speech for a surprise, and it came as a shock to white and black listeners alike:

> Every soldier's grave made during our unfortunate Civil War is a tribute to American valor, and the time has now come, in the evolution of sentiment and feeling under the Providence of God, when in the spirit of fraternity we should share with you in the care of graves of the Confederate soldiers.

Convulsive applause seized the audience as if it would not let them go.[26]

It was a brief love affair, but it cost him the unstinting loyalty of his black constituency. In the election of 1900, the African Methodist Episcopal bishop Henry McNeal Turner of Georgia declared he would vote for Bryan "five times before I would vote for William McKinley once." Even apart from such disillusionment, the machinations of white supremacists working to disfranchise blacks reduced turnout and Republican counts throughout the South, and Georgia was no exception. McKinley took only 35,832 votes to Bryan's 81,700. The rest of the South went likewise for the Democrat even as the country restored McKinley to office. The President's diligent attentions to the South had failed to win the fickle white vote and had alienated the faithful black vote.[27]

Falling heir to this Southern mess, Theodore Roosevelt knew precisely what he needed to do. When Booker T. Washington went to the White House, he discovered there a coolheaded President unlikely to be surprised by Southern politics. Washington knew Roosevelt never acted without carefully planning his moves, and his Southern strategy was no exception.[28] The symbolic message of Washington's visit was clear, to Southerners both black and white: the new Republican President was not going to woo white supremacists of the South, but intended to restore usual relations with African-Americans through a socially conservative and politically shrewd leader. As the *Washington Bee* exulted, "In one fell swoop Mr. Roosevelt has smashed to smithereens" the hopes of Southern segregationists for his support.[29] On the other hand, the substantive message Roosevelt gave Washington was equally clear, and elements of this "clearly defined policy" appeared soon afterward in both black and white newspapers. Roosevelt "quite frankly . . . did not propose to appoint a large number of coloured people to office in any part of the South," Washington reported.[30] Instead he would, as the *Washington Bee* read the tea leaves, discipline upstart Southern Republicans by "the appointment of Gold Democrats" to office—and "whipping into line" remaining complainers who might, if they learned to behave, "receive a share of the plums by way of consolation."[31] Having neutralized the South, which he did not expect to win, Roosevelt could turn his attention to the West, whose enthusiasm for Bryan had lessened since 1896.

This decision reflected hardheaded political calculation, but it also suited Roosevelt's quirky personal convictions. Not only could Republicans more easily win the West than the South but, Roosevelt believed, the West represented a more plausible vision of America's racial future because it had a more typical American past. Alongside his career as politician, Roosevelt carried on a career as historian, in the course of which he published his six-volume *Winning of the West* in the early 1890s. Roosevelt's story of Americans' move west recapitulated a common tale of human history: the "submersion or displacement of an inferior race" by "a superior one." The conquest of the American natives meant, he allowed,

> the infliction and suffering of hideous woe and misery. It is a sad and dreadful thing that there should be of necessity such throes of agony and yet they are the birth-pangs of a new and vigorous people. That they are in truth birth-pangs does not lessen the grim and hopeless woe of the race supplanted; of the race outworn or overthrown. The wrongs done and suffered cannot be blinked. Neither can they be allowed to hide the results to mankind of what has been achieved.[32]

McKinley had looked at the South as the site of Americans' bloody national rebirth as a people; Roosevelt looked to the West. There, a "mixture of races" from Europe fought to wrest the land from the Indians, and in so doing became a new people, a strong hybrid "mixed race."[33] The hybridization of peoples in new territories "very clearly" produced "great men," Roosevelt believed—that was the lesson he suggested one might draw from the strength of polyglot New York (with its Dutch, English, French, German, and Irish) over merely Puritan Massachusetts.[34]

In romanticizing the American assimilation of new races, though, Roosevelt kept African-Americans to one side of the story. The South had a peculiar place in his understanding of American history, and the centuries Southerners spent locked in a deadly embrace with the sin of slavery kept them out of the tale of expansion and racial mixing. He preferred to leave alone that backward culture and its people, whom he suspected could handle themselves. "The Negro, unlike so many of the inferior races, does not dwindle away in the presence of the white man. He holds his own," Roosevelt observed, and in saying so he seemed to agree with Booker T. Washington's plans for African-American advancement.[35]

It was a deal Washington could make. Born into slavery in 1856, like Jim Parker he had known emancipation and Reconstruction, and he knew now that Jim Crow was the wave of the Southern future. But unlike Parker, Washington was prepared to swallow his pride publicly and maneuver within the framework of segregation. Indeed he preferred that the South be left out of the progressive plan for immigrant-fueled industrial expansion across the West. If the South was not roiled by a new racial mix, he believed whites might learn to live with blacks there and allow them to earn their economic independence.[36]

Though the new President and the former slave shared little, they shared this much: the notion that the South and its blacks could be left to themselves. Rather than antagonize Southern whites by pursuing patronage policies that tended provocatively to emphasize the social accomplishments of blacks, the Republican Party would appoint sound whites to government positions. Barring an occasional, often less than vigorous remonstrance that lynching really ought to cease, the national politicians would not meddle in local affairs. In focusing instead on what Roosevelt called "the process of assimilating, or as we should now say, of Americanizing, all foreign and non-English elements," the agreement between Washington and the new Administration allowed the immigrant to displace the black man as the object of white Americans' fear and hope alike.[37]

A LEGAL LYNCHING

On September 13, 1901, a week after the shooting, Jim Parker learned that the North did not differ too much from the South in its brutal partisanship, at least where black men were concerned. The morning

Tableau of McKinley's murder by the artist T. Dart Williams, ca. 1905. Note Williams's rendition of Jim Parker accosting Czolgosz: some Americans continued to believe in Parker's heroism long after the Secret Service tried to discredit it. (Library of Congress)

brought news of President McKinley's sudden turn for the worse. By that afternoon the President was dying. That evening, the Secret Service issued a statement repudiating Jim Parker's story and its own earlier description of the shooting.

Under the headline "Did Jim Parker Do It?" the *Washington Evening Star* reported that agent Foster, the Secret Service man who had been on the lookout for swarthy men with mustaches, now denied Parker's role in subduing Czolgosz. It was, Foster now said, an Irish-American soldier, Private Francis O'Brien, who had first reached the anarchist and disarmed him. There had been no black man involved in this tragedy; it was now a story about the children of immigrants—the villainous Polish anarchist and the heroic Irish soldier—the one hopelessly alien and the other loyally Americanized.[38] Foster repeated the same story at trial. Samuel Ireland, the Secret Service agent who first reported Parker's heroism, did not testify and so was spared having either to contradict his colleague's testimony or his own earlier statements.

Parker quite naturally took offense at this twist in the narrative, which took him out of the story altogether, though in subsequent interviews he did not express surprise that the white officers were taking credit for his work. Indeed, he seemed to have expected as much. When he spoke to a reporter from the *Savannah Tribune*, he told him bluntly, "The twenty thousand white people there ought not to have expected a nigger to do it all."[39]

Parker had hoped his fellow citizens might help him lynch Leon Czolgosz. "He only regrets he was not allowed to kill Czolgosz," the *Savannah Tribune* reported. "I wanted to cut his throat," Parker said, "but they took him from me . . . Some of them ought to have helped me kill him." And then, with an ominous confidence that other Southerners would have recognized, he bragged, "We would have fixed him quick in Georgia."[40]

White men of the South practiced lynching to terrify black men into submission. But the custom had the side effect of creating a general enthusiasm for the swift administration of community vengeance for real or imagined violations of the social order. Blacks could not lynch whites, but it was not unknown for black men to wield the rope against other black men—indeed, the Thursday before McKinley's death the *Washington Evening Star* happened to have carried a story headed "Negroes Lynch Negroes," reporting how representatives of the black community in Wycliffe, Kentucky, broke into a jail and hanged, without the interference of white officialdom, a group of black prisoners who had robbed and killed "an old and respected negro." They had thus restored a sense of social order. "Everything was quiet in Wycliffe today and the bodies of the men were still hanging at noon," the *Star* noted. It was not the perpetrators of an extralegal execution who made it a lynching; it was the victim, who had to be an outsider—preferably a racial one—identified as a threat to the social order.[41]

When Czolgosz fired on McKinley and then claimed—even as Parker was trying to cut his throat—that shooting the President was his duty, he identified himself as an enemy of the social order and thus a safely lynchable criminal. The reporters recognized the crowd's mood; they wrote that in the moments after the arrest "an attempt was made to lynch the prisoner, but the police succeeded in getting him out of the grounds."[42] Afterward a mob of citizens milled around police headquarters, shouting "Lynch the anarchist!" while the D.A. interrogated Czolgosz inside.[43] When the crowd tried to break into the jail, the police pushed them back and sent them off, but they gathered at a nearby intersection, where a speaker inveighed against anarchists, concluding with the shout "To No. 1 [police headquarters] and lynch him!" Echoing the cry, the citizens of Buffalo charged the police cordon once more, only to be repulsed again.[44]

The foul smell of a lynching in the offing drew Booker T. Washington to the Czolgosz case. Never insensitive to opportunity, Washington believed the situation offered a chance to compare one lawless danger—anarchism—with another—lynching. "I want to ask," he wrote in a widely reported letter to the Montgomery *Advertiser*,

is Czolgosz alone guilty? Has not the entire nation had a part in this greatest crime of the century? According to a careful record kept by The Chicago Tribune, 2,516 persons have been lynched in the United States during the past sixteen years . . . A conservative estimate would place the number of persons engaged in these lynchings at about fifty per individual lynched, so that there are or have been engaged in this anarchy of lynching nearly 125,000 persons to say nothing of the many bands of technically organized anarchists . . . We cannot sow disorder and reap order.

To give Czolgosz a proper trial, Washington argued, would make a good lesson for the whole republic—but especially its Southern branch—in the efficiency of the justice system. "One criminal put to death through the majesty of the law does more, to my mind, to prevent crime than ten put to death by lynching anarchists."[45]

Washington played on a double parallel. On the one hand, anarchist murderers were lynchers. But on the other, even anarchist murderers deserved a fair trial lest they became the objects of a lynching.

The former theme appealed to the African-American press—the *Washington Bee* cried, "Wipe out Anarchy and Lynch Law," while the *Chicago Broad-ax* referred derisively to "anarchists—better known as lynchers."[46] If it was a morally sound parallel, it did not set the public conscience afire. In keeping with the deal Washington would strike with Roosevelt, the plight of Southern blacks receded from public attention, replaced by concern with the situation of immigrants and their descendants in America. The notion that immigrant anarchists were displacing blacks as a social threat preyed on the mind of Czolgosz's unhappy defense attorney, Loran Lewis.

In his address to the jury on Czolgosz's behalf, Lewis acknowledged that an anarchist—"a man who does not believe in any law"—was outside the social order and a danger to it. But, Lewis contended, foreign-bred anarchism posed less of a danger than "the belief that is becoming so common . . . that lynch law should take the place of a calm and dignified administration of law in our courts of justice." He compared Czolgosz to William Freeman, a black man accused of murder and defended by William H. Seward at trial in 1846. Seward insisted on a trial—"not that he cared anything for the negro," Lewis quickly added. "But he wanted to teach the people of the country the sacredness of the law." It was important that the accused have what Lewis called "the form of a trial."[47]

The form of justice did not guarantee the substance of it—this, too, was commonly known among critics of lynch law. "Legal lynchings"—trials carried out in unseemly haste—were proper ways of killing off racial threats in communities that preferred proceedings more dignified than the posse.[48] As Booker T. Washington noticed, the determined speed of Czolgosz's prosecution and the relentless characterization of the assassin as a racial outsider gave the case the flavor of a lynching even before the trial. The similarity grew stronger when the execution became a national public spectacle and the executioners systematically mutilated the body.

On the morning of Czolgosz's electrocution, the Edison Company set up cameras outside Auburn State Prison and filmed its exterior during what they calculated to be the moment of the killer's death.

They distributed this panorama in early November, spliced to a dramatization of the execution in which an actor, his face darkened by shadow, jerks cathartically in a prop electric chair. In the real death cell, the body went from the chair to the autopsy and then to the prison officials, who had decided that an ordinary burial, even with an application of quicklime, would not destroy the body soon enough for them. His guilt determined, his sentence carried out, his postmortem duly performed, the prisoner would not, Auburn officials were determined, become fodder for ghoulish medical second-guessing or even amateur souvenir taking. So they took what the press called an "extraordinary precaution"—they dug Czolgosz a special grave, with vents to carry out the gases of a speedy decomposition, and put in it enough sulfuric acid to dissolve the flesh and bones within twelve hours.[49]

To Doctors Channing and Briggs, mulling over the autopsy report in their Brookline offices, the rapidity of the trial, the brevity of the postmortem investigation, and the thoroughness with which the officials destroyed the body combined to suggest a miscarriage of justice. To the patrician Dr. Channing, that was all it spelled, and he meant to set it right (at least in principle) if he could; but Channing had little firsthand experience of racial difference and knew it chiefly as an abstraction. He tended to keep people unlike himself at a benevolent distance, supporting a private school for the separate education of "colored children," and favoring immigration restriction.[50]

Briggs, on the other hand, knew what a legal lynching looked like. He had seen one in Denver, in 1886. A confessed murderer named Andy Green—a black man—was hanged in public before a crowd of about twenty thousand representing, as Briggs wrote in his journal, the entire community:

> The crowd laughed and joked, as if this were indeed a gala occasion. All the small boys in town appeared to be there; there were of course a great many negroes, and the Chinese were well-represented. Large delegations of working men came, representatives of local industries; we noticed, for instance, the crowded wagons of the Denver Brewing Company and the

Continental Oil Company; there was hardly a prominent business firm in the city that had not sent its clerks in the firm's
wagons. There were people of all classes; many of the women
were well-dressed and looked like ladies.

Briggs watched his fellow Americans of all castes and colors jostle
each other happily as Green confessed his guilt on the scaffold and
then was hanged. In the moment before his execution, Green did
something to cast doubt on his sanity, gleefully leading an assembled
choir in the singing of "Nearer My God to Thee" and then shouting
"Farewell, everybody!" A shocked Briggs watched as Green jerked on
the rope, noting,

> It was twenty-five minutes before he was officially declared to
> be dead . . . The crowd watched his dying agonies with interest.
> The excitement among them was indescribable. As soon as the
> hanging was over, vendors of sandwiches, fruit, peanuts, lemon-
> ade and prize packages of popcorn, who had been quiet for a lit-
> tle while, set up their cries again, and the inhabitants of
> Denver began to wend their way home after their holiday, talk-
> ing it all over.[51]

Briggs knew what multicultural harmony meant when it focused on an
execution. It created a community by dividing people into two categories—Americanized citizens and others, or the lynchers and the
lynched. The execution of Andy Green was one of several hangings
that made a profound impression on Briggs, and persuaded him that
because public executions served the function of defining a community against its outsiders, people often rushed to determine a criminal
sane and worthy of execution—it comforted them to dispose of a definite outsider. "The day of execution, with a negro on the block, was a
day of hilarity, with drinks for every one," he remarked dourly in a
later book on the moral indefensibility of capital punishment.[52] When
he looked at the Czolgosz case, he saw what he had seen in Denver: a
community coming together to expunge someone whom it could regard as racially different, without too much regard for whether the

man was sufficiently sane to bear responsibility for his actions. The investigation into Czolgosz's unhappy life and death meant for Briggs a descent once more into the bleaker side of human consciousness, a prospect that weighed on him as he packed his newspaper clippings and his portable typewriter and took a train for upstate New York.

4

KILLER ANARCHISM

B y the second time Briggs was hurrying past the winter-bare branches of the elms of Auburn to the New York state penitentiary's high granite walls, he had begun to wonder if the whole population of the little prison town was not determined to foil his investigation. He had budgeted for only a day in the city where Czolgosz died; it was already afternoon and he had met only bland resistance to his inquiries.

Returning to the prison, he crossed the tracks of the New York Central Railroad, which ran cruelly close to the walls of the inmates' exercise yard. The boxcars, flatcars, and passenger coaches of the trunk lines carrying goods and people freely to and through the city clicked past, taunting the incarcerated. Briggs felt a similar frustration as he chased after elusive, critical clues.

That morning, January 7, 1902, he had hopefully stepped off the overnight train from Boston, brimming with plans for action. He deposited his bags and took his breakfast at a local lodging house, then made his way to the office of the clerk of Cayuga County. After looking over his notes and clippings on the train, he had decided to begin at the end: the autopsy. The report of MacDonald and Spitzka was the most sustained medical effort to establish Czolgosz's normality, filed by two of the most respectable skeptics of the M'Naghten test. Briggs wanted to see the raw material of their reasoning, and because New York state law required that autopsy reports be filed with the county clerk, he expected to find the postmortem notes in the recorder's office.

But no sooner did he make his routine request of the county clerk than he met with the cheerful blankness that would recur throughout the morning. There was no report on file, the clerk told him with brisk finality. Briggs patiently insisted there must be a report—the law demanded it—but the clerk and his associates, turning over the offices' papers, said they could find nothing. At Briggs's demand, they consulted their superior, who eventually emerged with a report—but it consisted of no more than the barest affirmation that a "Charles [sic] F. MacDonald" had under the supervision of Auburn State Prison physician John Gerin performed an autopsy on Leon Czolgosz. An incredulous Briggs asked if that was all the doctors had provided. The clerk, now recollecting MacDonald's visit to his office, allowed that he had noticed the slender commentary of the report—and that "the true report was folded up and carried away in the pocket of the physician." But as the report on file fulfilled legal requirements, he was officially satisfied.[1]

Stymied, Briggs decided to visit the prison officials who had authorized the autopsy, hoping they might remember something of the examination. Built in 1816 with single-occupancy cells for humane incarceration, Auburn State Prison remained a model for the nation's penitentiaries down through its acquisition in 1889 of New York's first electric chair. Its cells—three and a half feet wide, seven and a half feet long, seven and a half feet high—would not be condemned as "medieval" for a dozen years, nor would its custom of marching inmates in lockstep through the yard be seriously questioned until the progressive reform movement had gathered sufficient steam to focus public attention on the living conditions even of criminals. The prison provided Auburn with its major industry, and however cramped its accommodations, it harbored inmates more comfortably than its cousin at Ossining.[2] Its guards and warden took their jobs seriously, Briggs found—so much so that although warden Warren Mead agreed to see him, Mead immediately stoppered all inquiry.

LIFE IN THE DEATH HOUSE

On welcoming Briggs into his office, Warden Mead tilted back in his chair, lowered his gaze at Briggs, and said, "I do not know you and my mouth is shut to you, sir." A frustrated Briggs pleaded his case as a psychologist and invoked the cause of scientific inquiry, but the stubborn warden told Briggs he "had no idea how many scientific men and cranks of all kinds came to make measurements of different classes of criminals, casts of thumbs, palms of hands" and so forth, and what was worse he "had been pestered to death with . . . all sorts of people in search of information . . . after Czolgosz." Desperate to distinguish himself from this class of intellectual jackals, Briggs offered to give Mead some answers before he asked his questions, which was how he found himself rushing back to the lodging house for his notes, then retracing his steps to the prison for a last effort.[3]

Briggs's willingness to share his professional opinion interested Mead. The warden was keen to discuss the report filed by MacDonald and Spitzka because, he had to confess, he had not made friends with the doctors during their visit and so missed out on their opinion. After some discussion of the published report Mead said finally that if Briggs would not use his name, he would tell him all he knew—but that if anyone in the office of the State Superintendent of Prisons found out he had talked publicly about Czolgosz, his "head would come off in a minute."[4]

Mead thawed gradually, and in the end he talked to Briggs for three hours. Through the fading light of a January afternoon in upstate New York, they sat in the warden's office. Prison guards and doctors came and went, offering their observations as they recalled them, fitting together a collective picture of their celebrity inmate. It turned out the officials at Auburn shared a clear, and even somewhat sympathetic, opinion of his case. Czolgosz was not innately depraved, they believed: merely disappointed and fatally misguided, a victim of his unfortunate exposure to the poisonous philosophy of anarchism.

Czolgosz impressed them all with his calm. He was a hearty eater— a "gourmandizer," one of the policemen said—and a cleanly man who washed regularly. He kept to himself, "invariably maintaining a stolid silence," unless asked a question—and then he would pause a long while before answering. Mead remarked that Czolgosz rarely "gave them any information about himself other than often declaring he was an anarchist." He seemed always comfortable with his impending doom, and lost his composure only twice. Once, when he first arrived in prison, "he went all to pieces—he shook or shivered—trembled and was completely undone." He also betrayed surprise and dismay when a guard told him he would be electrocuted here in Auburn, rather than go on to the electric chair at Sing Sing—but even then he recovered swiftly and simply commented that in Ohio, where he had lived lately, they electrocuted in only one prison.[5]

One of Briggs's Auburn informants stated, off the record, that just before his departure Czolgosz had been tortured in Buffalo, which could have accounted for his shaky state on arrival. According to the informant, Czolgosz's interrogators hoped he would reveal a conspiracy to assassinate the President. "I understood the torture was what is called the 3rd degree and is by burning the eyes in some manner which few men can stand," Briggs told Channing. But Czolgosz "did not confess a word" that would "implicate anyone else" in the shooting.[6]

Mead and the prison physicians all noticed Czolgosz's unusual intelligence. The plainspoken warden said the assassin seemed to him "way above" the average criminal, so much so that "the murderers about him seemed down on him." Czolgosz played games with the warden, telling him he would see a priest and then refusing once the priest arrived. He claimed to be illiterate, yet he clearly knew a great deal about books. Dr. John Nelson Ross, who took measurements and made observations of all the criminals who came through Auburn, believed Czolgosz's mental development put him "away ahead and above the average of any class" of known felon.[7] When Briggs told Ross that Czolgosz could read and write after all, Ross upped his estimate of Czolgosz's intelligence even further: "How well he played his game while he was in the toils," he exclaimed.[8] When Leon's brother Waldeck came to see him in prison, the warden learned Leon had an unschooled talent as a skilled mechanic—Leon told Waldeck that after leaving the family farm in July he had made his way west, earning his living through the summer months by repairing threshing machines. Listening to the brothers talk, Dr. John Gerin concluded that "Leon was far above his family in intelligence."[9]

Indeed, the prison-keepers believed that his intelligence had been poor Czolgosz's downfall. Ross gave Briggs his theory of the crime: "he developed so far above his family and surroundings that he got into the habit of brooding and 'soured on the whole world' [and] feeling he was above his associates and having no place he adopted anarchy as a way out of it all."[10] The trouble with Leon Czolgosz, his last guardians believed, was that he was too smart to be happy as a workingman, and in his misery he fell prey to anarchism, which offered him an explanation for his unhappiness: the system of industrial life was rotting the whole world. Czolgosz's intelligence and social position had made him susceptible to the real villain: the corrupting ideas of political radicalism.

In the eyes of Auburn's minders, intelligence came as an awful curse to a working American, an inheritance of dubious value that lent itself more readily to a sickness of the spirit than to practical use. Laborers should have no more intelligence than they needed to do their jobs, for an underoccupied intellect grew discontented, and got to seeking reasons for its dissatisfaction. Anarchism preyed on such minds, seducing them into a perverted understanding of the world, whispering that only a society gone sour could have spawned such unhappiness.

These opinions could only foment further unhappiness, the prison-keepers believed, and were therefore better left unspoken: which was why Warden Mead refused Czolgosz his desire to make an "anarchistic speech on the scaffold in public," and why his guards forced Czolgosz into the electric chair and strapped his mouth shut while he was still talking. Those ideas were dangerous, especially with reporters in the room. If the three newspaper correspondents who witnessed the execution were to copy down Czolgosz's sick utterances, they could contaminate the world: it was better to force the prisoner's mouth shut.

And as far as Warden Mead was concerned, medical notions were nearly as dangerous. Like Czolgosz, doctors tended to overanalyze things, to see what a plain man knew was not there—or preferred not to know was there. Mead had to let MacDonald and Spitzka perform the autopsy, but he "stationed his most trustworthy guard over them," and left "instructions to 'run them out' if they attempted to secret or carry away an atom of the remains of Czolgosz." They did not like his terms: "they both 'begged hard' for the brain or a portion of it and were both perfectly confident of it at first but," Mead noted with satisfaction, "they were disappointed and got nothing." For the warden, dissolving the body in acid was simply the last step in keeping Czolgosz away from the sickness of too much intellect. Now no enterprising ghoul could return to salvage a portion of the corpse and subject it to unwarranted and excessive analysis.[11]

Mead had, in short, determined that as long as he bore responsibility for the assassin, Czolgosz would not become a martyr either to anarchism or to psychology. So he made sure the assassin went to his death without speaking and to his grave without too leisurely an inspection. And that, the gruff warden abruptly told Briggs, was all there was to say. If he wanted to know more about his anarchist, well, he should go on to Cleveland to meet the family. The police at Buffalo were "rather dull and stupid" and could scarcely tell him anything he did not already know.[12]

Briggs thanked Mead and the doctors, and went on to Buffalo all the same on another overnight train. But Mead had been right: he learned little there. He met the same obstacles of concealed or absent evidence and official disinterest. District attorney Penney made him wait all morning in his outer office and then told him "he cannot show me the confession made by Czolgosz as he has refused it to everyone who has asked." Penney said "plainly . . . that he wished to say as little as possible . . . believing as he did that Czolgosz was sane and an anarchist without question."[13] Police superintendent Bull was a little more forthcoming, chatting agreeably with Briggs about the case, but it proved in the end the prosecutors shared the prison-keepers' opinion of Czolgosz: anarchism had corrupted a mind at loose ends. It was a pity, they thought, but that was what happened when an idle intellect met a seductive philosophy.

The metaphor of seduction shaded into the real thing whenever the subject of Emma Goldman came up. Goldman, the fiery anarchist orator, was the only inspiration Czolgosz claimed in his confession. A lecture she gave at Cleveland stirred him, and smitten by her charms—philosophical or otherwise—he set out to follow her on her speaking tour through the industrial Midwest to Chicago. Superintendent Bull told Briggs "it was plain to anyone who heard him talk about Emma Goldman that he was in love with her."[14] Indeed, one of the Buffalo policemen told Briggs that sex was altogether the root of anarchy's attraction: a colleague in Chicago told him he "had surprised Emma Goldman in bed with three others, that she was there known as a common harlot, and it was there thought she used Czolgosz as a tool [in a conspiracy]."

Briggs had a hard time believing the story—with her hair in a bun and her corsetless dresses, Emma Goldman did not fit his idea of a seductress. "This is poor stuff I only tell you because it was told me," he wrote Channing—but it was the sort of thing that the Auburn warden and the Buffalo D.A. tended to believe about anarchists. In general, it was what anarchists believed about themselves. The seductive powers of freedom—extended even to free love—drew them and others to the philosophy. Perhaps more important, it was not far off what the new President believed, or said he did when he offered his rendition of the prosecution's argument in Czolgosz's case: the lure of anarchism would seduce the weak of will if they were not given some reason to keep their honor.[15]

RUNNING THE REVOLUTION

Looking back on Theodore Roosevelt's career, Senator Albert Beveridge of Indiana thought his political friend did no greater intellectual service to his fellow Americans than "in differentiating that species of anarchism which we popularly term 'Bolshevism' from that form of normal progress called liberalism." Progressive Republicans like Beveridge and Roosevelt believed the United States faced a crossroads at the turn of the twentieth century. Their country was suffering from the wrenching effects of industrial growth. In response to these growing pains, the nation could swerve to the political left, adopting socialism, communism, or anarchism; it could veer to the right—as some Republicans hoped—and altogether reject government regulation of the economy. Or, as the progressives wished, it could continue straight ahead on the path of democracy by somewhat increasing government power to lessen the destruction that always accompanies capitalist creativity. The greatest threat to progressive liberalism did not come from anarchism, which Beveridge and Roosevelt believed was a weak movement with few adherents. But progressives worried that if anarchism grew to frighten the populace, it might "throw liberal men into the ranks of reaction" and thus doom the possibility for liberal progress.[16] In consequence they had to steer clear of reaction on one side and radicalism on the other, keeping a close eye on both, especially when a crisis like the McKinley assassination roiled the already muddy waters of American politics.

The tide of industrialization set American political certainties adrift. The United States suffered and benefited from new techniques of production much as other countries did. All over the modernizing world—throughout Europe, the Americas, and Australasia—nations adopted new technologies that made possible large-scale mechanized production in factories and fields alike. Industrial agriculture put family farmers out of business with astonishing speed, and rural workers migrated to cities to find work in the new factories. Once workers began moving in search of higher wages, they often kept going, even if it meant crossing national borders. Between about 1850 and the start of the First World War in 1914, some fifty-five million people moved to new countries in search of better jobs. This mechanization, consolidation, urbanization, and migration made the world economy more efficient and made new factory-produced goods widely available to middle-class consumers, but in pushing millions of working-class people around, it created tremendous uncertainty, discontent, and even anger.

Uniquely among the industrializing peoples, Americans experienced industrialization as a problem of immigration, because as bad as factory conditions and wages were in the United States, they were markedly better than in other countries. So of the fifty-five million global migrants seeking a new fate, thirty-three million went to American cities. There they competed with less-skilled American workers for jobs, driving down wages and turning dispossessed American-born workers into migrants themselves, as they upped stakes and moved west. The vagabond foot traffic of displaced Easterners passed the weedy fields of failed family farms, filling the West with a population disappointed by the advance of global industry.[17]

The arithmetic of this desperation filled thoughtful heads with ominous statistics. The figure that loomed largest in the imagination of American thinkers was zero: the remaining acreage of frontier, calculated by the United States Census Bureau in 1890. Migration to the empty West had seemed a safety valve for overflowing Eastern industrial discontent, a reservoir to take up the tide of unhappy laborers. There they might find their feet, and in the wilderness regain their sense of individual independence—they could, in short, become Americanized much as the Dutch, English, French, and Spanish immigrants of the seventeenth century had. But as the open spaces filled, this opportunity vanished; Eastern cities could no longer easily export their labor troubles westward.

The end of the frontier meant that more mundane data increased in importance, and so the states created bureaus of labor statistics to estimate average wages and enumerate the unemployed. They found with some precision what the observant imagination could roughly sketch: in the suddenly urbanizing Midwestern and Western states, a third of the population still worked on the land, and over half worked in trades (including agriculture, construction, and transportation) with habitual seasonal unemployment. Thus a majority of Westerners knew they would spend about three months of the year out of work, scarcely daring to spend their meager savings against the uncertain day when work might begin again. When the economy slumped, as it did repeatedly and dramatically in the 1890s, workers' savings accounts gave out, and families went hungry.[18]

Amid these scenes of Western desperation a radical zeal grew. It took root in the culture of farm life, and sprouted agrarian enthusiasms for economic changes—greenbackism, silverism, populism: measures for a currency based on paper or debased metals or grain or anything that would reduce the pressure on debt-ridden farmers threatened with foreclosure. In the mines and on the factory floors of Western towns, it produced a set of union movements seeking to relieve the misery and uncertainty of industrial employment by measures ranging from eight-hour workdays to socialization of the means of production. And in the small, swiftly growing cities of the West, these ideas mixed with the socialist philosophies that accompanied immigration from Europe, turning railway hubs into entrepôts of political intrigue. Coalitions of farmers, immigrant workers, displaced native-born Eastern laborers, and college-educated political theorists favored regulation of railroads, banking, and interstate commerce, as well as municipal ownership of utilities and public health laws. By the end of the nineteenth century canny politicos knew that the allegiance of the West—and with it the electoral votes to win the presidency— would go to the politician who could squelch, buy off, or somehow satisfy these impulses.

The most outré of these political philosophies was anarchism. It had no Bible, no Decalogue or catechism, no church or even, properly speaking, leaders. After all, by definition, anarchists believed in no rulers. The traditions that fed anarchism ran through such a respectable American channel as the philosophy of Thomas Jefferson, who famously preferred newspapers without government to government without newspapers, and infamously told his friend James Madison that a little revolution now and then was a good and necessary thing. Defined in Emma Goldman's magazine *Mother Earth*, anarchism was a Jefferson-compatible "philosophy of a new social order based on liberty unrestricted by man-made law." But in its industrial form, anarchism professed closer kinship to Karl Marx than to Thomas Jefferson. *Mother Earth* also defined anarchism as "the theory that all forms of government rest on violence and are therefore wrong and harmful, as well as unnecessary" and associated anarchism with "free communism: voluntary economic co-operation of all toward the needs of each. A social arrangement based on the principle: To each according to his needs; from each according to his ability."[19] Late-nineteenth-century anarchists generally agreed that any considerable accumulation of property was theft, that capitalism therefore was theft with legal sanction, and that laws protecting property and property-holders were therefore immoral. The state—any state—existed chiefly to oppress individuals by upholding the rights of property, and only liberty from state power could free modern people. Whether this liberty would come through a peaceful withering away of the state or from a violent overthrow, anarchists could not all agree. But increasingly, as violent strike followed violent strike, as capitalists grew richer and the ranks of unemployed workers swelled, radical opinion tended toward the notion that an armed clash between classes was in the offing. This being the case, intelligent workingmen had every right to bear arms in case they had to defend themselves.

No American politician took this prospect more seriously than Theodore Roosevelt. "The time of the great social revolutions has arrived," he wrote in 1894. "We are all peering into the future to try to forecast the action of the great dumb forces set in operation by the stupendous industrial revolution which has taken place during the present century. We do not know what to make of the vast displacements of population, the expansion of the towns, the unrest and discontent of the masses."[20] Although he despised what he regarded as the "note of hysteria" in the campaign waged by William Jennings Bryan on the combined Democratic and Populist platforms of 1896, he supported much of the substance of the Bryan campaign.[21] Unlike Mark Hanna and the McKinley Republicans, who believed the Western problem would simply go away with the next economic uptick (at most it might require minor application of protective tariffs and trickle-down economics), Roosevelt thought the radicals were onto something and required Republicans' full attention. Most of all he worried that unless Republican leaders set about solving social problems in a systematic fashion and adopted some of the regulatory measures for which the Bryanites clamored, the voters would elect representatives who supported real revolution. He therefore set himself the task of implementing radical changes for conservative purposes. And to cast himself as the proper conduit for progress, he had to champion change while stigmatizing the politicians who had beaten him to it.

He got his chance not three months after taking office, and made the most of it. On December 3, 1901, he delivered his first annual message as President to the United States Congress. After the obligatory eulogy for President McKinley, he launched into a condemnation of anarchism as a simple "evil." The anarchist, he declared, "is a malefactor and nothing else. He is in no sense, in no shape or way, a 'product of social conditions.' " Anarchism deserved no credence as a political philosophy: it "is no more an expression of 'social discontent' than picking pockets or wife-beating." No serious person could believe it, for "the anarchist, and especially the anarchist in the United States," where social conditions tended more toward equality than anywhere else, was no more than a criminal,

> whose perverted instincts lead him to prefer confusion and chaos to the most beneficent form of social order. His protest of concern for working men is outrageous in its impudent falsity; for if the political institutions of this country do not afford opportunity to every honest and intelligent son of toil, then the door of hope is forever closed against him.[22]

No sooner had Roosevelt finished ridiculing critiques of American social conditions that would tend to elicit sympathy for Czolgosz than he offered his own critique of American social conditions. "The tremendous and highly complex industrial development which went on with ever-accelerated rapidity during the latter half of the nineteenth century brings us face to face, at the beginning of the twentieth, with very serious social problems."[23] Moreover, these problems could be addressed by something very like a Bryanite agenda: "Corporations engaged in interstate commerce should be regulated if they are found to exercise a license working to the public injury. It should be as much the aim of those who seek for social betterment to rid the business world of crimes of cunning as to rid the entire body politic of crimes of violence."[24] The new Republican President went on to praise labor unions. "Very great good has been and will be accomplished by associations or unions of wage-workers,"[25] he noted. He called for banking regulation and an elastic and regulated currency, to

President Theodore Roosevelt enjoying the use of the "bully pulpit." (Theodore Roosevelt Collection, Harvard College Library)

damp the "deranging influence of commercial crises."[26] He asked Congress to regulate railroads, holding out the ominous possibility of socialization in the implicit threat "The railway is a public servant."[27]

Had any other politician delivered the same message, Roosevelt would have accused him of giving aid and comfort to the anarchists by calling into question the justice of basic American social institutions. But by opening with his round condemnation of anarchism, Roosevelt inoculated himself against the criticism he himself freely dished out, and skillfully turned the Republican Party into a potential home for what he and Beveridge called progressive liberalism. If, as Beveridge said later, Roosevelt had successfully distinguished unacceptable radicalism from normal progressivism, he had done so by observing two major distinctions: first, revolutionaries and anarchists favored political murder, while he did not; and second, criticism of industrial conditions aided anarchists, eroding national unity and resolve—unless Roosevelt himself uttered the criticism.

Czolgosz gave Roosevelt a precious tool, one that he could never have crafted for himself: a badge of legitimate infamy, signifying a terrible threat, to bestow on his political opponents. So the new President could piously condemn not only the "professed anarchist, inflamed by the teaching of professed anarchists," but suggest that the susceptible Czolgosz had been corrupted "probably also by the reckless utterances of those who, on the stump and in the public press, appeal to the dark and evil spirits of malice and greed, envy and sullen hatred."[28] With this single graceful insinuation, Roosevelt implicated the Democratic Party and the newspaper industry in the President's murder. The nation was now on notice: the President spoke for progressive liberalism, and anyone who spoke against him in this time of crisis was aiding the agents of terror.

THE ANARCHISTS AND THE OUTSIDER

In the course of his investigation, Briggs was beginning to learn that policemen needed stricter definitions of anarchism than the President's if they were actually to arrest anyone for illegal activity. His most reliable informants were working cops: they took a practical interest in anarchist philosophy, trying only to distinguish what was criminal from what was harmless.[29] Setting out their plan of inquiry in January 1902, Channing and Briggs agreed that their investigation would reap the best returns should Briggs seek Czolgosz's family and youthful origins in Cleveland and Detroit. At the same time, Channing advised Briggs to keep up a correspondence with "someone out there" to track the anarchist connection in the Midwest.[30] Through letters and telegrams, Briggs pieced together a story from policemen and police reporters, with whose help he began to tap into the small but complex world of urban anarchism in America.

As New York City Police Commissioner Michael Murphy remarked, "There are only about 200 Anarchists in this city . . . and on the whole they are a harmless lot." Murphy displayed a more pragmatic familiarity with radical political theory than Roosevelt (who had once held Murphy's job as New York's top cop): "The majority of the so-called Anarchists in New York are Socialists. This class has among its number some great minds." Murphy expected no trouble from Manhattan's radicals, but reassured New Yorkers that his men would "keep them under close surveillance, as they have always done."[31] While the press depicted boatloads of bomb-bearing anarchists rowing into New York harbor under the nose of the Statue of Liberty, the police demurred. Murphy's Chicago counterpart, chief of police Francis O'Neill, showed similar restraint in dealing with the radicals of his city. "I am bound by the law just as they are . . . If a number of persons holding ideas adverse to our form of government gather in a house and discuss this matter among themselves, I cannot arrest them . . . They must violate the law before we can reach them."[32]

Chief O'Neill was under special pressure, for the nation looked grimly on Chicago as the cradle of political dissent. Fed by the populism of the farmers to the West and by the socialism of the immigrants from the East, Chicago radicalism offered a variety of views opposed to the status quo, and made the city more than once the site of fierce protests. Chicago hosted the 1896 national convention that erupted at Bryan's "cross of gold" speech, and threw the Democrats into the arms of the Populists. It witnessed the Pullman strike in 1894, when President Cleveland sent troops to restore order, and it had been at the center of the national railroad strike in 1877.

But the Chicago clash that loomed largest in Americans' memory and whose legacy surfaced again in the wake of McKinley's assassination came in the first week of May 1886. It began innocently enough, when a coalition of Democrats, labor leaders, socialists, and anarchists lined up behind a strike on May 1 to support the eight-hour working day. Even Chicago's mayor, Carter Harrison (a Democrat), supported the demonstration, which—despite dire warnings from the conservative press that no such radical effort could come to any good—went off without a hitch. In Chicago, forty thousand workers put down their tools; nationwide, about three hundred thousand did the same. It was a powerful demonstration of working-class might, and of the coalition that stood behind the strike.

Trouble came two days later when a continuing strike at the McCormick Reaper Works, fueled partly by anarchist pickets, broke out into a fight between strikers and scabs. Policemen arriving to stop the fight met a hail of stones, and fired their revolvers into the crowd, killing two protesters. A rally convened the next day at Haymarket Square to protest the killings. Mayor Harrison, sympathetic to the cause, attended and made himself conspicuous in the crowd. August Spies and Albert Parsons, local anarchist leaders, addressed the assembled citizens. Harrison listened for a couple of hours till he convinced himself "there was no suggestion by either of the speakers for the immediate use of force or violence toward any person that night."[33] Then he went home. No sooner had he got in the door—about fifteen minutes after he left the square—than he heard an explosion. A thrown bomb had landed among the policemen stationed at the square. The assembly broke up into chaos, with shooting and fighting for five minutes. It left seven policemen and a much larger (though to this day unknown) number of civilians fatally wounded.[34]

The Haymarket bombing led to the murder trial of Spies, Parsons, and six other accused anarchists. None were charged with actually throwing a bomb or shooting a policeman. They were on trial on the presumption that the expression of their general views on the coming revolution made them accessories to the specific crime of murdering police officers. All were convicted and seven sentenced to death. One committed suicide in prison. Four, including Spies and Parsons, were hanged in 1887. Of the remaining three, the two condemned had their sentences commuted by governor Richard Oglesby; all were pardoned by the newly elected governor, John P. Altgeld, in 1893.

The Haymarket episode provoked Theodore Roosevelt, then running a crew of cowboys at his Dakota ranch, to contemplate the possibility that good, loyal workers like his own might have to take up arms against violent anarchists: "My men here are hardworking, labouring men, who work longer hours for no greater wages than many of the strikers . . . I believe nothing would give them greater pleasure than a chance with their rifles at one of the mobs."[35] Roosevelt's assessment mirrored the anarchist analysis of industrial crises. Anarchists like Spies and Parsons had for years been predicting class war, and advocating that the working class arm itself in preparation. In their minds it was simply a matter of self-defense. Employers "everywhere and always fall back on the use of *force*," they reasoned; workers must prepare to do the same. The law would not protect them. In language that closely paralleled Roosevelt's later call to action, Parsons declared, "The economic forces are at work incessantly, generating the forces of the social revolution. We can neither retard nor hasten the result, but we can aid and direct its forces."[36] To Parsons, this meant preparing to fight the bourgeoisie to the death; to Roosevelt, it meant arming the bourgeoisie but also attempting to stave off the conflict through politics that lessened the pressure on workers—which was what Roosevelt and Beveridge would call progressivism.

For most Americans, Haymarket taught no such precise lessons. The affair left instead a fearful wound on the political consciousness of Chicago and the country, a scar irritated by every new appearance of anarchist opinions. Listening to the anarchist orators before the bomb blast, Mayor Harrison thought that they said nothing unusual—and indeed they had not, but he was used to hearing their critique of society: "The law is only framed for those who are your enslavers . . . You have nothing more to do with the law except to lay hands on it and throttle it until it makes its last kick."[37] After the explosion, Chicagoans no longer treated such public utterances as a simple matter of ordinary politics. The city suddenly seemed a tinderbox in which rhetorical sparks could not safely fly, lest it burst into flames once more. One businessman's daughter remembered that when her father built a house just after Haymarket, the new must-have security feature was a direct wire from the local police station to a push button in the front hall labeled "Mob."[38]

And it was because of Haymarket that in the autumn of 1901, suspicion of a conspiracy in the shooting of President McKinley turned immediately to Chicago. "We have a bad lot of Anarchists here," mayor Carter Harrison II—the son of the previous mayor, Carter Harrison—confessed on the evening of the shooting, and on little more than this suspicion the city's detectives were looking for a Chicago connection to Czolgosz.[39] Secret Service men based their Chicago hunch on "the name of the man"—which they at that time believed was Nieman—"and the fact that he is probably from the same general section of the country"—that is, the industrial Midwest—"as some of the Haymarket participants."[40] One Chicago police captain, Hermann Schuettler, had a "distinct recollection" of an anarchist family of the name of Nieman in his precinct, "during the Anarchist troubles of 1886," and set forth to pound the pavement till he turned them up.[41]

The Chicago connection rested on no stronger reed than the city's radical reputation. Captain Schuettler's lead took him nowhere—it was cousin to the urge that led Detroit policemen to rap on the doors of two Nieman families on September 6, only to discover the two local men named Fred Nieman—one a gardener, one a laborer—innocently at home.[42] Yet it turned out there was something in reputation and rhetoric after all: by the next day the Chicago police had rounded up at least five anarchists who knew Leon Czolgosz.

Chief among them was Abraham Isaak, an immigrant from Russia who now edited an anarchist newsletter called the *Free Society*. A former Mennonite who fled tsarist persecution in the late nineteenth century, Isaak had experienced the oppression of a real police state and appreciated the comparative tolerance of the United States.[43] As he told police when arrested, there was no need for American anarchists to meet in secret, because their rights to express their political opinions were respected. Indeed, this openness allowed Isaak to make a modest living publishing his opinions and arranging public political meetings. It was after one such meeting, on July 12, 1901, that he met Czolgosz.

The occasion for the meeting was the visit of Emma Goldman. She had been touring throughout the Midwest, making a little money by selling stationery and addressing various radical groups. In July she stayed with Isaak for a short while, and afterward took a trip to Buffalo with his sixteen-year-old daughter Marie to see the Pan-American Exposition—two months before the President was shot. On the eve of her departure from Chicago, Isaak and a group of anarchist friends went to the Lakeshore station to see her off, only to find her already speaking (albeit with an impatient air) to a well-dressed, clean-shaven young man who introduced himself as Leon Czolgosz. While Isaak's friend Hippolyte Havel spoke briefly to Czolgosz, Goldman complained to Isaak that "the fellow had been following her around wanting to talk to her, but she had no time to devote to him. She asked me to find out what the fellow wanted."[44]

As Isaak later wrote, Czolgosz sounded like an unusually inept police spy trying to infiltrate a group of philosophical anarchists in the hope of discovering some terrorist connection. The young man nodded to Isaak, calling him "comrade," then immediately asked if he could attend the "secret meetings." Isaak told him the anarchists had no secret meetings—that he had attended some secret gatherings in Russia, but in America there was no need for them. Czolgosz told him he had been a socialist for seven years, but his socialist discussion group spent its energies in innumerable doctrinal quarrels, over which they finally split. He "was looking for something more active," he said. Isaak thought nobody but a cop could possibly be this clumsy, but as he spoke to Czolgosz, he "could not help thinking that his eyes and words expressed sincerity." Czolgosz said he had heard Goldman speak in Cleveland and followed her to Chicago to learn more about anarchism. Czolgosz and Isaak spoke for almost an hour, and after a while Isaak grew nearly persuaded that Czolgosz's bluntness was rather a product of naïveté than of ungainly guile. Czolgosz sounded as though he had come to a painful, and simple, radical political awakening through disillusionment with the McKinley Administration. He explained that the "outrages committed by the American government in the Philippine islands" upset him. "It does not harmonize with the teachings in the public schools about our flag," he said.[45] They spoke of the increasing number of violent strikes and other signs of social revolution in progress. It turned out finally that Czolgosz had no money. Out of sympathy, Isaak booked him a room, and offered to see him the next morning, buy him breakfast, and help him find a job.

Isaak never saw Czolgosz again. He wrote his colleague Emil Schilling in Cleveland, who replied and reported he had the same experience with Czolgosz: his "desire to become an anarchist was so strong and intense," Schilling said, "he was immediately put under suspicion."[46] With Schilling's corroboration, Isaak concluded his first instincts had been correct, and published a warning describing Czolgosz and identifying him as a spy. "His demeanor is of the usual sort, pretending to be greatly interested in the cause, asking for names, or soliciting aid for acts of contemplated violence," the announcement read. It appeared in Free Society on September 1, five days before the shooting.[47]

As Emil Schilling later told Briggs, the shooting seemed to prove Czolgosz's authenticity, and made the anarchists feel guilty. They had shut Czolgosz out, thinking him a gawky misfit, his enthusiasms misplaced and ill informed. Schilling said, "I thought that [Czolgosz] wanted to be smart enough to find out something as a secret detective, and I thought he was not smart enough to do what he wanted."[48] Havel, Isaak's friend, dismissed Czolgosz as "a little child. No, I don't believe he was insane, but he asked such foolish questions . . . He wanted to know all about the 'comrades' in Chicago and about the secret meetings of the local Anarchists."[49] Yet he had turned out to possess a single-minded capacity to act. "Then I did not think he had a plan—afterwards I did," Schilling remarked ruefully. Max Baginski (who, with Isaak and Havel, also met Czolgosz at the train station) wrote, "I reproach myself for having indifferently passed by, without a kind and tender word, an outraged and deeply wounded soul."[50]

But even putting his wounded sincerity aside, they were not quite sure he qualified as an anarchist. "He had not read any Anarchist literature but the 'Free Society,' " Schilling noted.[51] Isaak remembered

Czolgosz's saying, "I know nothing of Anarchism, excepting what I know from one speech delivered by Emma Goldman in Cleveland."[52] Baginski noted, "He was unknown to [the revolutionists and anarchists]; he seldom frequented their gatherings."[53] Most of all, Isaak thought, the anarchistic nature of Czolgosz's assault on the President remained unclear. "I don't believe in killing rulers, but I do believe in self-defense," Isaak said, trying to clarify the role of violence in anarchist philosophy.[54]

Indeed, the only anarchist who entertained no doubt about Leon Czolgosz was his inspiration and alleged love interest, Emma Goldman. She herself had undergone a sudden conversion to anarchism unaided by the established literature, and believed Czolgosz could, too. Born in Lithuania, then a province of the Russian empire, in 1869, Goldman came to the United States in 1885 and worked in sweatshops. She attended socialist meetings and studied the literature. But it took the Haymarket trial to make an anarchist of her—it "brought me to life and helped to make me what I am."[55] What was more, she alone of the anarchists connected to Czolgosz was known to have promoted political violence and to have been "closely connected" with an assassination plot.[56]

In 1892, under the influence of their common philosophical inspiration, Johann Most, Goldman's lover, Alexander Berkman, tried to murder Carnegie steel executive Henry Clay Frick. During a strike at the Homestead plant in Pennsylvania, Frick offered to hire former employees as nonunion labor, and the door of his office was open. Berkman walked in, shot Frick in the head and the neck, and, while struggling with the company's vice president, stabbed Frick four times in the side and back. Despite the injuries, Frick recovered quickly, continued to run the plant, and broke the striking union.

Berkman went to prison for fourteen years. Johann Most repudiated the assault on Frick at a public anarchist meeting, in response to which Goldman produced a horsewhip and struck him repeatedly, stalking off to become her own philosophical inspiration. She went on tour, stumping up and down the country like an itinerant minister, publicizing Berkman's martyrdom to the cause, and promoting anarchism as she understood it.[57] And—also like an itinerant minister—

she depended on her personal charisma to win converts. She was, even her great admirers believed, "very vain" and—despite Dr. Briggs's skepticism on this point—"an oversexed personality [who] made all sorts of advances to men," which was part of her charm.[58]

Once Czolgosz had shot the President and claimed he did it for admiration of her, Goldman suddenly had a great deal of time for the man she now called "poor Leon."[59] She had heard Isaak and Schilling express skepticism about Czolgosz's commitment to anarchism and, she said, she was appalled by their certitude—"they have done an injustice to the young man." As far as she could see, the only honest position on Czolgosz's alleged anarchism was agnosticism: "No one can with certainty say, that the man was an Anarchist, since he was but little known, and since he has never made a public statement to that effect. Still less can one prove that he was not one."[60]

More to the point, Goldman believed, his action spoke louder than his inarticulate yearnings or lack of anarchist learning. "There is nothing in his act by which one can deny him the right of being an Anarchist." Whereas Isaak distinguished between Czolgosz's attack and the asserted anarchistic right to self-defense, Goldman blurred this line. When, in the course of his investigation, Dr. Channing pressed her to explain the relation between anarchism and Czolgosz's act, she replied, "It is true, the Philosophy of Anarchy does not teach Invasion, but it does teach self defence, and Czolgosz's act was an act of self defence and nothing else. You may question this, since Czolgosz was not personally attact [sic] by McKinley, quite true, but Czolgosz belonged to the Oppressed, the Exploited, to the Disinherited Millions, who lead a life of darkness and despair owing to those, of whom McKinley was one, therefore he was personally attacked by the President"—here she backed off, realizing she had lost her train of thought, and perhaps had contradicted herself—"or rather he was one of the victims of the McKinley regime and those McKinley catered to." Thus, she said, rallying to her point again, "I insist [the assassination] had nothing unanarchistic about it."[61]

What was puzzling Goldman was not the violence of the action, but the target. She echoed Theodore Roosevelt, who pointed out that of all his conceivable offenses, McKinley had never accumulated wealth of his own. Likewise, Goldman later wondered, "why had he chosen the President rather than some more direct representative of the system of economic oppression and misery?" The only answer that seemed plausible to her was the one Czolgosz himself had suggested to Isaak: "Was it because he saw in McKinley the willing tool of Wall Street and of the new American imperialism that flowered under his administration? One of its first steps had been the annexation of the Philippines, an act of treachery to the people whom America had pledged to set free during the Spanish War."[62] But though she clearly would have thought it more logical to attack another capitalist like Frick, she was prepared to make room for Czolgosz's decision in her definition of anarchistic action. As she wrote, "Anarchism claims the right to Defence against Invasion and Aggression of every shape and form and no one who has his eyes open will and can deny that those in Power are the Invaders, and McKinley certainly was one of them."[63]

Goldman's determination to claim the assassination as an anarchistic act put her in agreement with Roosevelt. It made political sense to both of them that the murder should have been an expression of anarchism. It gave each of them a martyr to exploit—never mind that one valorized the killer and the other his victim—and a moral tragedy with which to illustrate the abstract wrongs wrought by industrialism. However politically neat, this interpretation satisfied neither the police nor the psychologists.

A CONSPIRACY THEORY EXPIRES

President Roosevelt and the press played an important part in using the assassination to define what was properly American and what was not, but so did immigrants and their descendants. From the moment Private O'Brien replaced Jim Parker as the man who (albeit briefly) rescued McKinley from Czolgosz, the struggle between Americanism and anarchism was a struggle between good ethnic Americans and bad ones. And at the front lines of this fight, the issues had less to do with abstract ideologies than with which groups held political power. Goldman and the Chicago anarchists found themselves unwittingly caught between two such groups.

In the autumn of 1901, two factions struggled for control of the Chicago Police Department. Chief O'Neill, who described himself as Mayor Harrison's man, was appointed in April to clean up the department, and was working with an independent civil service commission to combat corruption. This effort paralleled other anticorruption campaigns in American cities. Throughout the country, independent bodies were appointed to draft and oversee meritocratic standards for civil service. Most notably, the commissions implemented competitive civil service exams, making performance rather than patronage the measure of advancement. The commissions were bipartisan bodies (Democratic President Grover Cleveland kept Theodore Roosevelt on the national Civil Service Commission) and were supposed to prevent politics from corrupting essential public services—public safety chief among them.

When civil service reformers spoke about corruption, they often saddled immigrants and ethnic populations with an undue share of the blame. There was some truth in the finger-pointing: political operators did truly meet boatloads of immigrants at the docks, soliciting their loyalty, offering them jobs, and giving them places in organizations that asked of them only that in return they vote early and often. But as politicians and journalists of the period also knew, the involvement of immigrants in partisan machines told only a small part of the story of American industrial politics. Sensitive to stereotypes and conscious of the more complex truth, some ethnic politicians at the turn of the century tried to combine loyalty to immigrant communities with stainless political careers.[64] No population stood accused of political misbehavior more often than the Irish, whose pattern of assimilation to American society imbedded them in police and fire departments and other essential institutions of urban politics. As English speakers who had begun migrating to the United States early in the nineteenth century, they had an advantage over other immigrants as they gained access to political institutions.[65] By the turn of the twentieth century, Irish-Americans already wielded tremendous and largely unchallenged influence in the city politics of New York and Boston.

In Chicago, the Irish ascendancy came slightly later, and was still taking shape in the fall of 1901.[66] Hence Chief O'Neill's commitment to cleaning up Chicago's police. He was waging a war for the integrity of American Irishness against a faction of Irish-Americans with fewer qualms about wielding patronage power.

Born in County Cork, O'Neill came to America in 1869 and joined the Chicago police in 1873. He benefited from civil service reforms, excelling at the competitive exams and rising through the ranks on merit. Nobody was a more dedicated scholar of Irish culture than O'Neill, who in his spare time collected, arranged, and published thousands of Irish folk melodies lest they vanish in the diaspora.[67] But the chief would not let his Irishness signify his corruption, and so showed a conspicuous zeal in anticorruptionist efforts, even—or perhaps especially—when it pitted him against other Irish cops. He had one invaluable ally—Mayor Harrison, who was trying to hold on to a coalition of progressive Democrats that would enable him to win a fourth consecutive term—and one enemy close to home.

Captain Luke Colleran ran the city's Central Detective Bureau, and so he had charge of the interrogation of anarchists arrested in the McKinley shooting. He was politically connected to Robert E. Burke, the city oil inspector and head of the local Democratic Central Committee. There was no Democrat the mayor would rather bring down than the Irish fixer Bobbie Burke, and there was no Irish cop O'Neill would rather bring down than Colleran. The Civil Service Commission had already interviewed Colleran in August in an investigation that forced the resignation of some key detectives under him. And although Colleran himself escaped censure on that occasion, O'Neill was hot on his heels. Before news of the assassination attempt broke, the early edition of the September 7 *Chicago Tribune* carried in its lead story the Civil Service Commission's interest in Chief O'Neill's charges of evidence tampering against Colleran.[68]

The shooting of the President gave Colleran a reprieve and a chance to prove his worth. On the evening of the arrests, he could promote the heroism of his detectives to the press, maintaining that his investigation would soon uncover the details of an anarchist conspiracy to assassinate the President. But even this early in the case, one highly placed source in the police department told a *Chicago Tribune* reporter, "The general opinion outside Captain Colleran's office is that no special reason exists to connect the would-be assassin with the local Anarchists except the general character of their teachings and agitations."[69] Shortly afterward, the *Chicago Journal* identified the chief as the source of skepticism: "Chief of Police O'Neill is frank in saying it does not look as if the anarchists under arrest were involved in a plot. On the other hand, Capt. Colleran—who usually likes to 'swell things up' more or less—maintains an air of mystery, as if he had something up his sleeve."[70]

When Czolgosz shot McKinley, Emma Goldman was in St. Louis, in the midst of a speaking tour. When she saw newspaper headlines reporting a dragnet out for her, she decided to go to Chicago, where she would confront the policemen who had fired on strikers at Haymarket and who now held her friends captive. Captain Schuettler arrested her on a conspiracy warrant on September 10, and threatened her: "If you don't confess, you'll go the way of those bastard Haymarket anarchists." Colleran's detectives starved her, burned her eyes with a bright light, and goaded her with threats—but she had nothing to confess.[71]

On September 11, Chief O'Neill concluded there was nothing in the conspiracy case, and that Colleran must stop trying to force a confession. He told the press that Colleran could not hold Goldman and the other anarchists any longer unless Buffalo police offered some evidence that there had been a conspiracy, and sent Buffalo a telegram stating tersely, "You must prove your case."[72] O'Neill also made a personal call on Goldman to conduct his own interrogation. He asked politely her version of events, and had his stenographer take down what she said. After she finished, he told her, "I think you are innocent, and I am going to do my part to help you out." Goldman was, she said, "too amazed to thank him; I had never before heard such a tone from a police officer." O'Neill made good on his promise: Goldman had good treatment from that point onward.[73]

News of McKinley's death, accompanied by a plea from the Buffalo police for more time, delayed the anarchists' release. But O'Neill treated it as a foregone conclusion. "It is reassuring to think that we are unable to discover any evidence of a plot," he told the press on

September 15.[74] At the same time, Roosevelt was strenuously expounding on the global terrorist threat, expanding the circle of anarchism to encompass a shadowy, omnipresent network. Washington politicians were feeding press reports of a "war on anarchism," conducted with a coalition of European nations, targeting evildoers throughout the world. But the Chicago police chief, who knew some actual anarchists, was quietly suggesting that though, to be sure, anarchists held reprehensible political opinions, their plotting extended mainly to the scheduling of meetings to air such opinions, and only the slenderest of threads—certainly not a casual link—connected those meetings with Czolgosz's fatal action.

Colleran's effort to cook up a conspiracy was not part of a national red scare; it was a decidedly local effort to prevent the progressive faction under Mayor Harrison from sacking him and his patron Bobbie Burke while gaining control of the Democratic Party in Cook County. No sooner did O'Neill end Colleran's inquiry into the conspiracy than the war between factious Democrats returned to the fore. On September 23, O'Neill released Isaak and his housemates, and on September 24 let Goldman go as the conspiracy charge was dismissed.[75] The same day, the chief brought Colleran before the Civil Service Commission on charges of evidence tampering in a robbery case. The hearings ballooned into a public dispute between reform-minded Democrats and the traditional party leadership. Mayor Harrison sided with O'Neill, and Burke backed Colleran. A source in the mayor's office told the Chicago Tribune it was shaping up to be a battle between "Burke and his clansmen" on one side and Harrison and the civil service reformers on the other.[76] The reform forces won: Colleran was convicted and fired, and Burke was indicted for embezzlement and bribery (he had pocketed money from the Standard Oil Company) and forced to resign.[77]

Chicago's progressives had no political use for a conspiracy in the Czolgosz case, and so on Chicago's local stage it died. The usefulness of Czolgosz's connection to anarchism lay elsewhere, with the anarchists themselves and the national parties who could stigmatize them.

The Chicago press reflected this split opinion in the national debate concerning the influence of anarchism on Czolgosz. In the course

Emma Goldman, anarchist, as depicted in a week's worth of the *Chicago Tribune*: demon, seductress, or innocent bystander?

of six days, the *Chicago Tribune* offered three different pictorial repre-
sentations of Emma Goldman's relation to the crime. In one, she appeared as the devilish priestess of a hellish philosophy that owned
damned souls, surrounded by tongues of fire, surmounted by the portrait of a demon. In a second, she seemed the full-lipped languid embodiment of bespectacled intellectual sex appeal, a woman who, if she
seduced Czolgosz, did it not with philosophy, but the old-fashioned
way. In a third, the cartoonist let her off the hook altogether, showing
Czolgosz blaming a befuddled, even matronly Goldman for his mis-
deed, under the caption "The Oldest Excuse on Record."[78]

This last explanation gained force as the first two waned: the problem lay not with anarchism or its prophetess, but with the specific
history of Leon Czolgosz. Attending an anarchist meeting in the
countryside near Boston once he returned home to Massachusetts in
the summer of 1902, Briggs swung around to this conclusion. The anarchists were more festive than fiery, he thought: "their games and
their music . . . held their interest much more than the speech making."[79] It was not an environment to create an assassin. For Czolgosz
to murder McKinley, and martyr himself, he must have had problems
in his earlier environment. Curiously enough, Emma Goldman came
late in her life to the same conclusion. Well after writing her memoir,
she added a psychological layer to her understanding of Czolgosz the
martyr, saying, "I know definitely [that his childhood] must have been
a perfect hell." If an investigator wanted to understand "the beginning
of his revolutionary awakening and his hatred of all injustice and all
authority," then he would have to look at Czolgosz's upbringing.[80] It
was under this same conviction that Briggs traveled to Cleveland in
the winter of 1902 and sought out the assassin's family.

5

ALL-AMERICAN

On January 9, 1902, four months after Roosevelt took office, Briggs finally found his way to the Czolgosz house on Fleet Street in Cleveland. He had to fight his way into the parlor, past stacks of packed boxes and piled furniture: the family, pestered by journalists since the assassination, was moving out. The father, Paul, had found a new place still comfortably within the extensive confines of Cleveland's Slavic community. Briggs caught up with them on the last day they lived in a house Leon knew, and despite the commotion managed to get a few questions in as the Czolgosz sons were busy getting their possessions out.

For his voyage into the Polish parts of the city, Briggs engaged an "interpreter and guide."[1] Such resources were easy to find in early-twentieth-century Cleveland: like most industrial American cities in the 1890s, it had several German-language newspapers, and owing to the German empire's recent consolidation, the German language had become a necessity for eastern Europeans. The migrants brought their official language with them to America, and the distinctive sound of German consonants filled marketplaces and offices alongside or even to the exclusion of English in industrial towns throughout the United States. German grew swiftly to become the second-most-published language in the nation, reaching hundreds of thousands of readers.[2] It was a simple matter, then, for Briggs to call at the offices of *Wachter und Anzeiger*, a local German-language newspaper, where he found a linguistically talented reporter named Ludwig Darmstadter to arrange and interpret his meetings with the Czolgoszes.[3]

With the parents and the boys stacking boxes and moving sofas, Briggs had nobody to talk to but Leon's youngest sister, Victoria. She ordinarily worked as a maid for a family on Cleveland's Broadway, but during the move she was minding the young children of Paul Czolgosz's second marriage. Eighteen years old, Victoria had no firsthand recollection of Leon's childhood—he was ten years older than she— but she was easy to talk to and, Briggs noticed, to look at: "Victoria was a comely girl with light hair, fair skin and hazel eyes and a well developed figure."[4] She spoke to him while her brothers carried furniture, glowered at the conversationalists, and growled at her in Polish—trying to get her to help, she noted, as she continued to chat with the stranger.

In plying Victoria and the other Czolgoszes, Briggs was hunting for clues to the cause of Leon's presumed insanity. He asked after unhealthy environmental influences, bad family dynamics, acquired disease, and hereditary mental disorder. He looked for patterns of strange behavior and odd ideas. Briggs and Channing hoped and expected to find evidence to back the theory of the defense at trial: that anyone who sacrificed his own life to kill the President for a cause like anarchism must suffer from some form of madness. At the same time they had not committed themselves to any particular theory of madness, believing that insanity could have many different causes. So Briggs did not confine himself to any single avenue of inquiry, but asked about everything. Through the course of Briggs's interviews he seized on the smallest hint of an oddity, and he underlined and emphasized even the most indirect hint of eccentricity in his quarry. Although he found a few peculiarities, the cumulative force of the detail he piled up tended overwhelmingly to illustrate the opposite point—the utter, and often depressing, typicality of Leon Czolgosz's family and upbringing.

Victoria said she knew that her father, Paul, came to Michigan from Prussia in the early 1870s. His wife, Mary Nowak, followed some months later with their three sons, and Leon was born soon after. Once in America, Mary bore a child approximately every two years

till she died in childbirth, about ten years later. Paul married Katren
Metzfaltr a year and a half after Mary's death.

Katren brushed past Briggs and Victoria where they sat in the front
room, and at his request Victoria stopped her and asked her a few
questions in Polish. She did not smile or say much, but she rested, red-
faced with her exertion, willing to talk a little. She said Leon had attended Catholic school in Michigan, public school in Ohio. And
beginning at the age of sixteen he worked, first in a glass factory in
Pennsylvania, then a wire mill in Ohio, and then, toward the end, not
much at all, as far as she could tell.

As Katren returned to her labors, Victoria admitted to Briggs that
she herself had thought her brother lazy (though she was fond of him).
But Katren's dismissive attitude, she assured Briggs, reflected more
that Leon had fought constantly with his stepmother—"they were always nagging each other, and while he never swore he came pretty
near to it in talking with her."[5]

Leon's brother Jacob and father, Paul, also paused to speak to
Briggs, but neither could tell him much more about the family history
or health. Apart from having lost a finger while in the army ordnance
department at Sandy Hook—from which he received a pension of
thirty dollars a month—Jacob was hale and hearty. So was Paul,
though Briggs thought him "rather a rough looking man." Paul told
Briggs he "could never remember dates," but figured Leon's mother
was about forty when she died; otherwise his relatives lived long lives.
Only one—his mother's sister Ann, who remained in Prussia—might
have been mentally ill; she behaved oddly just before her death. Briggs
treasured this slender hint of insanity in the family, though it rested
on meager evidence. Paul had learned of his sister-in-law's odd behavior in a letter from the old country. Like most immigrants, he kept up
correspondence with family left behind, but it was a slow medium and
awkward for a class of people who worked mainly with their hands, so
such letters tended toward pith rather than detail.[6]

With the family's move still under way and the evening progress-
ing, Briggs agreed to meet them again the next day. He hoped to talk
a little more about Leon's childhood and have photographs taken. So
he bid them good-night and went to a hotel. And as he did through-

out his trip, he spent his evening going over his notes, preserving every detail of each encounter in the reports that he mailed back to Channing in Brookline. "I have decided to write out every minute of my time and every thing I learn or that is said to me," he told Channing. "It makes more work for you but you will be able to choose all that may be important to you in your conclusions."[7]

By compiling this meticulous record, Briggs accidentally established an evidentiary foundation for Leon Czolgosz's ordinariness. If experience and inheritance made the assassin insane, then the same factors were hard at work maddening millions of other Americans.

PEASANTS INTO PUNCH CARDS

Nineteenth-century migrants felt pushed about by mighty forces herding them off the land, lumping them together into cities and factories. These forces did not build over time; they simply announced themselves by the sudden drop in the price of wheat. Thinking back, an American farmer might reconstruct a slow progression: the introduction of chemical fertilizers and reaping machines, the land around being bought up and put under intensive tillage. But in Europe, a landsman would never see these things or be able to identify their effects unless he went down to the docks and saw the ships unloading grain from countries where it grew unimaginably cheaply.

Those few clever or lucky men—bankers like J. P. Morgan, manufacturers like Andrew Carnegie, shippers like George Pullman—who saw what was coming made great fortunes off investments in consolidation. These princes of capital seemed to move mountains; they certainly moved populations. They made it possible to personalize the abstract statistical facts that shaped the era. As one Polish nationalist wrote, "It is a fact . . . that almost a half million Poles have gathered in America. This fact cannot be reversed. This situation was created . . . by the miserable and criminal politics of our enemies, who took as their purpose the ruin of the Polish nation."[8] It was easier to blame these criminals than historical forces tending blindly toward industrialization.

Swept up in these same forces, the Czolgoszes saw the same faces on them as everybody else. They lived in a section of Cleveland called Newburgh, where Leon and his older brother Waldeck worked at the steel-wire factory. Newburgh was once a separate village built around its iron mill, founded by Welshmen and worked by British immigrants. Cleveland Rolling Mills incorporated the Newburgh Works in 1863. The city of Cleveland annexed Newburgh township in 1873. The Cleveland Rolling Mills corporation used Polish immigrant workers to break a strike among the British workers in 1882, and the Polish and Czech influences soon swallowed up the Welshness of Newburgh. In an effort to pool the steel-wire market in 1899, Judge Elbert Gary and J. W. Gates's American Steel and Wire Company bought the Cleveland Rolling Mill's wireworks in 1899, and in 1901 the new United States Steel Corporation—a creation of Gary, J. P. Morgan, and Charles M. Schwab—swallowed the lot.[9]

To the millions of migrants who heeded the call of American capital, the corporate captains in the United States were only the last in a long line of princes who seemed happiest when persecuting peasants. Interviewing the Czolgosz family, local saloonkeepers and factory foremen, policemen and priests, Briggs discovered a miniature social history of the immigrant reaction to this world of great men and dehumanizing forces. Only Leon's determination to strike at one of these princes lifted his family's story out of the morass of the masses and put his face on another set of social forces—the frustration and anger building up from below the bootheels of an indifferent, or unknowing, class of oppressors.

With the interpreter Darmstadter's help, Briggs arranged for the family to be photographed the day after the move. Posing for his portrait, Paul Czolgosz smoothed his rough edges as best he could and put on a black coat. His collar fit loosely, and his calloused hand rested awkwardly on his chest. The back of his neck showed a deep tan, interrupted by the pale furrows of wrinkles in his skin. He had weathered hardships and it showed. He made a visible contrast with his sons: with combed and oiled hair, they shaved clean and dressed up for their pictures. This difference exemplified the yawning chasm between the generation who migrated and their children. Born in the

Paul Czolgosz, Leon's father, in
January 1902. Note the button
depicting Leon in his lapel.
(Massachusetts Historical Society)

New World, the younger generation had New World skills, incomes,
and appearances. They looked, lived, and worked like the native-born
Americans they were. Their parents kept to the appearances, accents,
and reduced livelihoods of their past. Whatever benefits accrued to a
family from the voyage to America usually fell upon the native-born
generation, rather than the migrants themselves.[10] Despite this generation gap the Czolgoszes, like their fellow migrants, stuck together as a
family. They lived in the same house in Cleveland, they pooled their
savings and contributed to the purchase and upkeep of a family farm
in nearby Warrensville, and in their lapels they wore medallions depicting their dead brother.

Paul Czolgosz could not understand how his family story took such
a tragic turn. His son had always been quiet, even bashful—certainly
peaceful and never a fighter. He did not drink or smoke, and had generally kept to himself. The Leon he knew could not have done this
terrible thing unless, of course, he had gone mad somehow. He cer-

tainly did not follow in the footsteps of his father, who stuck to a common strategy of migrate, adapt, and work.

The young, alienated Leon Czolgosz stood in many Americans' minds for the threat posed by the "new immigrants"—the migrants from southern and eastern Europe who began arriving in significant numbers in the 1890s, and who numbered some eighteen million arrivals by 1920.[11] Motivated by the lure of better salaries in the United States, 76 percent of them were young adults (between the ages of fifteen and forty), and 64 percent of them were men. They came singly, rather than in family groups. In short, like most voluntary migrant streams in world history, America's comprised mainly young single men seeking material betterment.[12] The new immigrants came from countries where modern industry was already changing traditional assumptions and livelihoods, and they knew enough about factory labor and world markets to see they could make more money doing the same jobs in America. Quite often, they had no particular intention of staying in their host country; among some new immigrant populations, the rate of return migration ran as high as 50 percent (although among Poles like Czolgosz it was never much higher than 30 percent).[13]

As a population of rootless young men with no interest in Americanization, these migrants seemed—to the growing number of immigration restrictionists like Channing—to pose a threat to social order. As some Americans grew increasingly uneasy about the new immigrants, they began to think of these Europeans as racially different, for as young single workingmen they resembled an earlier pattern of migration: the movement of workers from China in the 1860s and 1870s. Working-class white Americans in the West who competed with the Chinese migrants for jobs identified them as a racial threat. Thus construed, the Chinese migration so disturbed Americans that Congress voted to stopper it with the Chinese Exclusion Act of 1882. Aimed at Asians, exclusion barely troubled Americans who believed in the importance of racial difference. But now they confronted a group of apparently white immigrants who resisted cultural Americanization while gladly accepting economic Americanization. Exclusion began to look like an appropriate policy for certain kinds of Europeans whose competition for wages and resources was beginning to make them look racially suspect.[14]

But to think of Leon Czolgosz as an example of this threat was a category mistake. He was a native-born American, or at most what social scientists called a second-generation immigrant. His perception of American industrial civilization had nothing to do with the motives and fortunes of the new immigrants. On the contrary, his father and mother were very much a product of older immigration patterns and ambitions.

Paul Czolgosz left Prussia in 1873 for Michigan, fleeing the grinding effects of nation making. Chancellor Otto von Bismarck, seeking to secure the expanded borders of the new German empire, waged a *Kulturkampf* against Polish Catholics living within the boundaries of the new Reich. The chancellor believed active discouragement of Polish cultural practices was the only way to solve what he and his allies regarded as "the Polish problem."[15]

Being called an ethno-religious "problem" by the German Reich made Polish Catholics see migration as more urgent, and under pressures like these whole families decided to move as swiftly as possible, creating a refugee migrant stream that looked different from the opportunity-seeking new immigrants. The sources of "new immigrants"—Old World families who sent forth young single men with little to lose and much to gain—were pressured only by the economic squeeze of global industrialization. They might go or not; having gone, they might return. By contrast, those who fled oppression tended to move as families, and to seek a permanent home in their new country. Paul Czolgosz scouted Detroit for only a few months before sending for Mary and the children to join him. Then, torn by the American promise of opportunity and the memory of the communities they left, the Czolgoszes kept seeking out something better and more like home.

The earlier migrants who left Europe for the New World came mainly from rural origins. They worked the land, and their ancestors had worked the land before them. In turn they expected to go to America and work better, richer land there for happier returns. More even than satisfying a peasant's natural dream the plan to stay on the land seemed to make economic sense: the United States possessed immense acres of undeveloped country and proportionately few citizens to work it.[16] And greater even than migrant wishes or economic theory was the desire of the Republican Party, distilled into law in 1864: the Republican Congress had passed "an Act to encourage Immigration," which Abraham Lincoln signed on July 4, with the express intent of settling the West swiftly with free laborers. Although federal enthusiasm for immigration later waned, Western states like Wisconsin and Michigan continued to seek immigrant labor, establishing in eastern Europe permanent colonization bureaus to beckon workers to the New World.[17]

The combined pressure of the immigrants' wishes, economic logic, and the intentions of politicians could not overcome the forces that kept the immigrants in cities. Migrants weary from their journey and desperate for their daily bread found it easier to work on the docks where they landed or in nearby factories than to seek passage inland to unknown and isolated farmlands. And industrial employers wanted immigrants to stay in cities—hard-up travelers would work for a lower wage than native-born Americans, and a workforce speaking half a dozen languages was slow to unionize.

Working for subsistence pay and subject to cyclical unemployment, immigrants relied on the credit extended by grocers and landlords, who had little choice when their entire clientele needed help. This web of debt tied families to their urban neighborhoods. And as years went by with these forces in effect, more immigrants stayed in cities. This ethnic clustering became an added lure: it was comfortable to stay with a community preserving familiar folkways of language, religion, and food. It was also easier to start a business among people with familiar tastes. Although only a third of new businesses lasted more than three years, those that did could thrive. Ethnic communities devoted to preserving their culture made eager customers for olive oil, familiar spices, and other products of the old country.[18]

But the traps and blandishments of the cities could not wholly erase the desire for familiar landed security. So the migrants bought farms when they could, and then they experienced the hallowed American tradition of farm failure. It was, after all, the age of acceler-

ating agricultural mechanization and consolidation: one of the worst
times in U.S. history to establish a family farm.

The soil of the American West was largely uncultivated. Entrepreneurs of the earth were buying up unimproved acres by the hundreds,
rendering them instantly suitable for production by superfertilizing
them with imported guano. They harvested the proceeds with machines made by men like Chicago magnate Cyrus McCormick, whose
ability to meet the needs of a global commodities market accelerated
and guided the processes transforming agricultural production around
the world. These factors determined the price of farming for agricultural firms and families alike.

In the dry prairie country of the plains states, a farmer needed at
least 160 acres to make a go at success. At about $5 an acre, plus
money for the necessary buildings, machinery, and stock, it came to a
total investment of about $1,500. And then the farm might fail,
falling prey to locusts, floods, or drought. Few immigrant families,
however ambitious, could afford to risk capital on this scale.

Clearing forested land, despite the need to cut and take away trees,
was a safer bet, requiring only about $250 of investment. In the
wooded, wetter states a small farm needed only about forty acres. Even
so, it would take, on the average, three or four years' factory work to
save enough to start. And once farming had begun, the global com-
modity markets, driven to deflation by the high price of gold and the
increasing production of farm goods, pinched indiscriminately the
children of the Old World and the New. Even if everything else
worked well, the patterns of commerce, as global and unpredictable as
the patterns of weather, might yet drive a farm to failure.[19]

Thus driven from the industrial city to the industrial countryside
and back, a migrant family might finally invest a nest egg, avoid the
specter of farm failure, and make a place for themselves of their own
choosing. But to achieve this modest success would mean that women
and children must work, that all must live together and as cheaply as
possible, and that all must agree to defer their private dreams—and
some might give their lives—in the interest of the family's collective
good fortune.

From the time of their arrival in 1873, the Czolgoszes followed this pattern, seeking to bend a grinding cycle of uncertainty into a spiral upward to security. Paul worked in Detroit factories and dockyards for three years. He would have had to save a little longer to buy his own farm, but an early opportunity came his way: an employer nearby was recruiting eastern European workers for a lumber mill, and offered land in return. The price was life and labor in a company town named Rogers City.

The firm of Rogers & Molitor bought its lands in the Michigan woods in 1869 and laid out a town in 1870. The company founders, William Rogers and Albert Molitor, recruited German and Polish immigrants through the German-language newspapers of Detroit, offering lots and lumber to employees, who could build their own houses and bring their families. Like most company towns, it offered its citizens a stable, planned community in return for the privilege of insulating them from the labor market. Off in the woods of Presque Isle, depending on a weekly boat for its supplies, Rogers City kept its workers where they could not afford to strike, nor could they easily leave for another firm.

It was commonplace for lumber and mining companies to build housing and civic institutions in the forests and mountains of the West, where no town would otherwise flourish. The firms soon made profit of these necessities, supplying money at interest and credit at the company store to bind workers with chains of debt. More ambitious businessmen began to think about the company town as a social experiment, and, like George Pullman of Chicago, constructed planned communities with model housing. There were about twenty-five hundred such towns in the United States in 1900.[20] Whatever the beauty and order of planned communities owned by a single company—Pullman won an international award as "most perfect town"—their paternalist structures tended to collapse. The town of Pullman erupted in a strike in 1894, which ended only when President Grover Cleveland used federal troops to break it. Afterward, in 1898, the Illinois Supreme Court ordered the company to divest itself of the town, finding the corporation's ownership of the civic community a "usurpation."[21] Less-ambitious projects like Rogers City fell to similar, if less spectacular, fates.

William Rogers, who had no appetite for life in the woods, left the management of the town to Albert Molitor. A Prussian rumored to be the illegitimate son of King Wilhelm I, Molitor treated the town as his personal fief, winning elections by "peculiar means," issuing town bonds—and spending the proceeds—on his own authority. A lynch mob cornered him in 1874, but Molitor told them to go to a "warmer climate," and the citizens quailed before the man who controlled the city's food supply. But in 1875 a group of horsemen simply rode up to the window of his office and opened fire, killing him.[22]

If Briggs had been able to put the Czolgoszes in the region of another political assassination it might have helped his investigation, but Paul and his sons were quick to tell him the murder happened before the family lived there. The vagueness of their recollections made the timing of their move to Rogers City unclear, though when the murderers were finally named and convicted in 1891, there were no rumors that any Czolgosz had been involved. In any case, even in Molitor's unlamented absence, the town offered the Czolgosz family little opportunity beyond the ownership of a house. What was more, its community appeal did not extend to Polish Catholics like them: the tight-knit society was dominated, like the Prussia they fled, by German Lutherans. So after only a few months in the Rogers City woods they moved to Alpena, a port on Lake Huron serving the lumber mills of the Thunder Bay River. There, in a rented house, Paul supported his wife and family for five years, while the children increased in number from six to eight.

Loading lumber on the docks, Paul earned 30 cents an hour from a firm called Fletcher (equivalent to an hourly wage today of about $5.04).[23] If he worked between fifty and sixty hours a week year-round he would have made between $780 and $936 a year, in an era when an annual minimum living wage was often estimated at around $700.[24] But he would not have worked year-round: like almost all unskilled American workers, especially those in industries (like timber) afflicted by seasonal drop-offs, he would have spent a third of the year out of work. In late-nineteenth-century Michigan, workers routinely spent almost four months out of work. Paul Czolgosz's annual wage would therefore have been somewhere between $520 and $624—barely enough, if indeed sufficient, to house and feed his family.[25]

It would therefore have been extraordinary if in about 1877, when his older children began to reach the age of ten, Paul did not begin to depend on them to generate additional income. Michigan had no minimum-age legislation until the mid-1880s, and no state had a broad minimum-age law when the Czolgoszes moved to Alpena. Early, limited legislation had appeared by 1879, when seven states had passed laws. And even then, after the moral campaigns to preserve the welfare of children and keep them from toil, most states set the minimum age for manufacturing jobs at ten years old.[26]

Children were simply too valuable, both to families and to industry, to leave idle. Almost half of immigrant family incomes came from children's labor by 1880. Unskilled labor paid so little to an adult head of household that a family could double its income by sending children out to work. With the possibility of injury or unemployment always hanging over every easily replaced factory worker or dockhand, child labor provided a way for families to spread these risks around, ensuring that even in the event of catastrophe some kind of income would continue.[27]

Employers, for their part, valued the children as cheap, productive, energetic, and nimble workers. As industrial production expanded in the last three decades of the nineteenth century, the new factories drew in as many laborers as they could, and in the process they increased the American child-labor force by more than a million. The little workers added great fortunes to the mill owners' coffers and a few additional pennies per hour to the immigrants' purses.[28]

The savings tactics employed by the Czolgosz household in the 1870s and 1880s worked, and after a few industrious years at Alpena they could afford to buy a farm. They selected a plot in the nearby Polish community of Posen. The settlement there, cut from the same Michigan woodland as Rogers City, was new and isolated in the middle of the forest like an island in a sea of trees—but not because company managers had planned it for their purposes. Named after a Prussian city, Posen was established by Poles in an effort to create for themselves a "small Poland." Its land lent itself readily to farming—after the labor of clearing. Polish men set dynamite in the fields to explode stumps left from the trees felled by their children—sons and daughters alike—wielding axes. Laboring in concert, families and community extended the fields into the woods. Like all farming it was hard, but in the rainy climate of Michigan it was surer than the drier homesteads in the more distant West. Weighing the risks of the larger farms in the prairies against the work of clear-cutting forests, one land agent summed up the analysis simply: "no one ever fails who settles in the timber."[29]

Though their children worked here just as they did in the cities—often starting by milking cows when they were as young as eight—the farmwork of children seemed natural and even wholesome to the Poles and indeed to most Americans. Even once states began passing child-labor laws, they often exempted work done during school vacations—when farmwork was heaviest—or exempted agricultural labor altogether. In the New World as in the Old, the family on the farm was its own unit of economic production, and children were a customary part of the labor force.[30]

In the timberland of Michigan the American Poles built their new Posen and reached out from it to the wider world, constructing roads to the state highways and spurs to the railway trunk lines. But they tried to keep the world from reaching in to them. They established a Catholic church, and a parochial school with nuns to teach in it. They spoke their own language there—not German or English—and, singing their own hymns, worshipped their own Christ and His Mother. They farmed potatoes, kept and grazed cows, and manured the land with the products of their own livestock. The Czolgoszes stayed there five years, and might have remained happily forever, had not their mother's labor led to grief.[31]

Whatever work the Czolgosz children did on the homestead or in the factory, their mother had her own specific chore in the household. Mary Nowak Czolgosz's job was to generate more children and to keep healthy those she had until they reached working age. Birthrates among the immigrant population of the United States ran much higher than those of the native-born—from 35 percent higher in rural

A baby at play, photographed by Jacob Riis in a tenement in the immigrant-heavy Lower East Side of Manhattan—"its playground," as Riis wrote. (Collection of the New-York Historical Society)

areas to 90 percent higher in urban areas, which suggested that fertility varied primarily according to the way of life women expected.[32]

The fertility pattern of migrant women corresponded to their families' needs for productive workers: farm women, whatever their country of origin, needed children for work, and farm children tended to be producers. The more children, the better, so far as life on the farm went. By contrast, city women's children tended to be consumers, especially if they were native born to white-collar parents. Middle-class children being unlikely to bring in money rather than spend it, middle-class families were smaller. Foreign-born women, whether they lived in the rural or urban United States, preserved the farm pattern of fertility. After all, poor city families depended on child labor just like farm families. And children might die young—infant mortality rates ran high; as many as half the deaths in a rural immigrant community might be children under the age of five.[33] The Czolgoszes did not escape this probability; one of Leon's brothers recalled a child who died within weeks of being born. Beyond this loss the family was relatively lucky. In addition to the child who died in infancy, Briggs recorded the names of eight brothers and sisters for Leon, born over a period of about twenty years. A nursing mother might keep to about this rate, so it is possible Mary lost no other children in her years of contributing to the household workforce.

Catholic duty and custom corresponded to economic needs. Emily Greene Balch, a social scientist studying the Slavic communities at the turn of the century, learned from a priest that "our women despise American women because they have small families." Whether or not Slavic mothers agreed with their clerics, the fact and burden of large families was undeniable. Balch wrote of the women she observed that "they have as hard confinements as Americans, but . . . they recover more quickly. In Allegheny [Pennsylvania] a settlement friend went to see a neighbor and found her at nine o'clock, barefoot in the yard, hanging out clothes. She had borne a child at midnight, after which she had arisen and got breakfast for the men of her family and then done the washing."[34]

With a house full of children, Mary Czolgosz had these same tasks before her, and harder ones, too. As Balch further noted, "Even if a woman is physically able to do this sort of thing, she is aged by it—by that and the continuous child-bearing."[35] It aged them, and it also killed them outright. Foreign-born women were more than twice as likely to die from pregnancy as native-born women.[36] When Mary Czolgosz died in 1883, having just given birth to Victoria, she left her children one final legacy common to the immigrant experience: Slavic Americans of childbearing age were almost three times as likely to die as their native-born counterparts, and thus much likelier to leave orphans.[37]

Shortly after losing the wife, mother, and center of their household, the Czolgoszes gave up their family farm. Their years in Posen had been good ones, but now they would return to Alpena to start again their cycle of family saving and ambition. Paul meant to seek new work and a new wife. The children who could legally do so would return to the factories; by this time the state of Michigan required that children attend school to the age of fourteen.[38] Ten years old when the Czolgoszes sold their farm to another Polish family, named Rambuski, Leon duly enrolled in the Alpena public school. He proved able in class—"he was considered the best scholar of them,"[39] one of his brothers remembered—which explains why his family took the slightly unusual step of leaving him in school until 1889, when Leon reached the age of sixteen.

In 1890, for the first time, the U.S. Census Bureau recorded the social circumstances of Americans on punch cards. The 1880 census had been the first to record extensive sociological data, inquiring not only into the number and location of people in the United States, but their national origin, color, place of birth, occupation, religion, history of indigence, illness, and cause of death (if applicable). It took nearly a full decade—into the next census cycle—to tabulate the data. In response, census special agent Herman Hollerith developed a method of

A twelve-year-old boy working in violation of New York's child-labor law, as photographed by Jacob Riis. (Collection of the New-York Historical Society)

recording and collating this information mechanically. Hollerith remembered seeing a railway conductor in the West produce what was known as a "punch photograph"—using his pocket hole-punch, the conductor took a ticket and punched out a pattern indicating the hair color, height, skin color, and other defining features of a passenger, so nobody else could take his or her place in the coach. Hollerith applied the same profiling system to the census. Enumerators punched out the race, class, gender, religion, ethnicity, and other data of census respondents on cards that clicked through electric machines that generated neat columns of figures corresponding to the social categories. Americans could now be codified, cross-referenced, and compared to norms and means.[40]

If the punch card representing Leon Czolgosz in 1890—seventeen years old, American citizen, Catholic, eight brothers and sisters, both parents born in Polish Prussia, some public school, now working in a factory, living with the family, mother dead of pregnancy-related illness—were dropped into a chute with the cards belonging to the hundreds of thousands of other eastern European immigrants and their children and tabulated by Hollerith's machines, it would not stand out from the pack. Along all the axes definable by modern social science, the Czolgosz family was statistically rather ordinary, even normal. But (according to Americans from Emma Goldman to Theodore Roosevelt) that was the problem: in the late nineteenth century there was a great deal of hardship in normal American lives.[41]

Having company in this normal misery made for little comfort, especially when these numbers stood in newspaper columns next to other numbers like those of "the 400": the families who defined high society in Manhattan. Or a number like "1000%": the increase in the number of American millionaires in the decades around the turn of the century.[42] Or numbers like "one billion": the capital invested into the corporation that Morgan, Gary, and Schwab made from the country's steel holdings. These numbers went along with names the entire nation knew, names that no statistics could obscure, names denoting the tiny fraction of the population that controlled the bulk of the nation's wealth.

This gap, between the great number of the poor and normal and the small number of the rich and exceptional, appalled the Americans whose duty it was to compile and read the numbers. Even before they knew who the Czolgoszes were, these social scientists and social workers knew how they lived. The idea of Mary Czolgosz as a representative woman—a woman bound to bear children till she simply wore out, a woman harnessed to the family welfare as surely as a cart horse, whose children had no greater significance than as sources of income—inspired women of greater means and education to investigation and action. Even before the census could, they collected the numbers and began to tell each other and the rest of the nation what the new Americans' lives were like.

FROM SETTLEMENT WORK TO SOCIAL SCIENCE

When Luke Colleran's detectives of the Chicago Central Bureau arrested the Isaak family and their friends on the night after the McKinley shooting, their neighbors feared the worst. Rousted out of their row house by Colleran's infamously corrupt detectives—men who still bore grudges from the Haymarket bombing and enjoyed any opportunity to vent their anger at foreign-born anarchists—the Isaaks were sure to meet torture and grief in the city's dungeons. Or so the neighborhood, populated predominantly by eastern European migrants and their children, firmly believed, especially after the police refused their application to visit the imprisoned anarchists. Despairing, they turned to the only authority figure they trusted: Jane Addams.

No bond of debt or labor tied Addams to the predominantly immigrant Nineteenth Ward of Chicago: Addams lived among the migrants by choice. Alone among the ward's residents, she could—and immediately did—get an appointment to meet Mayor Harrison. Because of the unusual (though not unique) social position Addams held, only three degrees of personal acquaintance separated Leon Czolgosz from Theodore Roosevelt even before William McKinley's assassination.

Gracing the parlors of Chicago capitalists like George Pullman and

Marshall Field, applying pious Christian bromides on brotherhood to
the discussion of social problems, Addams looked and often sounded
like the Midwestern Republican housewife she would have become if
her family had had its way. Yet she studiously avoided what she called
the "family claim" on her life in favor of the "social claim": instead of
devoting herself to the service of a husband and children, she deliberately made a career for herself as the conduit between the rulers of the
country and its most destitute citizens.

Addams's family background gave little hint of her radical future.
Her father, John, owned a bank in Freeport, Illinois, and he helped to
create the Illinois Republican Party, which obliged by sending him to
the state senate. Jane herself was born in the year of the secession crisis and grew up on tales of Lincoln's martyrdom; as a girl she was
steeped in the Republican virtues of thrift, labor, and sacrifice. Her
own mother died when she was two, and her stepmother brought her
up with her three brothers, two sisters, and two stepbrothers. She received a Christian higher education at the nearby Rockford Seminary,
and returned home to find her stepmother asserting an unusually familial claim on her future: she thought Jane ought to marry one of her
stepbrothers and settle down to housewifery.[43]

Jane thought a domestic future a waste of her time and talent
and—what was more alarming to a thrifty Republican—a waste of
scarce social resources. Only about 4 percent of Americans could attend college at all, and well under half of those were women, making
for perhaps forty thousand women collegians in a total population of
some fifty million Americans. Even so, this number represented a
marked increase since the Civil War—an increase propelled by the
creation of state universities with federal funding under the Morrill
Land Grant Act, passed by the Republican-led Congress in 1862. A
simple economic impetus lay behind the increased numbers of women
in universities: taxpayers putting up money for education wanted their
daughters as well as their sons to benefit. But when these young
women reaped the dividends of Civil War education legislation, they
found few careers open to them. Business, law, medicine, engineering,
and the ministry—the fields that attracted their brothers—refused
them entrance. Four-fifths of this first generation of women university

graduates became teachers of one kind or another. And as rewarding as teaching could be, it offered little possibility of advancement. As one woman of the period noted, "When a girl comes back [from college], what can she do? She can teach, but after she's done that she finds that she has reached the top, that there is nothing more for her."[44]

Facing these limits, the highly educated and inventive women alumnae of the late nineteenth century invented a profession of their own: social work. They would apply their classroom learning to the laboratory conditions of the real world. They raised funds, pooled their inheritances and incomes, and bought houses in the hearts of industrial cities. Settling in the immigrant ghettoes, they made homes among the alien poor. They thereby made themselves useful—and just as important to them, they made themselves feel useful.

Addams pioneered in this field, establishing Hull House in 1889. The country house of industrialist Charles Hull—which once had been a settlement on Chicago's far frontier, a businessman's rural idyll—became, after the city expanded, a settlement in its new urban frontier. Addams had come up with the idea while avoiding marriage to her stepbrother.[45] Tinkering with the idea during a decade of idleness, as she toured Europe and spent family money seeing the great artifacts of Western civilization, she finally decided she must put her dream to the test. A graceful mansion filled with graceful ladies, Hull House stood as a bastion of Anglo-Saxon Protestant American domesticity amid the teeming tenements of Poles, Czechs, Germans, Italians, and other new immigrants who worked in Chicago's industries. The women inside knew Italy only as one might see it from inside the Uffizi or the Galleria dell'Accademia, yet they were determined somehow to bridge the gap between the Sicilian peasants on their doorstep and the privileged Americans in their parlor. By the early twentieth century, Hull House had some four hundred counterparts in American cities, housing a few thousand determined settlement workers.[46]

As Addams wrote in 1892, the settlement houses fulfilled an objective social necessity, but also a subjective need. On the one hand, they acculturated the new immigrants, at sea in a new language and legal system. Providing not only the latest information on hygiene, child rearing, and labor law but also an introduction to high culture, with lessons in music, art, and literature, the settlement houses offered resources that no other agency could or would, and offered them in a comfortable homelike environment. They also gave the educated young women without professions who directed Hull House's myriad activities a sense of purpose, and what Addams called "a recognized outlet for their active faculties."[47] If the daughters of corporate chieftains and political panjandrums were going to evade marriage—and among that first generation of university graduates, about 40 percent did—their fathers were willing to support them while they lived in a respectable house and served as a civilizing influence to these communities that appeared to need one.

Their efforts at offering civilization did not always work as intended. Not everyone who seemed to need civilizing necessarily wanted it. Among many economic migrants the idea of Americaniza-

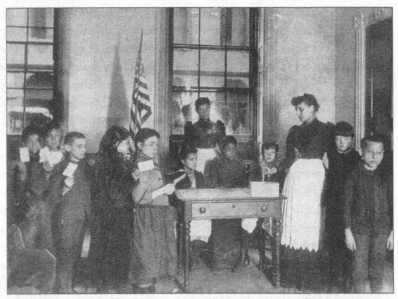

Immigrant schoolchildren stage their "first patriotic election" in this Jacob Riis photo documenting the process of Americanization. (Collection of the New-York Historical Society)

tion appeared a waste of time. As many as half of them were going to return, and wanted only to save their American dollars to reinvest in their home countries. Even among those who fully intended to stay in the United States, the Americanization that Hull House was peddling was not the one they wanted.

So immigrants developed a way of getting what they wanted from the settlement workers, often in spite of the settlement agenda. For example, Hull House started a boys' band with the intention of saving neighborhood boys from drunkenness and thievery by teaching these children of the eastern European shtetls music appropriate for civic meetings and even—nice Jewish boys though the band members tended to be—church picnics. Hull House's mistresses certainly did not intend their prodigies of musical salvation to develop proficiency with the music of the saloons and dance halls. Yet the Hull House Boys' Band alumni ultimately included some of Chicago's foremost jazzmen—Milt Hinton and Benny Goodman chief among them. They learned their skills from the settlement curriculum, but they dodged its substance.[48]

When the worried neighbors of the incarcerated anarchists appealed to Addams, she confronted much the same dilemma. She knew Isaak. He had often attended events at Hull House, even though he did not especially agree with Addams's reformist agenda. And he was welcome, despite Addams's lack of sympathy for his social analysis, which she described as an awkward cross between the revolutionary Mikhail Bakunin's and the conservative Herbert Spencer's. Isaak did not expect to convert to Hull House's genteel politics, but he found in the settlement a valuable resource. Addams invited speakers of all political stripes, including communist anarchists like Prince Peter Kropotkin, who held special interest for the Russian émigrés in the neighborhood. Indeed, Addams remembered Isaak's visiting Kropotkin at Hull House. Like the elder Mayor Harrison, Addams thought there was a civic duty in providing a forum for open debate. And she told reporters after McKinley's assassination that she had never heard Isaak or anyone offer "any utterances that would be classed as inflammatory." But in staying neutral and simply stating the case, she found herself held responsible for consequences she never intended.[49]

On September 8, 1901, less than forty-eight hours after the Isaaks' detention, Addams received an appointment with Mayor Harrison. Harrison, like his father, took a sympathetic view of labor—he himself had been called an anarchist when, like Jane Addams, he supported strikers against the Pullman Company in 1894.[50] Harrison told Addams that he would be happy to let her see the anarchist prisoners. As far as he was concerned they had been held incommunicado only to keep them safe from lynching vigilantes. Addams visited Isaak, who told her "he had not asked to see an attorney, and did not wish to see one unless we advised him to the contrary. Of course, I had no advice to give on the subject, for I was satisfied that the complaints that had reached me were unfounded." Reading between the lines of Harrison's and O'Neill's comments on the accused conspirators, she figured "it looks now as if they would all be dismissed."[51] Cross that Hull House "should have been even remotely mentioned in connection with the case," she returned to ordinary life, though she soon "discovered that whether or not I had helped a brother out of a pit, I had fallen into a deep one myself." Newspaper scolds took her to task for sympathizing with anarchists, and street critics threw bricks through some of Hull House's windows.[52]

Addams's invented profession put her at the center of all these personalities and forces. She rubbed shoulders with politicians like Roosevelt, industrialists like Pullman, and anarchists like Isaak. The Isaak story offered only the most condensed example of her career—and the careers of all settlement workers'—at the center of American industrial politics. Like all active social scientists, seeking like Briggs the sources of working people's discontent, she spent time in the factories and streets. She deliberately chose a life that would keep her in contact with the mean and the mighty, with the radical fringe and the pillars of power. Remaining constantly in such contact gave her not only what power she had, but also her sense of purpose and the basis for her social philosophy. It was the industrial environment that bound all these people together and made them who they were.

Addams realized early in Hull House's life that the purpose of settlement work was not for her to teach immigrants civilization, but was for the experience of living among the needy to teach both her and the immigrants what kind of society they were making together. It shocked her, she wrote, to become "the point of contact" between rich and poor: that connection with the 60 percent of Chicago's population who were foreign-born and who made the city run "reveals so clearly the lack of that equality which democracy implies."[53]

Addams did not believe in a theologically specific Christianity— she was religious for social reasons: "to adjust [men] in healthful relations to nature and their fellow men."[54] She learned two ways to preach the social religion of greater equality. One was to retell her own stories, making vivid moral points about inequality and injustice. The other was to prove these points with data. Nobody was better situated to accumulate scientific information on immigrant society than one who lived among it, and so Hull House became a social science laboratory, publishing in 1895 its first detailed study of the neighborhood and its people, entitled *Hull House Maps and Papers*. The settlement's residents produced a relentlessly scientific inquiry replete with tables, charts, and foldout color maps. It enumerated hardship and vice: seventy-five children living in a single city block; most families earning between five and ten dollars a week; eighty-one saloons within a third of a square mile; upwards of sixty "*declared* brothels."[55]

This application of science to society served activist ends. And just like settlement work generally, social science served both objective social needs and subjective personal ones. In its study of the conditions under which immigrants lived, it vividly suggested the need of social action to remedy the problems of American cities. In this respect, Hull House carried on a long-standing American commitment of politically practical social scientific investigation that stretched back to the early 1800s. The construction of national canals, roads, and markets began to demonstrate that Americans did not live independent lives on the frontier, but interdependent lives binding them each to another in a web of commerce, making them all parts of a complex society requiring careful and knowledgeable balance. Hull House's work also looked forward to the early era of modern feminism, when scientific investigation of humankind—often carried on by just such young women as populated the settlements—would begin to justify women's demands for suffrage and fuller inclusion in the public life of American society. The women of Hull House were among the first to use their lives as systematic case studies of the palpable political good that educated women could accomplish.[56]

Hull House Maps and Papers was a diagnosis of a social sickness, pointing to a course of treatment. It suggested Americans follow Hull House's example, and do as doctors must in the presence of the sick and hurt. "Merely to state symptoms and go no further would be idle; but to state symptoms in order to ascertain the nature of disease, and apply, it may be, its cure, is not only scientific, but in the highest sense humanitarian." In drawing her final lesson from the case, Addams directly addressed her readers: "The crucial question of the time is, 'In what attitude stand ye toward the industrial problem?' Are you content that greed and the seizing upon disadvantage and the pushing of the weaker to the wall shall rule your business life, while in your family and social life you live so differently? Are you content that Christianity shall have no play in trade?"[57]

Addams borrowed the "question of the time" device, complete with its social application of Christianity, from her friend and political ally Jacob Riis. Riis had framed his 1890 study of a New York neighborhood, *How the Other Half Lives*, by telling his readers:

> What are you going to do about it? is the question of to-day . . .
> Not long ago a great meeting was held in this city, of all denominations of religious faith, to discuss the question how to lay hold of these teeming masses in the tenements with Christian influences . . . Might not the conference have found in the warning of one Brooklyn builder . . . a hint worth heeding: "How shall the love of God be understood by those who have been nurtured in sight only of the greed of man?"[58]

A Danish immigrant whose major talent lay in handling a camera, Riis dramatically documented this case with his own photographs of tenement life. Like Addams, he bolstered the moral and illustrative argument with tables and figures. Riis had no more intrinsic interest in social science than Addams, but he quickly learned it could be a valuable tool. Like Addams he learned the use of the tool from someone else: Theodore Roosevelt.

FROM SOCIAL SCIENCE TO THE STREETS

The first time Jacob Riis tried to introduce Jane Addams to Theodore Roosevelt it did not go well. Addams was visiting Albany in 1899 when Roosevelt was governor of New York. She wanted to talk to him about the use of social science to improve living conditions for urban immigrants and specifically to discuss the possible involvement of her fellow Hull House resident Florence Kelley in a New York investigatory commission. (A Cornell University graduate, a legal scholar, and a veteran of federal commissions, Kelley had superb qualifications.) Riis, Kelley, and Addams found the governor unavailable—it turned out he was busily fastening himself into evening clothes while they were waiting in the parlor. Roosevelt raced downstairs in his dinner jacket only to find Addams's card on his hall table. He wrote Riis, "I . . . was merely informed that you had two ladies to see me and as I was late for an engagement and literally had not one second, I sent down the word I did. If I had realized who they were, I think I should have broken my engagement—I should certainly have been late for it."[59] Roosevelt knew Addams would someday prove an invaluable ally, much as Riis had. He often cited them in speeches as examples of the progressive reformers he liked. And they would provide him with a direct connection to the immigrant and ethnic neighborhoods who comprised half or more of the urban vote.

Jacob Riis knew Roosevelt as a social scientist before he met the man. When Roosevelt was Civil Service Commissioner in the early 1890s, he drew criticism for lessening the influence of immigrants on politics: by fighting the corruption of political machines, his opponents charged, he was really waging war on ordinary Americans. Civil service reformers wanted government appointments to depend on standardized, testable technical skills and knowledge, rather than on political connections. Critics took one look at the standardized tests and cried cultural and class bias. The meritocracy, they argued, was only a way to give the government back to native-born blue bloods like Roosevelt. Riis admitted he, too, "went about with a more or less vague notion that [civil service reform] was some kind of a club to knock out spoils politics with, good for the purpose and necessary, but in the last analysis an alien kind of growth, of aristocratic tendency, to set men apart in classes," until he began to read Roosevelt's reports himself.

Though Riis did not at first enjoy the bristling erudition of facts and figures, he soon realized they were weapons wielded for democracy. In a report on graft in the New York customs house Roosevelt pointed out that "political blackmail"—by which he meant the influence of patronage politics—cost an employee 3 percent of his salary. This did not sound like much till Roosevelt translated the numbers into illustrations: 3 percent to a customs clerk meant "the difference between having and not having a winter coat for himself, a warm dress for his wife, or a Christmas-tree for his children—a piece of cruel injustice and iniquity." It was, Riis said, the Christmas tree that did it: the little sketch drawn from the statistics brought home the injustice. So, far from being an inherently dry device to distance men from the facts they believed they knew, social science could bring them into immediate contact with the remote and indirect effects of their careless actions. "So I overcame my repugnance to schedules and tables and examinations, and got behind it all to an understanding of what it really meant."[60]

And the result—Riis's own tables and schedules, illustrated with pungent anecdotes and his immortal photographs, and published as How the Other Half Lives—introduced him to Roosevelt the man. Roosevelt accepted New York City mayor William Strong's appointment to serve as New York City police commissioner in 1895, and on assuming the post one of the first allies he cultivated was the man whose book showed he knew the hard neighborhoods best. One day Riis went to his office to find Roosevelt's card waiting on his hall table, with the message "I have read your book and I have come to help."[61]

New York police lodging room, photographed by Jacob Riis. Police custody was often the first stop for indigent immigrants, until Commissioner Roosevelt helped secure its elimination in favor of a municipal lodging system. (Collection of the New-York Historical Society)

Riis became Roosevelt's interpreter and guide to the immigrant neighborhoods of New York. Roosevelt needed to see in person what he had only read about in books, and Riis obliged him with tours of the tenement districts at day and night alike. "The midnight trips that Riis and I took . . . gave me personal insight into some of the problems of city life. It is one thing to listen in a perfunctory fashion to tales of overcrowded tenements, and it is quite another actually to see what overcrowding means, some hot summer night," Roosevelt wrote.[62] Like Addams, Roosevelt felt immeasurably transformed by his personal contact with the other half. "Looking back, I made my greatest strides forward while I was police commissioner, and this largely through my intimacy with Jacob Riis, for he opened all kinds of windows into the matter [of immigrant life] for me."[63] Roosevelt, with Riis, backed slum clearance and tenement reform, and elimination of the police role in taking custody of innocent homeless immigrants in favor of a municipal lodging system. And Riis believed Roosevelt stayed true to his belief in democracy even in the face of racial difference and alien culture, meaning every word when he "speaks nowadays about dropping all race and creed distinctions, if we want to be good Americans."[64]

As admirable as Riis found Roosevelt, he entertained few illusions about him. Riis was a reporter for the *New York Sun*, and he knew how useful his newly progressive political friend found him. Here was no bully cowboy, no impulsive boy-hero elevated by sheer energy and mere accident to the highest office in the land. No, Theodore Roosevelt was in Riis's measured assessment exactly what he seemed to Booker T. Washington: neither an unwitting tool of others nor a victim of his own myth, but a brilliant and calculating politician. "The fact is that he is a perfectly logical product of a certain course of conduct deliberately entered upon and faithfully adhered to all through life," Riis wrote.[65] Riis therefore took seriously even Roosevelt's most peculiar reaction to immigration: his preachments on "race suicide."

When Roosevelt looked at the data on immigration and child mortality, he saw not one but two social problems. The first, which immediately leapt out at Addams, Riis, and other progressives, was the appalling urban environment, and it was a lesson that echoed in his own experience of the New York streets. The poor living and laboring conditions of decent people needed, and got, Roosevelt's energy and compassion, and whatever public welfare legislation he could wring from city, state, or nation. But he also saw a second problem in the numbers, a problem in the more abstract category of race:

> The figures given for the Harvard and Yale graduates show that, taking into account the number of children that die before growing up, the number of adults that do not marry, and the number of marriages where for physical and natural reasons— that is, reasons presumably implying no moral blame in the parents—there are no children or only one or two children, it is necessary that the family physically able to produce children shall average over three or the race will slowly decrease in

numbers . . . Under any circumstances an average of one or two
children means rapid race suicide.[66]

The eccentric notion that the graduates of Harvard and Yale comprised
a race made some sense in those days when the New England colleges
took chiefly the sons (and in the case of Harvard's Radcliffe College, a
few daughters) of the nation's ruling Protestant caste. Yet it was a race
open to talent, as it took in some—though precious few—Jews, blacks,
and other outsiders. And this idea of a race as a selectively open class
comported perfectly with Roosevelt's other uses of the term.

At the turn of the twentieth century, whiteness did not belong
equally to everyone who was not dark-skinned. It denoted a racial pro-
clivity to independence, vigor, and an enterprising spirit—and as such
seemed to show up admirably among Anglo-Saxons. Italians, Irish,
Poles, and other Europeans might, depending on who was speaking,
possess some or no amount of racial whiteness.

The influence of Darwinism cut both ways in the matter of racism.
Some argued that immutable racial characteristics determined fitness,
condemning entire peoples to lifetimes in bondage. The U.S. Civil
War was supposed to have settled this question, but as the decades
passed after the conflict and Northerners let Southerners reassert
racial control over their region, the lesson faded. Others argued that
the influence of environment on individuals, and even whole peoples,
forced them to adapt, trumping inheritance: upbringing determined
whether they could exercise their independence.[67]

As a descendant of Dutchmen, Roosevelt could scarcely limit his
racial enthusiasms strictly to Anglo-Saxons, as some racial theorists
did, and he defined races loosely. Not exactly pure communities of inheritance, they required a certain hybridity to keep their vigor, and
he applied this notion of hybridity so generously that it drew contemporary mockery. Newspaper columnist Finley Peter Dunne had his
alter ego, the Irish barkeep Mr. Dooley, exclaim of Roosevelt's racial
Anglo-Saxonism,

I tell ye, whin th' Clan an' th' Sons iv Sweden an' th' Banana
Club an' th' Circle Francaize an' th' Pollacky Benivolent Soci-

ety an' th' Rooshian Sons iv Dinnymite an' th' Benny Brith an'
th' Coffee Clutch that Schwartzmeister r-runs . . . an' th' Hol-
land Society an' th' Afro-Americans an' th' other Anglo-
Saxons begin f'r to raise their Anglo-Saxon battlecry, it'll be all
day with th' eight or nine people in th' wurruld that has th'
misfortune iv not bein' brought up Anglo-Saxons.[68]

Roosevelt's liberality with his racial labels struck some critics as mere
political convenience—as Riis wrote, "When President Roosevelt
speaks nowadays about the necessity of dropping all race and creed
distinctions, if we want to be good Americans, some one on the out-
skirts of the crowd winks his left eye and says 'politics.' "[69] But Riis argued that it was more, that it was Roosevelt's "own sturdy faith in his
fellow-man. Men became good because he thought them so"—however their racial or cultural backgrounds might have made them otherwise behave. Still, when Roosevelt wished to say the same of Riis,
he used racial language: "He had a white soul."[70]

Roosevelt's concern with "race suicide" embarrassed Riis and other
progressives, especially those like Addams who strenuously worked to
see society from a variety of viewpoints. They tested the abstract powers of racial thinking against their own concrete experience, and saw
it fail. Nor were progressives alone in this observation: Roosevelt's peculiar racial ideas were often the subject of jokes in the press, where
he appeared as "the uncle of his country," encouraging women to
breed.[71] And the contradiction between his concern for the poor and
his zeal for more good children bore the brunt of a blunt thrust leveled
in the midst of an economic downturn:

> And when my eldest needed shoes,
> My baby needed milk;
> For this I would not have the blues—
> I'd feel as fine as silk.
> "Down with race suicide!" I'd roar,
> "Let grafters make complaint!"
> If I were sure as Theodore:
> (But then, you see, I ain't).[72]

Riis preferred to treat Roosevelt's racial fixation as an eccentric cousin to his virtues: "People laugh a little, sometimes, and poke fun at his 'race suicide,' but to him the children mean home, family, the joy of the young years, and the citizenship of to-morrow, all in one."[73] He admitted its presence in his friend, but suggested it was an unimportant quirk in an important progressive ally. Roosevelt himself acknowledged that his private concern with race suicide, though real, ranked well below the more pressing public concern with economic justice: "The diminishing birth rate among the old native American stock, especially in the north east, with all that that implies, I should consider the worst. But we also have tremendous problems in the way of the relations of capital and labor to solve. My own belief is that we shall have to pay far more attention to this than to any question of [Anglo-Saxon] expansion for the next fifty years."[74]

So there the matter rested: when he worriedly scanned the population data, Roosevelt tended to talk about the abstraction of racial descent as if it were a real quality in the blood. But as a matter of public policy and of personal conduct, he pushed to define American citizenship as inclusively as possible. In person he made himself irresistible to immigrants. When he enforced Sunday saloon closures as police commissioner (though he was not a temperance crusader, he objected to the saloons as engines of political corruption and police bribery), German-Americans turned out for an anti-Roosevelt rally—and so did Roosevelt, deflecting their ire by clambering to the reviewing stand, waving and applauding floats. When a disbelieving demonstrator cried, "Wo ist der Roosevelt?" he replied, "Hier bin ich," and the suddenly won-over crowd collapsed with laughter.[75] More important, Roosevelt found ethnic Americans irresistibly deserving of his own fellow feeling. His "concrete" encounters with struggling families brought the population tables into sharp relief, and overrode the abstractions he had been trained to consider. When he stood with real immigrants in the tenements and factories of the Lower East Side—putting himself at the sharp, shocking point of contact that Addams described—he felt the sting of social injustice. These repeated meetings were, he said, "how I became a progressive." And, conscious of their value both politically and personally, he repeatedly put himself into immediate contact with the poor throughout his career.[76]

But there were some immigrants who definitely lay beyond the pale in Roosevelt's imagination; under no circumstance could they become Americans. They were few, but important to identify, and chief among them in the weeks after McKinley's assassination were anarchists. In his first message to Congress he said that anarchists "should be kept out of this country, and if found here they should be promptly deported to the country whence they came." He committed himself to "war . . . against anarchists," in cooperation with other civilized nations, and to making anarchism an international crime like piracy or the slave trade. Congress did not follow him in all these leads, but it did append a clause to the immigration law in 1903, prohibiting the immigration or naturalization of "anarchists, or persons who believe in or advocate the overthrow by force or violence of all governments, or of all forms of law, or the assassination of public officials." It was the first time since it had required a loyalty oath for Confederates at the end of the Civil War that Congress defined eligibility for Americanness in terms of a belief. Under an extended version of this law, the United States would deport Emma Goldman along with 248 other anarchists, communists, and radicals during the red scare of 1919.[77]

When Roosevelt thought about the new immigrants as they appeared in his personal experience, he argued the general case for Czolgosz's defense: that the other half suffered from an appalling environment, and fell into vice and violence because of it. Only a wholesale reform of the industrial environment—which only state agencies could undertake—would prevent such lapses in behavior among the overwhelming numbers of the American urban poor. But when he thought in terms of abstractions—like racism or anarchism—he sided with the prosecution. The race needed protection; anarchy needed stamping out. Enemies of the social order, considered as ideal types, deserved deportation or death.

This fatal flaw in social scientific thinking—the tendency to take patterns in the numbers, give them names, and then treat the names (like "race," or "unskilled labor") as if they had the power to cause the patterns—was what the philosopher William James called in 1890 "the psychologist's fallacy par excellence." The need to categorize observations led to the belief that the category itself had the properties of the observations. But to collect a set of symptoms and call them madness did not mean that madness caused the symptoms. Nor did a set of observations about the shrinking family size of Harvard graduates necessarily correlate to the behavior, let alone the existence, of a race whose character had begun to favor smaller family size.[78]

Avoiding the psychologist's fallacy in favor of the lessons of experience was the essential impulse of the progressive movement, bringing together the interests of rich and poor, native-born and immigrant alike. Philosophical progressives kept themselves alert to the fallacy, and sought to expel it where they found it: but it was a feat of self-awareness not easy for less-introspective personalities to accomplish.

Jane Addams knew Roosevelt's weakness in this respect, and like Riis relied on the evidence and influence of personal experience to sway him to the more generous side of his nature. She had, her nephew diplomatically said, "the advantage over him of the perception that goes with a mind both imaginative and logical," which was to say that she attended carefully to the one subject to which Roosevelt never applied his formidable powers of analysis: his own personality. He knew exactly what he thought about everything except, it appears, himself. He loathed thinking about himself because it led him to depression. When he was young and first married, loss hit him hard and paralyzed him with doubt: his mother and his wife died on the same day in 1884. He then fled to the West, which became his own personal safety valve. He wrote of his feelings at this time that "black care rarely sits behind the rider whose pace is fast enough, at any rate, not when he first feels the horse move under him."[79] Speed alone could not save him; he needed innovation. Only the golden sense of starting something new kept him from his grief and doubt. So he thought and spoke about everything but his personal tragedies, which accounted for what, in Addams's view, was his "kaleidoscopic" vision. Understanding his character better than he did, she played on what she believed was the "genuineness . . . of his desire to 'do good.'" She did so by guiding his relentless energies to the logical conclusions of immediate experience with the poor, and at all costs by avoiding abstractions.[80]

Addams believed in social science only insofar as it made an effective argument for political action. When it created categories that divided people one from another—categories like capital and labor, or native-born and immigrant—it robbed them of their humanity. She abhorred this kind of social science with all its mighty abstractions. There were no real antagonisms between mighty interests. "The antagonism of institutions was always unreal," she wrote; "instead of adding to the recognition of meaning, it delayed [and] distorted it." This was the essential insight she gleaned from her experience at Hull House, and it was the basis for what became the progressive movement.

Contemplating the collapse of the company town at Pullman, Illinois, in 1894, Addams wrote that merely providing better material conditions for workers could not solve the problems of an industrial society. Democratization of the political process must also come, and swiftly. "The new claim on the part of the toiling multitude, the new sense of responsibility on the part of the well-to-do, arise in reality from the same source. They are in fact the same 'social compunction,' and, in spite of their widely varying manifestations, logically converge into the same movement," she wrote. For social reform to occur, and for it to stick, it must come from constant contact between governors and governed, to ensure it was what everyone truly needed. "The most unambitious reform, recognizing the necessity for this consent, makes for slow but sane and strenuous progress."[81]

As long as she pushed Roosevelt to think in these terms—in the terms of a shared (Riis would say familial) interest among all Americans, a shared interest made evident through shared personal experience—she might keep him on her side. When he visited Hull House in the course of political campaigns, she took private time with him to lobby for women's suffrage, for labor reforms, and for whatever measures she could concretely illustrate during his time in Chicago. Riding in a car on the way to a speech, they could talk about the city they saw around them and its immediate, evident needs. He proved eager for such arguments.[82]

Because Addams kept her thinking clear of the psychologist's fallacy, she could argue, a few years after McKinley's assassination, the explicit case for Czolgosz's defense:

> In the millions of words uttered and written at that time, no one adequately urged that public-spirited citizens set themselves the task of patiently discovering how these sporadic acts of violence against government may be understood and averted. We do not know whether they occur among the discouraged and unassimilated immigrants who might be cared for in such a way as enormously to lessen the probability of these acts, or whether they are the result of anarchistic teaching. By hastily concluding that the latter is the sole explanation for them, we make no attempt to heal and cure the situation. Failure to make a proper diagnosis may mean treatment of a disease which does not exist, or it may furthermore mean that the dire malady from which the patient is suffering be permitted to develop unchecked.

Again using the language of medicine, Addams argued that Leon Czolgosz's affliction was not his alone, nor even that of immigrants—those were false distinctions. If his malady resulted from the social environment, then all Americans bore responsibility for it:

> And yet as the details of the meager life of the President's assassin emerged, they were a challenge to the forces for social betterment in American cities. Was it not an indictment to all those whose business it is to interpret and solace the wretched, that a boy should have grown up in an American city so uncared for, so untouched by higher issues, his wounds of life so unhealed by religion that the first talk he ever heard dealing with life's wrongs, although anarchistic and violent, should yet appear to point a way of relief?

Addams believed that only "a sense of fellowship"—that immediate, personal sense of commonality and belonging she spent her life fostering—could dissolve the false and fatal abstractions of social antagonism and "break into the locked purpose of a half-crazed creature bent upon destruction."[83]

The specificity of Addams's experience of fellowship and the abstractions of Roosevelt's indulgence in the psychologist's fallacy remained in competition for the spirit of social science in part because neither could predict or explain a particular case like the McKinley assassination. Either the war on anarchism or healing the industrial environment might prevent future acts of terrorism, but neither anarchism nor artificial antagonism—neither the argument of prosecution or defense—could yet explain why among all the innumerable and unassimilated "other half" Leon Czolgosz alone should have become a presidential assassin. Social science could explain trends and tendencies and at its best prescribe ameliorating solutions, but it could not account for the singular case. All Briggs's data on Czolgosz's environment and upbringing made him statistically normal, but his action made him an outlier. Millions of migrants experienced hardship, rootlessness, and social injustice; some smaller but not insignificant percentage of them were exposed to anarchism. Something peculiar—or perhaps some peculiar confluence of ordinary things—must have happened to Leon Czolgosz. Briggs did not begin to know what this could be until he tracked down and spoke to Waldeck Czolgosz, who alone among the siblings had worked day by day alongside Leon and knew how he had developed in his political thinking over his short, dismal adult life.

As an alienist, Briggs was especially susceptible to the psychologist's fallacy par excellence. But for his career as a sometime journalist and his consequently meticulous note-taking, we might have no record of the details that set Czolgosz's case apart from the categories. As it is, Briggs all but missed the story.

6

THE INTERPRETATION OF DREAMS

After finishing his interviews at the Czolgosz family house, Briggs drove up Cleveland's Broadway to find Leon's older brother Waldeck, who was trying to avoid reporters, doctors, and other investigators interested in his story. Waldeck spoke English, so Briggs went alone to the simple workingman's house on a side street where Waldeck was staying in a converted attic. In the cold January weather Briggs climbed a set of stairs outside the house to the upper story, where a one-eyed man answered the door and let him in. The apartment was a small room whose ceiling sloped with the roof, furnished only with a stove, a makeshift bookshelf, a table, and three chairs. Waldeck and the one-eyed man sat in two of them and were in no hurry to let Briggs have the third.

Waldeck asked Briggs his business. Briggs explained what he was after, and said he wanted to know about Leon's life, health, and motives. Waldeck said he had no interest in helping another medical investigation—they all seemed utterly to miss the point of Leon's life. He said that he "had had all he wanted of doctors; they had treated him badly in Buffalo and Auburn."[1] In the awkward moment that followed Briggs appraised Waldeck, who looked stubbornly out from under the heavy-lidded gray eyes and light hair typical of his family. Like them, he also wore a photograph of Leon affixed to an oval button in his lapel. Briggs felt at an impasse until the one-eyed man intervened on his behalf, prevailing on Waldeck to try one more time to explain his brother.

Waldeck began at the beginning, telling Briggs once more the story of his family's exodus from Prussia and its wanderings in the American wilderness. He stumbled a few times over details—he could not remember exactly when his mother had died—but it was substantially the same history. Only when he reached Leon's working years did he have something new to add.

Leon's first job, at the age of sixteen, was in a glassworks near Pittsburgh, Pennsylvania, where the family moved from Alpena in 1889. There he carried the red-hot bottles from the fire to the cooling ovens. The work was hard, and for the first time since he started school Leon had no time to read. But it paid well for children's work—he made 75 cents a day at first, then received a raise to a dollar. Paul worked at a nearby chemical plant. With perhaps four children working, the family took in a goodly income—in any case, it provided sufficient excess that they could within two years afford not only to move to a house in the Newburgh district of Cleveland, but also to build a saloon, which Paul operated himself for a few months before renting it to the Findlay Beer Company.[2]

On their move to Cleveland, Leon began work in the Newburgh Wire Mills. He made fence wire at first; then, when he showed enough talent the foreman had him move to finer wire work. He worked a month's rotation, ten hours of day work for two weeks, then twelve hours of night work for two weeks. He received $17 for his fortnight on days, and $24 for his night stint. It brought in $492 for a year, if he remained employed year-round—which in this line of work was a reasonable expectation while a boom lasted.

By moving into the liquor industry as a saloon operator, Paul Czolgosz had found an income stream proof against the turn of the seasons, the weather, and even the economic climate. Leon's move into the steel industry made his income almost as secure. Owing to the nature of steel manufacturing, the plant owners believed their best strategy, even if demand started to fall, was to keep the mills running all out, twenty-four hours a day. It meant working the men around the clock, and running high risks. For if a downturn did prove significant, it could sink whole companies and their excess inventory overnight. In this era of industrial construction, it was rare for a recession to hit steel that hard unless some political factor pushed the economy down a steep slope. But with federal revenue depending on import tariffs, and with monetary policy controversially tied to the gold standard, political factors came rushing into the industrial mix. They combined to create a recession, and incidentally to put Leon Czolgosz out of work in the panic of 1893. The process began with the political ambitions of William McKinley.

STEEL AND SILVER

In 1888 William McKinley started his seventh term as an Ohio congressman. He returned cheerfully to Washington that spring, as did most Republicans: Congress and the White House belonged solely to them. Grover Cleveland, the first Democratic President since before the Civil War, had been dispatched home by the victorious Benjamin Harrison. McKinley had helped the Harrison campaign, and raised his national profile in the process, and now he stood a good chance of becoming Speaker of the House of Representatives. It was a fine time to occupy a senior position in the Republican Party: not only did it run the government, but the government was running a surplus, so there were no difficult fiscal decisions to make.

All this would go sour before two years were out. McKinley was going to lose the speakership contest, and indeed, he was going to lose his seat in Congress. Before doing that he was going to help turn the surplus into deficit. But disastrous as this term would prove for the country, the losses would turn out lucky for him. McKinley had a knack for remaining unscathed in the course of ordinary politics.

McKinley's principal opponent for the office of Speaker was Thomas Brackett Reed, a Maine congressman backed by the Northeastern element of the party. The two of them represented opposite approaches to American politics. If McKinley ever entertained the slightest doubt that he stood for anything less than the implementation of divine principle, he never let on. He remained simple piety incarnate to the day of his death, radiating the moral righteousness that accrued to him from his service to the Union Army in the Civil War. By contrast, Reed never let his listeners forget that politics was about power, and he meant for his team to win it. Reed mastered parliamentary rules and treated politics like a game, using procedural tricks to get his way and declaring that anyone who said politics was simple was telling, at best, half-truths.

Reed looked askance at McKinley's enthusiasm for being called "Major," and privately referred to McKinley as "Napoleon." It was an apt, and not uncommon, comparison: McKinley embodied a Bonapartist version of the American dream. Instead of rising from rags to riches—he was never a successful businessman—he ascended to imperial glory from the noncommissioned ranks of the army. Indeed, McKinley's military renown rested principally on his proof of Napoleon's dictum that an army travels on its stomach. Commissary Sergeant William McKinley had won the hearts of his fellow soldiers at the Battle of Antietam, when he dashed to the front with hot coffee and cooked rations to greet the men returning from the enemy's murderous fire. The deed won him his officer's commission, and he looked back on this time as an army cook as "a formative period of my life."[3] Reed, who had been a U.S. Navy paymaster during the Civil War, did not invoke his military service to justify his politics, and had little regard at all for any politician. Reed was, his friend Senator Henry Cabot Lodge said, "a good hater and he detested shams, humbugs, and pretence above everything else."[4] McKinley responded primly to Reed's private barbs, complaining, "Everybody enjoys Reed's sarcastic comments and keen wit except the fellow who is the subject of his satire."[5]

Perhaps nothing better illustrated the difference between Theodore Roosevelt and the man he replaced as President than Roosevelt's enthusiasm for Reed over McKinley. Choosing between the man of piety and the master of procedure, Roosevelt backed procedure. As the nation's newly appointed Civil Service Commissioner, he supported Reed against McKinley in 1889, and he would again in 1896, when the two men fought over the Republican presidential nomination. The acidic honesty of Reed appealed to Roosevelt as evidence of strength and toughness, while McKinley's mind struck him as weak; his "firmness I utterly distrust," Roosevelt wrote.[6]

Reed beat McKinley in his bid for the speakership in 1889, and in so doing set the stage for his later loss to the Major. Victory did not suit Reed. His cynicism did not play well on a national scale. And in accepting the speakership he took (along with President Harrison and the Republican Senate leadership) responsibility for what turned out to be a disastrous era of Republican stewardship. Meantime, he yielded to McKinley the chairmanship of the Ways and Means Committee, putting him in charge of tariff legislation and making the staunch Major a prominent public figure.

McKinley's ability to serve as a handmaiden to American manufacturers while claiming simply to represent principle offered Reed ample reason to regard the Ohioan as a sham. Throughout the tariff debates Reed ruthlessly enforced parliamentary rules and kept the legislation on track, running over opposition without pause and drawing cries of "Czar!" and "Tyrant!" from the Democrats. Meantime, McKinley sailed smoothly in Reed's wake, smiling his smile of refusal and silently smoking his cigar as he said nothing to lobbyists or reporters. He spoke solemnly in the House chamber about his "deep conviction[s]" while making the American manufacturers in general and the steel industry in particular as happy as was humanly possible. The abstract majesty of the markets, of national greatness—these were McKinley's favorite themes. He dwelt little on the quotidian details of life or legislation.[7]

In an era with no income tax, drafting the tariff legislation meant setting economic policy. Traditionally, politicians who supported putting a tariff on imports argued that although this tax raised retail prices, it was a necessary evil to allow the United States to gain its national economic independence. The tariff provided affirmative action for underdeveloped industries, and it was supposed to end when the industries achieved competitive levels of productivity.

Applying a tariff to industries in which the United States was not as efficient as other countries would make foreign goods too expensive to buy, thus letting American manufacturers sell their inferior products at a profit without worrying about foreign competition. This would theoretically give Americans time to improve their production methods. Tariffs were especially important, their proponents argued, in those industries vital to the national security, like agriculture and steel.

The tariff legislation that McKinley proposed to Congress went beyond these established principles of protection. First, it treated protectionism as a permanent policy, to persist even after American industries became preeminent in the world. Tax rates on steel were cut, but for steel any protection was a gift of public money: their product

OUR INFANT INDUSTRIES.

The infant is "protected," but how about the workingman and farmer!

William McKinley as Napoleon, promoting the tariff for "infant industries," depicted in this Cleveland *Plain Dealer* cartoon of 1893 as grown fat on protective pap and crushing the farmer and workingman.

was already good enough to compete in the world market. Second, the law set out a hypothesis and an experiment that would also benefit steel: if tariffs could protect infant industries, perhaps they could create nonexistent ones. The McKinley law put a tax on tinplate—which was sheet steel covered with tin, for use chiefly in canning—to see if it could create a domestic tinplate industry by making foreign tinplate prohibitively expensive. Third, it eliminated the tariff on sugar, helpfully reducing its cost to consumers in an election year. And overall, it raised rates to their highest levels ever.

The McKinley bill came at a steep price: the Republicans could not get the votes for its protective measures unless they pacified the silver interests. Since the silver discoveries of the middle nineteenth century, the white metal had fallen in value so that it no longer rivaled gold as a basis for national coinage. But in the United States, two Western factions wanted silver kept in circulation. Silver miners wanted a big, reliable market for their product, and nothing fit the bill better than the U.S. government. Debt-burdened farmers, forced to buy expensive machinery on credit if they wanted to stay in business, wanted any kind of inflation they could get. Together these groups had enough representation in Congress to prevent the McKinley Tariff from passing unless they got something in return.

The result was the Sherman Silver Purchase Act. It provided a double subsidy to the silver interests. First, it bound the federal government to buy 4.5 million ounces of silver each month using paper money called legal-tender Treasury notes.* Second, the law also provided that the Treasury had to do its best to defeat the free market, and keep silver trading at parity to gold. The practical effect of this second provision was that when anyone presented the Treasury with one of the paper notes it had used to buy silver, the Treasury would have to buy it with gold, to keep up the pretense of market parity.

Once appeased by the Silver Purchase Act, the Western interests

---

*The Sherman Silver Purchase Act augmented the provisions of the Bland-Allison Act of 1878, which under similar pressures obliged the U.S. Treasury to buy a much smaller, and variable, quantity of silver—$2 million worth—per month.

swung into line behind the McKinley Tariff, and the two laws together defined the economic policy of 1890. Under the high McKinley Tariff the volume of goods imported from overseas fell, reducing income to the federal government. The Sherman Silver Purchase Act required the federal government to spend its dwindling resources to subsidize the silver industry. The combined drain on the government's resources was only sustainable given indefinite economic growth and foreign investment.[8]

Looking back later, it was easy to say that 1890 marked a turning point in American economic history. In the course of a single legislative session and with only two laws, a Republican Congress and a Republican President ensured that a federal surplus would vanish overnight as soon as a sufficiently large group of creditors—say, the banks of the City of London—decided to exchange its dollars for gold. Whoever happened to be President at the time could do little more than stand slack-jawed as the gold rushed out of the Treasury, settling the economy onto a rocky bottom.

By the time that happened, the Republican leadership was long gone from Washington. Cleveland defeated Harrison in 1892, returning to the White House just in time to preside over the panic of 1893. He did what he could, but it was not enough, and in the time-honored fashion of American Presidents he took the blame for the economic downturn that occurred on his watch, thus virtually guaranteeing that whoever the Republicans nominated in 1896 would win the presidency.

McKinley also managed to be out of federal office when the panic hit in 1893, though not through any design of his own. In the spring of 1890 the Democrats won the Ohio statehouse and gerrymandered Congressman McKinley into a district with a three-thousand-vote Democratic majority. McKinley went to defeat in November 1890, but won the Ohio governorship in 1891 and put himself informally in line for the 1896 presidential nomination. His colleagues marveled at lucky Major "Mack," and how things always seemed to right themselves for him.[9] His friends who invested in the steel industry seemed also to weather the storm. The steel industry's employees were not so fortunate.

WIRE AND WATER

The Cleveland Rolling Mill Company, which starting in 1892 employed Leon Czolgosz, was the most reliable steel-wire firm in the country. Under executive Henry Chisholm (a friend and business associate of Mark Hanna), the company pioneered the use of the Bessemer process in the 1870s and became one of the biggest wire mills in the world. Unusual among American steel mills, it remained competitive with British wire firms through the 1880s. Chisholm developed a method of making wire from Bessemer steel ingots without having to cool and reheat the steel in the middle of the process, which cut the price of production sufficiently to keep the wire production division in business and to allow further innovation.[10]

The early 1890s brought a new twist to Cleveland Rolling's fortunes as an increase in demand drew new money and new players into the steel industry. After a depression in the early 1880s, demand for steel ballooned in the latter half of the decade, owing largely to increased railroad construction. The United States now turned in earnest to the exploitation of its natural resources in the West. Just as the Civil War made possible the extension of Northern industry into the South, so the Indian wars were clearing the way for expansion into the West. As a youthful Lloyd Vernon Briggs, then touring the West, remarked, "All seemed confident that if the Indians were exterminated business would increase tenfold, as capitalists, who were now afraid to come into the territory, might then do so with impunity." The army did its job, the capitalists came in their wake, and travelers followed—some few, like Briggs, aware of the whole story: "The railroad runs immediately in the rear of the position held [by the army] . . . and every foot of ground has drunk the blood of brave men."[11]

Between 1885 and 1890 the nation added almost forty thousand miles of track, of which 57 percent were built in the Western states. This construction boom created tremendous demand for steel, doubling production of steel rails, and more than doubling production of Bessemer steel ingots. The consequent increase in the price of steel made the industry more profitable, which attracted competitors to challenge Cleveland Rolling's lonely eminence. The fortunes of steel became the heart of the American economy, driving a significant overall financial expansion: the annual listing of new stock issues on Wall Street increased in value over 900 percent between 1885 and 1890.[12]

The increased profitability of American manufacturing created an enthusiasm for steel, the railroad it served, and the new national network it made. The protection afforded by the tariff schedule helped, allowing the steel industry to pad its profit margins unperturbed by foreign competition. Investors flocked to steel, looking for the chance to get in on the ground floor of something big. The sudden demand for investment opportunities pushed stock prices even higher, which suggested to optimists drunk on the vision of a new economy that stocks might actually be worth these inflated prices—so they poured yet more money into the market. Creative men thought up ways to justify demanding more dollars, usually by selling a story about a new technology that was going to change everyone's life. One such technology was the steel-wire nail.

Up to the late 1880s, most nails used in construction were cut nails made from sheet steel. It was of course possible to make nails from steel wire, and wire nails were less likely to split wood when a carpenter hammered them in. But wire was too expensive for this common use, until advances in manufacturing technology in the 1880s—some made by Cleveland Rolling Mill—reduced the price of production. Suddenly the wire nail became the emblem of high-tech construction, and production quadrupled within five years at the end of the decade.[13]

The expansion of the steel-wire industry coming on the heels of an overall expansion in the economy drew capital investment out of all proportion to the actual demand for wire nails. The same was true to a less-spectacular degree of steel production and railroad construction, which also ran ahead of demand. Investment in the American economy in the late 1880s went well beyond necessary growth into a speculative bubble, expanding in volume on hope and hot air.[14] It was going to pop—but canny businessmen, knowing an opportunity when they saw one, seized on the chance to turn this coming disaster to their advantage.

The usual method of skimming excess speculative investment was overstating capitalization—or, as it was more humbly called, stock-watering. The term derived from an old ranchers' trick: unscrupulous cowboys would salt cattle feed just before taking a herd to market. The thirsty livestock would drink up an enormous quantity of water just in time for it to register on the scales for sale. Then the cows would do what cows do with excess body water, and the money paid in excess of their usable weight would likewise vanish down the drain.

Given the Western origins of the practice, it was fitting that a steel-wire corporation would be watered by a man who made his name in the Texas cattle country. John W. Gates was better known as "Bet-a-Million"—though he might actually bet perhaps half a million while calling it a million on the balance sheet. He started small, as a barbed-wire salesman for the industry cartel. He distinguished himself as a promoter and salesman, but found little room for advancement within the established firms. So he struck out on his own to make unlicensed barbed wire in defiance of the patent holders. While keeping one step ahead of process servers, Gates devised a simple plan to undermine the cartel: combine independent wire makers into a new firm, sell watered shares—representing more capital than the combine actually had invested in it—and then live off this excess capital while underpricing the old manufacturers, betting they would go under before Gates ran out of money. If it worked, Gates's new firm would prosper, and eventually grow to be worth what the balance sheet said.

Gates put his plan in action, creating Consolidated Steel and Wire in 1892 by pulling together five firms whose combined output made them the largest manufacturer of barbed wire and steel-wire nails in the world. He gathered the firms' owners at his Chicago offices in an eleven-story building called the Rookery. There, in a ninth-floor suite from which they could see the new neoclassical buildings of Chicago's White City—the World's Columbian Exposition of 1893—the founding members of the new combine decided on an initial capitalization of $4 million. It was an amount believed to be well in excess of the constituent firms' capital endowment at the time, and it gave Consolidated Steel and Wire a treasure chest suited for the price war Gates planned. But he had scarcely swung his new galleon of a combine onto its charted course when the economic winds drastically shifted.[15]

MARKETS AND MEN

Waldeck Czolgosz's smoky garret off Cleveland's Broadway could not have looked less like John W. Gates's Rookery, yet the same breezes had blown both men to their vastly differing perches. The collapse of the U.S. economy in 1893 sent the price of steel products plummeting. The drop in demand revealed the extent to which speculators had overinvested in promising new technologies as the industry press glumly figured that "if all the wire mills in the country were operated to full capacity for four months, the consumption of the whole country for an entire year could be met."[16] The falling prices played into Gates's hands: in recession, big was the thing to be, and his firm was big and flush with cash from the sale of watery shares. He bought out his competitors as they faltered, and Consolidated Steel and Wire grew fatter. Other firms scrambled to cut costs to stay afloat, and like Cleveland Rolling Mill had to lay off workers—the Czolgoszes among them.

When the business cycle turned down in 1893, the economy tumbled into a crash. The dominoes the Republican Congress had lined up in 1890 fell in predictable patterns. The Sherman Silver Purchase Act sent gold trickling steadily from the Treasury, and put millions of dollars in legal-tender notes into circulation in exchange. People tended to spend the paper money and to hoard gold, keeping the yellow metal out of circulation and also out of the Treasury. Under the McKinley Tariff, a lower volume of taxable imports came into the country, reducing the amount of gold the Treasury brought in through customs duties. The 1890 failure of Baring Brothers, a British bank, set London financiers scrambling to recoup bad investments, and the flow of British investment capital into the United States fell off as the City of London liquidated its dollar assets, sending yet more gold out of the

United States. Finally, in April 1893—one month after the hapless Grover Cleveland returned to the presidency he had vacated four years before—it became known that the U.S. government now held less than $100 million in gold, about half what it had held three years earlier.[17]

The drop below $100 million triggered a panic. The outflow of gold, and the increase of legal-tender notes in circulation, fostered a suspicion among financiers that the U.S. government was going to succumb to Western radicals and abandon the gold standard in favor of a silver or paper currency. The herd of investors that had rushed in to graze on the green fields of new economic growth in steel and rail now turned tail and fled the American market. Western railroad stocks fell to one half or one-third of their former value. Corporations had to pay their debts with currency other than their own stock certificates, and many could not. When a company failed, the money invested in it often simply vanished; banks and other creditors were left holding worthless paper. When this happened too often, banks themselves failed; more than eight hundred collapsed in 1893, which was more than in any other depression in American history except that of 1929.[18]

Much like many another American, William McKinley, now governor of Ohio, found himself in financial trouble. Unable to meet upwards of $100,000 in obligations, he faced the possibility of an embarrassing and career-ruining bankruptcy. But he had resources not available to the wider public. Mark Hanna volunteered to help and called on some friends, including the reliable H. H. Kohlsaat and Cleveland banker Myron Herrick. When they began working out McKinley's debts, they found to their dismay that the governor owed much more than they could handle. So they called on more powerful friends to bail McKinley out. Many were steel barons, Andrew Carnegie and Henry Clay Frick among them; one was the chief executive of the Cleveland Rolling Mill Company, William Chisholm (son of innovator Henry), whose shrewd management kept his accounts sound.[19]

The recent expansion of the steel-wire industry, led onward by the promise of the technologically superior wire nail, suddenly reversed itself. Twenty-one wire nail firms failed or halted production, leaving their workers idle and so contributing to the unemployment rate, which swelled to 20 percent. The big firms, like Consolidated Steel and Wire, and the established firms, like Cleveland Rolling Mill, survived to fight over the scraps. With the plunge in prices, Gates's great stories about new technologies evaporated, replaced by a ruthless chasing after what little actual business remained. The legendary creativity of the expansive, visionary marketplace yielded to close-fought struggles between a few powerful men.

Their first response to the crisis was to continue running their mills all out, each desperately trying to undersell the other. They ran their factories so hard even in the teeth of depression that, despite the failures and production halts at other plants, the total industry output actually increased. Increasing production in a depression while waging a price war meant increased pressure to cut production costs—which meant cutting wages.[20]

"Running full" seemed the only thing to do in steel, whether in good times or bad. The lure of a protective tariff brought huge sums of capital into the industry for those seeking an easy profit under the government's sheltering wing. The steelmasters could only hope to recoup the investment by running their mills continuously. Consequently they put their money into whatever innovations would allow the mills to run more smoothly and quickly. This strategy invariably entailed substituting new machinery and processes for the labor of skilled workers. Getting rid of skilled workers had the added benefit of allowing mill owners to exert a greater degree of control over their workers—unskilled workers, who were easily replaced, could not strike as effectively as skilled ones.

Cleveland Rolling Mill, one of the more innovative companies of the 1880s, learned this lesson well. Henry Chisholm's innovations in production methods kept it at the forefront of wire production, and William Chisholm's management techniques kept its costs down. During the recessions of 1882 and 1885, workers at Cleveland Rolling struck in response to the lower wages. William Chisholm beat the strikers both times by taking advantage of ethnic and skill divisions in his workforce. In 1882, when the mostly skilled, British-descended labor force struck the mill, Chisholm implemented technological advances that allowed him to fire the skilled workers and rely more heavily on unskilled ones, who were mainly Slavic immigrants. Union men muttered darkly that Chisholm sent a boat to Europe to bring strikebreaking foreigners over, but the truth was more prosaic, and cheaper: Chisholm sent a man named Charley Frank, who spoke five languages, to the immigrant-receiving offices at Castle Garden, New York, to bring hungry workers back to Cleveland.

When the recession of 1885 brought layoffs and wage cuts of 50 percent, the new, unskilled Slavic workers struck Cleveland Rolling. They gathered to listen to angry orations and armed themselves with guns and clubs to blockade the mills. After Cleveland's mayor persuaded Chisholm to restore some of the wage cuts, the factory owner used an even simpler solution to maintain control of his workforce: he blacklisted the strikers and hired replacements, and the mill resumed operation.[21]

Steel-mill owners commonly opposed unionization, believing that organization of the men would rob them of their ability to control the speed of manufacture essential to profit. In steel-wire manufacture, the favored technique of stopping unionization was the "ironclad" agreement. Adopted by J. W. Gates in 1891 and commonly used throughout the industry, the agreement bound workers to accept fines or termination if they should "enter into or participate in any manner in any strike or labor trouble." The American Federation of Labor's efforts to unionize wire workers stumbled on this obstacle in the early 1890s, and though the AFL lobbied to have the agreements made unlawful, they remained a useful tool for steel men.[22]

The Cleveland press supported the steel men, snarling that the foreign workers were "Communistic scoundrels [who] have hoisted the red flag of Agrarianism, Nihilism, and Socialism," but the immigrant strikers of 1885 actually gathered together under the Stars and Stripes to stake their claims.[23] For them the American flag represented a right to stable work. The majority of them had come to this country to make money and then to return to Europe. They wanted only the guarantee of employment that recruiters like Charley Frank had sold to them. "If I don't earn $1.50 a day," one immigrant figured, "it would not be worth thinking about America." But for even a small regular wage it was worthwhile for a migrant to think about America. For a small regular wage was what they expected, and indeed it was all they expected. They had no illusions about their temporary home and they dreamed no American dream of democratic destiny.[24]

But in this the Czolgoszes differed from most of their immigrant fellows. Like the minority of migrants who came to America fleeing persecution, they had no intention of returning. They had bought into the American dream, and had—Leon especially—spent time imbibing it in the public schools. If he had not drunk so deeply of its promise he could never have fallen so far into disillusionment.

The price war in wire following the 1893 panic again sent profits spiraling downward. A major wire firm, Baackes, failed because, in the words of its operator, "unreasonable creditors" were "slaughtering" them. The Newburgh works of the Cleveland Rolling Mill took advantage of the business slowdown to shut up shop and upgrade its machinery. William Chisholm anticipated reopening at the lower wages then prevailing in Pittsburgh, the city that led the steel economy. When his workers then struck again, his company did again what it had done in 1885: it blacklisted the strikers and hired replacements. Leon Czolgosz went out with the strikers. The tide in the industry soon turned, and Gates, with his rivals, established a price-fixing pool for wire nails. However, for his sin of striking, Leon could not get back in the door of the mill because he was a troublemaker, with a black mark against his name on the list in a foreman's hand.

But the effectiveness of these lists depended on names and faces sticking together. Six months after the labor trouble, there was a new foreman at the Cleveland Rolling Mill works, who had the list of strikers but no memory of their faces. So Leon changed his name, and began calling himself Fred Nieman. "Fred" was a silly name they called him within the family, his sister-in-law said; his father said Leon had appropriated it for his middle initial because he liked the idea of having one. And Nieman meant "nobody." It was a thin enough disguise, but it was enough to get him rehired, and he went back to work at his old wage. But the depression of 1893 had rattled Leon Czolgosz. He had lost his work and his good name, while the mill owners and political men prospered, whatever the economic weather. It was not long before he lost his faith, too.

Waldeck remembered how hard Leon took the depression. "He got quiet and not so happy," Waldeck said. Leon could not understand how everything he had learned—about obedience to God, about equality and democracy in America—had no effect on economic justice in the United States. He prayed. Indeed, Waldeck remembered, they "both prayed very hard but they got no answer." Their priest told them "they would be helped if they would pray," but, Briggs wrote, "they were not." Leon talked and talked about his unhappiness to Waldeck, and they set about teaching themselves a new set of principles. First they stopped going to church. They bought a Bible in Polish, and for the first time in their lives they read through the Scripture on their own. In itself this was an education. Leon concluded that Catholic priests " 'told it their own way' and kept back most of what was in the book." After a few more rereadings, he "believed the priest's trade was the same as the shoe-maker's or any other," and that the Church had little to do with what he regarded as Christianity. Waldeck and Leon began to spend their extra money on books and pamphlets concerned with religion and society, reading them over and over together.[25]

After a year and a half, Waldeck lost interest in their private study group. He tended to a more practical frame of mind: if Christianity or democracy, as he learned them, did not much account for the way the world ran, then he would learn to live in keeping with the world as he found it. He became a hardheaded, money-minded man—after all, fiscal concerns seemed to serve politicians and businessmen admirably, whatever they professed to believe.

But Leon persisted in his self-made course of study, pursuing ideas about American society through one text after another till, Waldeck said, he found one that especially fascinated him. Briggs wanted to see what it was, so Waldeck scraped back his chair and shuffled off to a corner of the attic where the roof sloped down and bit into the living space. He dug into a trunk and pulled out a well-thumbed Polish translation of Edward Bellamy's 1887 novel Looking Backward.[26]

Bellamy had written nothing of distinction in a long career till he burst suddenly into bestsellerdom with *Looking Backward*. A Massachusetts preacher's son who rejected his father's religion, he struck out as a writer in the 1870s. He plugged away at newspaper writing and romance novels until 1886, when the Haymarket bombing inspired him to inflect his next book with a full-throated critique of industrial society. The timely result was *Looking Backward*, which electrified all America and the whole industrial world, selling through hundreds of thousands of copies and dozens of editions in five years. Translated into a wide variety of languages and selling for as little as fifty cents, it swiftly became one of the most accessible books in the United States. Its story of Julian West, a well-off Bostonian who goes to sleep in the strike-shattered world of 1887 and awakens in a utopian America of 2000, contrasts the industrial war of the late nineteenth century with a future in which social classes do not war with one another but work together in peaceable recognition of their common interest.

Looking Backward echoed all manner of industrial disillusionment, but it resonated specially with a young man who had just lost his identity in the wake of a strike. Bellamy's protagonist comes to a crisis when he too loses all "[clue] to my personal identity." Alienated from himself, he endures a "mental torture . . . eyeless, groping for myself in a boundless void," and adds, "No other experience of the mind gives probably anything like the sense of absolute intellectual arrest from the loss of a mental fulcrum, a starting point of thought, which comes during such a momentary obscuration of the sense of one's identity."[27] In the course of the book, Julian West comes to realize that this dislocation from himself was a necessary step on the way to an appreciation of the brotherhood of all men—a revelation that underlies Bellamy's American utopia of the late twentieth century.

In Bellamy's novel, the revelation comes painlessly, accompanying the inevitable economic development of society. Americans suddenly apprehend their common interest, agree to end all competition, and turn over their factories to one big government-owned trust. In this sudden sea change there is no struggle, and indeed Bellamy's characters despise anarchists and "followers of the red flag." The critique of industrial antagonism impressed middle-class Americans, as one set-

tlement worker wrote, with the "brutalities and stupidities of the capitalist order." In exchange it offered revolution without violence, an
evolution of the collective mind, a peaceable dream.[28]

Leon Czolgosz loved it. He studied his copy of *Looking Backward*
steadily for eight years, leaving it only when he departed home for the
last time in 1901. Like Bellamy's Julian West he had awakened to a
terrible alienation from himself and found himself adrift in the fantasy
of his native country. The land of freedom had failed him, reneging on
its promise of equality. He had learned that the great abstractions of
democracy and individualism served mainly to hide bids for power.
The markets were rigged and the churches corrupt. But he held out
hope that like West he might turn this abandonment of his old de-
luded self to his advantage, and he hoped to find a new brotherhood
in community with his fellow Americans.[29]

Bellamy's book inspired Americans to think about their obligations to each other. They started Bellamy Societies and joined mutual
organizations to hasten the process of self-socialization. Community
stood as a bulwark against competitive capitalism, they believed, har-
boring an alternative—though no less American—set of values.

Leon Czolgosz's American dream rested on these values, replacing
formal religion and allegiance to ideals with a sense of belonging to
something concrete and local. He joined the Knights of the Golden
Eagle, a benevolent fraternal society whose credo asserted that the
"association of mankind for the purpose of improvement and advancement is a Divine arrangement. Men are made for companionship. No
life is, or can be, entirely self-existent. We depend upon each other."[30]
He joined the Socialist Club (whose members distanced themselves
from anarchism) and went to its meetings. He saved his money. After
work he would perch in the window of the saloon owned by his father,
read the day's paper, and refuse to drink or gamble. "No, I have use for
my money," he would say.[31]

In 1897 the Czolgosz family started its own cooperative venture,
pooling their funds to buy a fifty-five-acre farm near Warrensville, not
far from Cleveland. Leon put in $46, the sum of his savings.[32] He
cared little for the heavy lifting of the barn or field, but liked doing
skilled work on the farm, which he managed around his ongoing work

at the steel mill. He hunted throughout the fall and winter, shooting rabbits with a shotgun or revolver. He tinkered, too. Fixing boxes or wagons, repairing fence wire, taking machines apart and putting them back together—his brother said he "could do anything in the way of fixing up." He had taken a shattered china pitcher and wired it so tightly it would hold milk again.[33]

He was "a nice boy," who literally would not hurt a fly—"he would brush them off or perhaps catch them and let them go again, but never kill one," the landlady at the saloon said.[34] He never lost his temper, or got into a fight. His Bellamyite socialism bothered only the foreman at the mill, who complained that Czolgosz "talked too much to his men," but as Briggs added in his notes, "there being nothing tangible in this direction it seems . . . that it was a notion of the manager's mind; every body else gave him the reputation of being a dreamer, always a dreamer."[35] His family came uncomfortably to feel that it was precisely this gentleness that was going to make trouble for Leon someday. Lived outside the pages of utopian fiction, life did not work along the lines of brotherhood, and Leon had little or no experience of more worldly matters.

Sometime about 1899, Leon Czolgosz stopped working at the wire mill, and went to live permanently on the farm in Warrensville. The family never knew fully why, though it happened around the time Leon's brother Michael came back from the Philippines, and when there was a change of ownership at the steel plant: J. W. Gates formed a new combine, the American Steel & Wire Company, and swept Cleveland Rolling Mill's wireworks into his holdings. Leon would have no more to do with the steel business. He tinkered full-time, fished and hunted rabbits, and continued going into the city to attend meetings of his clubs, till the Socialist Club disbanded in 1901 and he began making new plans.

EARTH AND FLESH

Conspicuously absent among the reactions to William McKinley's murder was any significant expression of surprise. Most public reaction stuck to sentimental cliché, bemoaning the loss of a man who exemplified success through discipline and virtue. Harsher opinions usually stayed private. The historian Henry Adams characterized the deceased as a "supple and highly paid agent of the crudest capitalism."[36] William James snorted, "The old humbug now adds the martyr's crown to the rest of his luck," and believed McKinley was getting away with something even in death: "He ought to have lived to experience the inevitable 'reaction'—he stood for absolutely nothing but 'success' and could no more have survived failure than a Napoleon."[37] Every so often someone publicly blurted out, as one Wisconsin man did, that "McKinley was not worth the bullet that laid him low."[38] Temperance crusader Carrie Nation shouted that "he deserved what he got." The mayor of Marietta, Ohio, said, "He ought to have been dead a long time ago."[39] Even before the event, some commentators saw it on the horizon. After the assassination of Kentucky governor-elect William Goebel in January 1900, journalist Ambrose Bierce wrote, in one of William Randolph Hearst's newspapers,

> The bullet that pierced Goebel's breast
> Can not be found in all the West;
> Good reason, it is speeding here
> To stretch McKinley on his bier.[40]

The millions around the country who read Hearst's newspapers were used to seeing daily caricatures of "Boss Hanna" wearing suits decorated in dollar signs and dangling a puppet McKinley on its strings. In the spring of 1901, a Hearst paper printed an editorial remarking darkly of the nation's leadership, "If bad institutions and bad men can be got rid of only by killing, then the killing must be done." Even Americans who did not share the excitability of the yellow press had a sense that violence was in the offing. Only half an hour before the shooting, the Buffalo Exposition organizers James Quackenbush and Louis Babcock were having a beer when Quackenbush commented "if it would not be just Roosevelt's luck for someone to shoot the President."[41] There was a widespread feeling that the bullet had been a long time coming, propelled by irresistible pressures building up in the industrial West, whose workers dreamed of liberation. In those parts Leon Czolgosz became an instant folk hero, legendary for behavior completely at odds with the evidence of his life.

Nowhere did reports of his travels persist more stubbornly than in the coal country of West Virginia and Pennsylvania. Miners told reporters in 1901 that they recognized Czolgosz's picture in the papers, that he had "made a tour of the anthracite regions about six years ago," and that he was a fiery agitator, who "insisted on doing all the talking" at any meeting.[42] The rumor grew into a lasting myth; in 1907 the Secret Service had to investigate a report that "the same gang that had egged on Czolgosz to the assassination of President McKinley was aiming at the life of his successor and had its headquarters in the Pennsylvania coal regions."[43]

If any region needed this dream of Leon Czolgosz it was the anthracite country. Anthracite fueled the blast furnaces of the iron and steel industry, and its efficient use helped make American factories more productive than their competitors around the world.[44] The men who mined it, like the steelworkers, comprised a workforce once wholly British in ancestry, but now largely eastern European and immigrant. Their union, the United Mine Workers, tended to sympathize with the mine owners. UMW president John Mitchell had little use for immigrants and hoped fervently to ingratiate himself with Mark Hanna, the statesman he most admired. Mitchell repeatedly counseled his workers to accept worse terms than they wanted, and in turn they surprised him by showing spontaneous solidarity and going out on strike without his approval. It was little wonder that the idea of an aggressive Polish anarchist with a gun in his hand appealed to them.

Much as they might have wanted a fighting Leon Czolgosz, the miners got a compromising Theodore Roosevelt. When the anthracite workers struck without Mitchell's guidance in the summer of 1902, asking for an eight-hour day and a wage increase, the syndicate of mine owners organized by J. P. Morgan refused to negotiate. Stalemate settled over the coal fields, and with a coal-less winter looming, the intransigence of management tipped public sympathy to the strikers. Indeed, the union had Mark Hanna's momentary sympathy, too.

Returning as Ohio's senator in 1902, Hanna looked to many McKinley Republicans like a good presidential nominee for 1904. If he could work with Mitchell to end the troubles in anthracite, he might emphasize his sympathy for labor rather than his friendliness to capital. Mitchell was happy to work with Hanna. He declared the miners were willing to negotiate, and even volunteered that they did not demand recognition of their union. The House of Morgan, unmoved, suggested the miners go back to work and trust that management would soon come around of its own accord to a more beneficent way of doing business. Mitchell demurred, but rather than up the ante he—with Hanna's effusive approval—declined to foment a sympathy strike in the bituminous (soft coal) fields, thus quarantining the discontent and limiting its impact.[45]

With the two parties at this impasse, the contretemps in coal country demanded the President's attention. He could not let the strike drag on into the winter months, nor could he let Hanna gain credit for ending it. Above all, Roosevelt could not stomach the businessmen flouting his authority.

Roosevelt tried to reason with management, but to no avail. One mine owner, George Baer, had declared along imprudently McKinleyesque lines that "the rights of the labouring man will be protected and cared for—not by the labour agitators but by the Christian men to whom God in His infinite wisdom has given the control of the property interests of this country."[46] In a meeting with Roosevelt, Baer and the other mine owners demanded that the President use federal troops to "put an end to the anarchy in the coal fields."[47]

The suggestion brought Roosevelt up short, infuriated by the owners' "wooden-headed obstinacy and stupidity."[48] Less than a year before, he had declared himself an unremitting enemy of anarchists. But he had in almost the same breath identified "real and grave evils" on Wall Street, the worst of which were stock-watering and combination. "Great corporations exist only because they are created and safeguarded by our institutions; and it is therefore our right and our duty to see that they work in harmony with these institutions," he insisted.[49] Soon afterward, he developed a suit—keeping it secret from Elihu Root, the corporate lawyer McKinley had made Secretary of

War—against a J. P. Morgan–created combine, the Northern Securities railroad company. The case brought him an agreeable publicity, distinguishing him in the public mind from the Hanna-led elements of the party. Now he found himself about to butt heads with another Morgan creation in the anthracite fields. Little as Roosevelt liked unions, and much as he loved to talk about summarily shooting the enemies of social order, these strikers had kept the peace and made reasonable demands. Identifying anarchist enemies was his prerogative, and he would not overuse it.

Against the advice of his cabinet, Roosevelt did threaten to send in troops—not to break up the strike, but to socialize the mines. Under this pressure Morgan and the mine owners agreed to arbitration. They ended by agreeing to higher wages and shorter hours—but still refused to recognize the union, in part because of Mitchell's early signal that the UMW was prepared to yield on this point.[50]

Roosevelt turned the anthracite strike to his advantage. It allowed him to distinguish his leadership from McKinley's. Where previous Presidents had responded to industrial crises by siding unquestioningly with capital over labor, he had positioned himself as a neutral authority between the two, representing an overall public interest. Hanna's effort to cast himself as the benevolent capitalist willing to take a cooperative union under his wing had failed, displaced by Roosevelt's vision of the executive branch as a power independent either of Wall Street or labor.

The miners had less cause for happiness. Without recognition their union still depended on an outside authority, like President Roosevelt, to bestow legitimacy upon it. Ill served by Mitchell, the men may well have yearned for a stronger leader. They had an alternative already among them, in Mary Harris "Mother" Jones. An independent organizer affiliated with the UMW, Mother Jones bitterly criticized Mitchell for yielding on the point of recognition. She was the real fiery agitator roaming from mine to mine and inspiring the men in 1901. She slept in the mining camps, collected the miners' stories, and lived their lives alongside them.[51] But she was also an Irish immigrant, a native English speaker, and a woman who fought with her words. The persistent myth that Leon Czolgosz had been abroad in the land suggested that the Slavic workmen of Pennsylvania and West Virginia wanted a leader who looked like them and would wield a gun for them. The tale of Czolgosz's time in the coal country grew and flourished. It incorporated a story, printed in the West Virginia papers, that he had lived a vigorous life there, allowing himself to be roped into marriage only because a constable tracked him down and held him to account for making a woman pregnant. He had become a legend.[52]

Repeatedly throughout Briggs's investigation, people told them not to believe what they read in the newspapers about Leon Czolgosz, and this warning applied to the tale of his crusade through the mining country and his roguish ways, culminating in a shotgun marriage. A reporter who went to find a marriage certificate in West Virginia triumphantly turned one up: but it was made out for a Frank Nauman, not Fred Nieman—let alone Leon Czolgosz.[53] Anyway, it simply did not sound like Leon: Waldeck Czolgosz told Briggs, "He was sure Leon never had any girl with whom he associated; he was quite sure he, Waldeck, would know if it had been so."[54] Leon's brother Jake said flatly, "Leon never looked at a girl."[55] His brother Joseph said Leon "never talked to girls and when he met or saw those he knew, when they were going home from church and at other times, he would cross the street rather than speak with them; that he was 'always awful bashful.' "[56] The landlady said that "he was plagued in and about the saloon about the girls whom he never seemed to have the courage to speak to."[57] He was nursing an obscure hurt, but it was not the ache of an abandoned West Virginia sweetheart.

Sometime in about 1897, Leon Czolgosz came down with an illness. He went to one doctor, then another—at least four that Briggs could find out about from the family. Leon collected prescriptions. "He did not look sick," Joseph said, "but he was always taking medicine, and sent a long way off for an inhaling machine and used it about two months."[58] Jake's wife told Briggs, "If you said anything to him about his sickness he would get mad."[59] The saloon landlady said, "He was always taking medicine, having a bottle in his pocket and a box of pills."[60] Briggs walked to the druggist around the corner from where Leon lived, where the pharmacist readily told Briggs that he "knew [Leon] quite well and . . . he bought a good many things there."[61]

He would not tell his father about his illness, or say "what and how many kinds of medicine he was using." His stepmother said he would take herb tea and cod-liver oil. She would find him using her kitchen to make preparations: "He never used cigarettes but he would grow some kind of a plant that, when sprouted, would give forth big leaves. These he would gather, dry them in the oven, and then crush and smoke them in the pipe."[62] Whatever he was taking, he grew dreamier and sleepier all the time.

He grew particular about his eating, taking simple meals to the fields or the barn, or dinner up in his room. "[H]e would not eat anything at the table," Jake's wife said.[63] He acted the same when he ate his meals at the saloon.[64]

Scanning reports of Leon's symptoms, Briggs concluded, "It would seem that about 1897 Leon to a certain extent became a hypochondriac."[65] Waldeck came to something like the same conclusion early on, rounding on his brother and saying Leon should go to the hospital if he felt so ill. But Leon only said, "There is no place in the hospital for poor people; if you have lots of money you get well taken care of."[66] Once Leon quit work, his suffering and self-medication became his principal hobby, continuing right up till it spurred him suddenly to leave the farm, beset by a premonition of his mortality.

In the spring of 1901, he told his family he wanted to take his investment out of the farm so he could leave. They dragged their feet, but he kept up his demands, saying he needed the money because "he was going west." Waldeck told him the money would not carry him far, but Leon waved off this objection, saying "I can get [a] conductor's job or [work] binding wheat or fixing machines or something." Waldeck wanted to know what the hurry was. "Look," Leon replied, "it is just the same as a tree that commences dying, you can see it is'nt [sic] going to live long."[67] Finally Jake's wife decided "it would be a good thing for him to go away," so she gave him $70 as his share of the farm at its estimated value, and bid him go.[68] He left in July, writing Waldeck from Fort Wayne, Indiana, on July 14, "I am on the road to

West. It is hard for me to tell you where Ill be so I can write you again. Hoping this will find you as well as it leaves me at present I remain yours, Leon F. Czolgosz."[69] The next the family heard of him was that he had shot the President.

Briggs's lengthy interview with Waldeck almost finished his business in Cleveland. He went around to the doctors who were supposed to have seen Leon, but none of them could remember treating him. As for the final disposition of Leon's body, Briggs learned from Waldeck and Paul that they had not knowingly asked Warden Mead to destroy the corpse. Waldeck wanted to take the body and have it cremated, but Mead told him that a mob would surely attack the corpse if it left the safety of Auburn State Prison. Mead telegraphed Paul to say that Waldeck had consented to the body's destruction, and received Paul's consent in exchange. Then Mead told Waldeck the same. "It was all fixed up," Waldeck said bitterly.[70]

At a last meeting with the family, Briggs bade farewell to Waldeck, who conveyed Briggs's thanks in Polish to Paul. Then Waldeck pulled Briggs aside, saying "he had something important to say to me: that the doctors in Auburn did not understand the sickness of Leon." And he said he could explain it to Briggs, but wanted $100.

Briggs was leery of the proposition. "I told him I was not buying anything I did not know the value of." Waldeck hinted that his information "was only valuable to a doctor." Now it was Briggs's turn to conduct his own third degree. "I got him into a room by himself and spent nearly an hour trying to get this secret from him."

Waldeck would not give up his whole secret without the money, but he threw out a few more hints in an effort to sell his story:

It related to and explained a scar that was on Leon's body; to prove his statement he said the doctors could have found it if they had looked for it; that it was in no way connected with a woman; in a way it was an accident and in a way it was not, that to doctors it explained his sickness; that if the doctors saw it and knew how he got it and told him correctly he would give back the money; from it they could date the beginning of all his trouble.

Briggs looked at Waldeck and thought he "told me the truth in the above facts." But Briggs had been on the road for a week. He had compiled seventy pages' worth of typed notes. He was tired of asking questions and he was short of cash—he owed Darmstadter $20 for his work as an interpreter. He wondered about the value of Waldeck's story, and he knew Waldeck needed money. "I decided to let him keep his secret," Briggs wrote. Waldeck flung after him that the story "was [in] no way connected with anarchy and that he never knew his brother to associate with anarchists."[71]

If Briggs had paid Waldeck, and if Waldeck had kept his word, Briggs might have been able to get his money back per Waldeck's guarantee. The doctors at Auburn did find a scar on Leon's body, and they decided they knew how he got it, and from what sort of sickness. Dr. Carlos MacDonald, examining Czolgosz on behalf of the state, wrote, "The external genitals were normal, excepting two small, flat, unindurated cicatrices on the mucous surface of the prepuce, probably the result of previous chancroids." He added, "There were no signs of specific nodes or periosteal tenderness over the usual sites of these lesions." Alerted by the genital scarring, he was looking for signs of syphilis, and he was not finding any.[72]

MacDonald knew it was important that he dispel any doubts on this score. Apart from a tumor, syphilis was the major known organic and visible cause of mental illness. If Leon Czolgosz had it in its tertiary phase he might have been incontrovertibly insane and irresponsible for his actions. Assisting MacDonald, Edward Spitzka examined Czolgosz's brain and found it healthy, although Warden Mead's insistence that he keep the autopsy short and carry away no tissue samples prevented him from performing a microscopic examination.

In 1901 syphilis, like most diseases, came from unknown sources and submitted to no sure cure—German doctors discovered the microorganism that causes it in 1905, and developed Salvarsan "606" as the first effective treatment for it in 1909. It was a plague that first afflicted Europeans shortly after they explored the New World in the fifteenth century, and it spread swiftly on the fuel of desire for the flesh. The unhappy victim noticed it first as a sore at the point of contact. Developing beyond that, it entered the secondary stage, or "great pox," of an overall rash. Then it seemed to vanish, though it was quietly infesting the whole system. In the tertiary stage, the bones and organs erupted in great soft tumors, or gummata, as the spirochete bacteria multiplied and consumed the tissues. Eventually the disease ate the host's brain. Medical studies in 1901 suggested it could sometimes prove self-limiting—but if it did progress it caused a prolonged, painful, and morally indefensible death.

Progressives identified the transmission of syphilis as the worst among the bad effects of the industrial environment. Regulation was unlikely to solve the problem—medical inspection of prostitutes too often failed, and anyway, prostitutes presented only the most obvious threat. Jane Addams blamed the crushing alienation of urban life: "loneliness and detachment which the city tends to breed in its inhabitants is easily intensified . . . into isolation and desolating feelings of belonging nowhere . . . The instinctive fear of solitude will send a lonely girl restlessly to walk the streets . . . where her desire for companionship in itself constitutes a grave danger."[73] Only reform of social relationships, the humanizing of cities, could help. Otherwise the absence of community could literally kill.

MacDonald and Spitzka found no evidence of syphilis in Czolgosz's body, or in his brain. Spitzka wrote that "the results of the necropsy can be summed up by saying that Czolgosz was in excellent health at the time of his death."[74] When another doctor criticized Spitzka for not performing a microscopic examination of the brain, he replied that it would have been "valueless," given the "possible clinical forms [of insanity] consistent with the patent, uncontested facts in re Czolgosz."[75] Spitzka believed it was impossible, given the otherwise healthy body, that the brain could have hidden evidence of syphilis undetectable to the naked eye. The evidence of soft scars on the genitals from a case of chancroid—a disease caused by a different sexually transmitted bacterium—had nothing to do with syphilis, whose chancres left hard (indurated) scars.

But the doctors were looking for organic evidence of syphilis—not for psychological evidence of the fear of syphilis. Progressive physicians inveighed against quacks for spreading fear and ineffectual cures—or worse—through newspaper advertisements claiming to offer easy and permanent cures for syphilis. One syphilologist wrote he had "seen young men who have had no syphilis go . . . to the advertising quacks. They were frightened in regard to their condition, and were treated for some time for a disease they never had."[76] It was a commonplace observation in glassworks of the late nineteenth century that syphilis could be passed on, worker to worker, from the common-use blowing-rods for bottles.[77] Syphilis and chancroid often occurred together and could be confused. Though a good physician should not be fooled, poor ones commonly were, and quacks—fooled or not—might take advantage of the mix-up to sell their treatments.

Leon Czolgosz was acting like someone who believed he had syphilis, and who had consulted a doctor for treatment of the disease. As a point of public health, doctors impressed syphilitics with the ease with which they could infect someone else. Czolgosz was avoiding all sexual contact, even to the point of brushing off advances. His family remarked on his odd refusal to eat at the table with them: but it was a common warning to syphilitics that they must not share "forks, spoons, glasses, towels, etc." lest they spread the disease through an innocent secretion.[78] He was also taking just such "herbal decoction[s]" as quacks often prescribed. He was also, it turned out, taking potassium iodide on the prescription of a Dr. Rosenwasser, who wrote Briggs after he left Cleveland to say that though he still did not remember Czolgosz, he had found a record of seeing him on April 28, 1898, in his files.[79] Potassium iodide was a common treatment for syphilis prior to the advent of Salvarsan. Some doctors would prescribe only potassium iodide if they believed the patient had entered the tertiary stage, although others believed mercury and the iodides had to work together.[80]

The treatments for syphilis often caused other symptoms—especially, in the case of potassium iodide, "a stubborn flow of mucus from the nose," or even a swelling of the respiratory tract.[81] This was the symptom Leon's relatives noticed: "catarrh (of nose)," they called it, and Leon's complaint to Dr. Rosenwasser was of catarrh and wheezing.[82] The effects of potassium iodide were sometimes, syphilologists noted, mistaken for those of syphilis itself.[83] When Leon returned to Dr. Rosenwasser in the fall of 1898, telling him he felt "worse" and had "aches all over," even though Rosenwasser recorded "Examination negative," Leon may well have had subjective evidence that syphilis had indeed infected him all over—never suspecting his pains came instead from his purported treatment.[84] Once in prison after the shooting, he was unable to continue his extensive medication, and whatever symptoms it caused him would have cleared by the time of the autopsy.

In the interview with MacDonald before his trial, Czolgosz "admitted having had sexual intercourse with women, but denied masturbation or other unnatural practices," and told policemen that a girl he loved had betrayed him.[85] When Paul Czolgosz told Briggs that Leon never had a girl, Briggs asked him about the one who "went back on him."[86] Paul shrugged it off, but as one interviewee after another told Briggs that Leon had never seemed sexually normal, he stopped looking for evidence of Leon's fickle girlfriend. The word around the saloon was that Leon might perhaps be an "onanist."[87] And if, as was Briggs's hunch, Waldeck was telling the truth about his secret, including his suggestion that Leon had a scar and a disease that had nothing to do with a woman—well, same-sex contact was commonly known, especially among an immigrant population that skewed heavily male. In many working-class contexts, it was not even especially stigmatized if a man was the penetrator, as the location of Leon's chancroids indicates he was.[88]

Another doctor who wrote about Czolgosz's case noted that his plan to shoot William McKinley was not only homicidal, but suicidal. This corroborated what Czolgosz himself told the police—that we must all die of something, and he might as well be hanged—and even being electrocuted might well have appealed to him given the alternative of having a dread disease dissolve his brain. If he did think, as he told Waldeck, that he was going to die soon anyway, then he had nothing to lose.

After all, by 1901 the foundations on which Leon Czolgosz rested his hopes after the crisis in 1893 had crumbled. The Bellamyite clubs, and Edward Bellamy himself, had pitched in with the Populists, only to see them go down to defeat before McKinley. The Socialist Club, to which Leon belonged, split over the formation of Eugene Debs's Socialist Party of America in 1901. Some went with Debs's party, which was led mainly by native-born Americans. Others sought immigrant or ethnic socialist groups to join. Czolgosz had no private life, and indeed was avoiding acquiring one. He belonged to half a dozen despised social classes—working-class, ethnic, Catholic, striker, freethinker, and so on. Every little community he loved had failed. So he set out to seek the company of the anarchists in 1901—and they pushed him away. And yet over the whole country presided the titans of industry and politics, untouched by the crises they helped cause, headed by lucky Major McKinley, President twice over, an American Napoleon who had just scooped up the nation's first colonies. For a self-identified nobody with no home in his own country, doomed soon to die, the prospect of taking an emperor with him beckoned seductively.

7

AN IRRESISTIBLE IMPULSE

On October 14, 1912, Theodore Roosevelt walked out of the Hotel Gilpatrick in Milwaukee on his way to deliver a speech at the city's Auditorium. He climbed into his waiting car in front of the hotel. A crowd had gathered to see him, and they cheered as he took his seat. Roosevelt could not resist bouncing back up again to wave his hat with his right hand. As he did so, a man stepped forward from the applauding onlookers and fired at point-blank range into Roosevelt's chest. Elbert Martin, a stenographer traveling with Roosevelt, tackled the shooter and bore him to the ground. Henry Cochems, a progressive politician from Milwaukee, threw himself over Roosevelt and asked if he was hurt. "He pinked me," Roosevelt answered.

It looked bad: there was blood on Roosevelt's shirt above his heart. But he gathered his strength, stood up, and saw Martin trying mightily to break the man's neck. "Don't hurt him," Roosevelt said, "Bring him to me!" Martin obliged, handing the pistol to Roosevelt and twisting the assailant's head so Roosevelt could see into his eyes.

After a brief glare at the man who shot him, Roosevelt sat back down and ordered the car to the Auditorium over the protests of his companions. He batted away the attentions of a doctor who had been administering to his sore throat, and refused all demands to see the wound. He coughed into his own hand and, seeing no blood, concluded he was well enough. "You get me to that speech," he ordered. "It may be the last one I shall ever deliver, but I am going to deliver this one." Alive to the political possibilities of even this moment, he said, "This is my big chance, and I am going to make that speech if I die doing it."[1]

Arriving at the Milwaukee Auditorium, he allowed a doctor to determine that though the bullet had lodged in his chest, it appeared not to have pierced his heart or lungs—though nobody could be sure under such circumstances, and his entourage urged him to go to a hospital. Instead he walked out onto the stage and told the audience he had been shot, but that he was going to give his speech anyway. Only when he pulled his notes from his breast pocket did he finally betray surprise: the bullet had passed clean through the fifty folded-over sheets of paper before it hit him. On this occasion his loquacity had literally saved his life. Shaking slightly, he began to explain why, in 1912, he was running for President yet again.

THE PROGRESSIVE MOVEMENT

In 1912 Theodore Roosevelt was, for the first time in his life, not a Republican. Having served nearly a full eight years as President, he left the White House at the end of his term in 1909. He declined to run for what would have seemed a precedent-setting third term, and decided instead to choose and campaign for William Howard Taft for the presidency. Taft's policies pushed Roosevelt further from his old party, turning the Republicans away from progressive politics and back to a more business-friendly conservatism.

Roosevelt enjoyed tremendous popularity as President. Apart from a relatively brief financial panic in 1907, his presidency coincided with eight years of general prosperity. Notwithstanding his often bellicose rhetoric, he had avoided war and indeed, acting as arbitrator, had made peace between the belligerent parties of Russia and Japan—an effort that earned him the Nobel Peace Prize in 1906. And he called with increasing heat and frequency for reforms that would regulate the U.S. economy in the interest of the public rather than allow-

ing the free market to take its natural course and consolidate wealth
and power in the hands of a fortunate few. Yet though he said much he
did little, and seemed to accomplish less as time went on. Apart from
his own caution, two obstacles stood in his way: the Senate and the
Supreme Court.

During Roosevelt's presidency the Senate was still a body of men
appointed by their state legislatures. The eighteenth-century framers
of the U.S. Constitution contemplated an upper house enjoying a dis-
interested and public-spirited independence from the whims of the
mob. The Senate's independence appealed more in theory than in
practice. Its remote inhabitants adopted customs that allowed a minority of members to block a vote altogether, or even a single man to
forestall it as long as he could speak, and they wielded these rights for
reasons that often corresponded with the interests of big business. Ag-
itation for the popular election of the unreachable senators, sporadic
throughout the nation's history, grew to a fury in the 1890s and early
1900s as more and more senators acted as though they worked for major corporations rather than for the people of the states. John Hay
remarked in despair, "There will always be 34 per cent of the Senate
on the blackguard side of every question that comes before them"—
enough, under Senate rules, to block legislation.[2] The popularly
elected House of Representatives responded to public sentiment, passing a constitutional amendment for the direct election of senators five
times between 1893 and 1902, only to have the Senate itself demur.
Not until 1911 did the Senate finally yield—and then only because
twenty-nine states had already short-circuited the federal Constitution by mandating popular votes that either advised or bound the
state legislature in choosing a senator.

But during Roosevelt's time in the White House this reform was
still coming, a mere cloud on the political horizon. It would not burst
until four years after he left office. As President he had therefore to
spend time and energy arbitrating between elements of the federal
government just as he did between capital and labor in the coalfields.
He worked especially strenuously as a referee between Democrats in
the House and conservative Republican senators in seeking passage of
the Hepburn Act of 1906. The act strengthened federal railway regu-

lation, though not nearly as much as Roosevelt or the congressmen would have liked.

And even when legislative obstacles yielded, the Supreme Court stood like a brick wall between the American voters and the regulatory state they sought. The Court declined to apply antitrust law too vigorously to corporations, but applied it with a will to labor unions. Citing everyone's freedom to make contracts—even for debilitatingly long hours and humiliatingly low pay—the Court struck down minimum-wage and maximum-hours legislation. In cases like *Lochner v. New York* and *Adair v. United States*, the Court ruled in favor of employers and against labor unions and legislatures seeking to regulate working conditions in the interest of labor.[3] Once more, as with Senatorial reform, rebellion brewed in the states. Movements to make possible the electoral recall of judges and judicial decisions appeared in local jurisdictions. Roosevelt sympathized with the effort to thwart the independence of courts which defied popular demand for labor legislation. The President wrote exasperatedly in 1908 that "if the spirit which lies behind these . . . decisions obtained in all the actions of the . . . courts, we should not only have a revolution, but it would be absolutely necessary to have a revolution because the condition of the worker would become intolerable."[4]

Roosevelt's strategy for overcoming these obstacles was threefold. First, he accrued to himself as much authority as he possibly could. "The Executive is the steward of the public welfare," he wrote.[5] Unlike Congress or the judiciary, the President was accountable to a national constituency and could claim to speak for national interests. Second, he used the press to circumvent the legislative process by a direct appeal to the voters. Like no President within memory, he not only perceived but enjoyed his job as center of media attention: "I've got such a bully pulpit!" he exclaimed to a friend.[6] And third, after working the public and the press, having got all the leverage he could, he compromised without apparent qualm or principle.

The method worked: not only did he secure the Hepburn Act, which gave the Interstate Commerce Commission authority to set maximum shipping rates, he used the press and public furor to his advantage in getting the Meat Inspection Act and Pure Food and Drug

Act passed in 1906. Perhaps most significantly, he lobbied for and saw through an employer liability law in 1906, only to have it struck down by the Supreme Court in 1908 and passed again in weaker form later that year.

One of Roosevelt's genially critical admirers, the political scientist and activist Charles Beard, remarked shortly after the close of Roosevelt's presidential career that "the social legislation passed during Mr. Roosevelt's administrations is not very extensive, although it was accompanied by much discussion at the time." Most of the discussion, Beard noted, came in the form of a rather repetitive monologue from Roosevelt. "The same notions recurred again and again, often in almost identical language and frequently in the form of long quotations from previous messages."[7]

Another contemporary of Roosevelt remarked shrewdly that all this talking had itself constituted the President's principal accomplishment. The journalist Stuart Pratt Sherman noted President Roosevelt was in reality a consummate compromiser, a man who denounced "the impossible better" as "the enemy of the possible good." But he had also constantly invoked impossibly high ideals. The tension between what he wanted and what he would accept made him, as Sherman said, "the greatest concocter of 'weasel' paragraphs on record." But his insistence on constantly calling and campaigning for more than he would ever get was his principal public service. "I should say that his most notable achievement was creating for the nation the atmosphere in which valor and high seriousness live," Sherman wrote.[8]

Roosevelt inspired better than he could know, and sped on their way reforms that outran the man he chose as his successor. Early in 1908, he held a dinner at the White House. The guests included his physically imposing Secretary of War, William Howard Taft, and Taft's wife. After eating, the company retired to the library. Roosevelt flung himself dramatically into a chair, closed his eyes, and intoned, "I am the seventh son of a seventh daughter. I have clairvoyant powers. I see a man standing before me weighing about 350 pounds. There is something hanging over his head. I cannot make out what it is; it is hanging by a slender thread. At one time it looks like the Presidency—then again it looks like the Chief Justiceship."

"Make it the Presidency," Mrs. Taft shouted. "Make it the Chief Justiceship," Mr. Taft rejoined.[9] Roosevelt followed Mrs. Taft's wishes, though he ought at that late date to have found alarming Taft's enthusiasm for a position on a Court the President regarded as an impediment to progress. Roosevelt got Taft the nomination, helped him get the presidency, and then left not only the White House but the country for a hunting trip in Africa followed by a tour of European capitals.

In Roosevelt's absence, Taft proved he was more temperamentally prepared for the Supreme Court than the presidency he inherited. (He would in time ascend to that bench, there to assist in striking down progressive legislation.*) Taft lacked Roosevelt's confidence that the President could, or should, speak for the whole people. He preferred the cautious conservatism of the judiciary, and under his presidency the reform impulse to which Roosevelt gave voice had no home in the Executive Mansion.

Yet even without presidential support or Roosevelt's rhetorical influence, progressivism not only survived, it flourished. It gathered force in the states, bringing direct democracy—the initiative, the referendum, and the recall—to bear against corporate influence on government. It bubbled through new civic organizations—not only those close to Roosevelt, like the National Civic League, which he helped in its mission to reform cities, or the National Consumers' League, which his niece Eleanor helped in its effort to organize consumers just as capital and labor were organized—but also those organizations whose concerns represented causes more antagonistic than his compromising spirit was prepared to accommodate: the National Association for the Advancement of Colored Persons, the Sierra Club, and the various women's suffrage organizations. All of them in one way or another followed Roosevelt by laying claim to speak on behalf of the public interest, in a manner untainted by business or partisan corruption. They lobbied for new laws intended to wrest power from corpo-

---

*Notably, Taft would vote with the majority in *Federal Trade Commission v. Curtis*, 260 U.S. 568, a 1923 case in which the Court appropriated to itself the FTC's presumed right to determine when a corporation was violating antitrust law.

rations and return it to the voters. As with the reform of the Senate, these progressive reforms percolated upward from the local to the federal level. Measures including corporate regulation, labor legislation, and women's suffrage gathered steam under state constitutions, putting pressure on federal lawmakers that even the most obdurate could not forever block.

When Roosevelt returned from his travels in 1910, he found a country increasingly alienated from the Republican Party that had nurtured him, while the progressive movement he had nurtured grew increasingly strong outside the party system. There were progressive Democrats and progressive Republicans, and soon there might simply be only progressives.

The presidential election of 1912 posed a temptation Roosevelt could not resist. Returning to the stump, he took back from Senator Robert La Follette the leadership of progressive Republicans, then challenged William Howard Taft for the Republican nomination. A bitter fight ensued, made worse by progressive reforms to the party: nine states had established primary elections, trying to dethrone party insiders who gathered to choose candidates in notoriously smoke-filled back rooms at convention hotels. This democratizing reform forced Roosevelt and Taft to take their differences to the public. Intraparty rancor, usually kept private, erupted onto the pages of the newspapers, revealing an ungracious side of the statesmen. Roosevelt rebuked his successor, saying, "It is a bad trait to bite the hand that feeds you." Taft finally retained his incumbent position as Republican leader only by working those smoky back rooms so that the party's committees awarded him all disputed nominating delegates. In a fury, Roosevelt broke with the party. Taft took the nomination in the face of accusations—not altogether unfair—of delegate theft. Amid fistfights on the convention floor, Roosevelt led his supporters out to found a new Progressive Party, whose mascot became the Bull Moose.[10]

The presidential race of 1912 became a four-way contest. The Republican candidate, the incumbent President William Howard Taft, stood for conservatism and respect for the judiciary. Roosevelt ran on the Progressive ticket, pulling together a platform of reforms that included direct democracy, progressive taxation, conservation, abolition of child labor, and women's suffrage. The Democrats, gleefully looking upon a split Republican Party, nominated New Jersey governor Woodrow Wilson. A conservative political scientist and a Virginia-born supporter of states' rights, Wilson's exasperation with party corruption and his sound political instincts pushed him to adopt increasingly progressive positions in 1912—though he still clung to an older-fashioned localism, which led him to oppose national legislation on issues like the minimum wage, child labor, and suffrage. And the Socialist Party nominated Eugene V. Debs, the union leader who had struck at Pullman in 1894 and who had run on the Socialist ticket in each of the two previous presidential elections. Indeed, it was the increasing success of the Socialist Party that made Roosevelt's candidacy more than a pipe dream. In coming to Milwaukee that October, mere weeks before the election, he was seeking to pick off some of the Socialist vote with what Charles Beard called a "socialistic platform."[11]

The success of American Socialist candidates in the local and congressional elections of 1910 provided concrete evidence that the impulse for substantial change had exceeded the voters' traditional party loyalty. Somewhere between four and five hundred Socialists held office in the nation in 1911. By itself, Wisconsin accounted for almost a quarter of them. The number of Socialists holding office rose with the elections of 1911, and the Socialist vote spread throughout the industrialized part of the country—running ominously through the states that normally voted Republican.

The electoral success of the Socialist ticket did not portend great enthusiasm for Marxist socialism, or even for municipal ownership. A Socialist in Pennsylvania looked with skepticism on a victory there: "I would not call the large vote polled in ——— a victory for Socialist principles because there isn't fifty in the town that understand the Socialist principles." Looking at one township, he wrote, "I would stake that not one of the sixty-three that voted the Socialist ticket knows anything about 'Surplus value' or 'Economic determinism.' [That] people are tired of being humbugged by the Democratic and Republican parties is the real cause of the Socialist success." One victorious Socialist mayor promised, oddly, "an honest, clean, business administration."[12] Socialists who understood Marxist economics and quarreled with their comrades over the desirability of a proletarian dictatorship found discomfiting their enthusiastic constituents who told them nobody needed even to read to be a Socialist: "All a fellow needs to know . . . is that he is robbed."[13]

Appealing to this same vague but heartfelt discontent, former Republican President Roosevelt, running as a Progressive, presented a much more plausible candidate than the revolutionary Socialist Eugene Debs. Along the campaign trail leading into heavily Socialist Milwaukee, Roosevelt had to cancel a string of speeches owing to a sore throat. But he was determined to make the Milwaukee speech, sore throat or no—it was critical to the campaign—and when it came down to the evening itself, he was still determined to make the speech, despite the bullet in his chest.

Roosevelt burst onto the stage to tumultuous applause, and told the audience with grim glee, "I don't know whether you fully understand that I have just been shot or not, but it takes more than that to kill a Bull Moose." He launched then into a heartfelt impromptu speech. "I want to take advantage of this incident," he said, as if being shot were simply a golden political opportunity, too good to be missed. "I cannot speak to you insincerely within five minutes of being shot. I am telling you the literal truth when I say that my concern is for many other things. It is not in the least for my own life. I want you to understand that I am ahead of the game, anyway."

Roosevelt used the moment to forswear any personal ambition. "I am in this cause with my whole heart and soul. I believe that the Progressive movement is for making life a little easier for all our people; a movement to try to take the burdens off the men and especially"— here he appealed, as Riis suggested he always did, to the ideal of family—"the women and the children of this country. I am absorbed in the success of this movement."

He went on to explain that he held much the same opinion of this would-be assassin as he did of the man who shot McKinley. "I don't know anything about who the man was who shot me tonight. He was seized at once by one of the stenographers in my party, Mr. Martin, and I suppose is now in the hands of the police. He shot to kill. He shot the shot, the bullet went in here—I will show you." Here he opened his vest, and the crowd let out a gasp of horror at the spill of blood on his shirt. "Now, friends, of course, I do not know, as I say, anything about him; but it is a very natural thing that weak and vicious minds should be inflamed to acts of violence by the kind of awful mendacity and abuse that have been heaped upon me for the last three months by the papers in the interest of not only Mr. Debs but of Mr. Wilson and Mr. Taft." To Roosevelt, gripping the podium with a bullet in his chest, just over a decade since a similar bullet made him President, the cause of political violence remained what it always had been: the insidious influence of demagoguery on the susceptible minds of society's unfortunates.

"Now, friends," he continued—and here one of his aides, Oscar King (O. K.) Davis, pleaded with him to stop speaking and go to the hospital. The wounded Bull Moose rounded on him ferociously. Biting off unusually clipped sentences, Roosevelt hissed, "I am not sick at all. I am all right . . . Don't you pity me. I am all right," and then, with a flash of humor, "I am all right and you cannot escape listening to the speech either."

Turning again to his audience, Roosevelt made the evening's assault on him into a homily on progressivism. "And now, friends, this incident that has just occurred—this effort to assassinate me—emphasizes to a peculiar degree the need of this Progressive movement. Friends, every good citizen ought to do everything in his or her power to prevent the coming of the day when we shall see in this country two recognized creeds fighting one another, when we shall see the creed of the 'Have nots' arraigned against the creed of the 'Haves.' " Jane Addams would have been proud—indeed, at least publicly, she was proud of Roosevelt, whom she endorsed for President at the Progressive Party convention. And now, even under these trying circumstances, he was expounding her view of American society, explaining that social divisions resulted from artificial antagonisms that threatened to tear apart a society that shared real common interests.

The idea of shared interests came in two varieties, the conservative and the radical. The conservative version of the shared-interest theory held that Americans all shared an interest in the continued profitability of the existing system. It espoused an enlightened capitalism, coupled with a reasonably generous amount of trickle-down wealth. It amounted to a purely materialist version of the American dream. Apart from assuring greater material rewards to workers, the invocation of shared interest posed no threat to the social status quo. It was a vision that Mark Hanna could have shared. The more radical version of the common-interest argument held that Americans shared an interest in the fulfillment of democratic principles. Capitalism, though an invaluable mechanism, had license to operate only insofar as it served this end. Government—acting as the steward of the common interest—had rightfully to regulate the engines of economic productivity in the interest of distributing not only wealth, but enlightenment and power, widely and democratically throughout society.

The Progressives of 1912 tried to obscure the distinction between these two visions of the common interest so they could attract voters from any of the other parties. The Progressive Party leadership yoked Addams and Roosevelt together with J. P. Morgan partner George Perkins. They hopefully, but uncomfortably, shared space on the Progressive platform, each wondering how the national interest would look if any two of the others could go it alone.

In November 1912, Addams aired her misgivings about the Progressive dedication to the public interest, albeit couched in an optimistic appraisal of the party's potential, in an article for the NAACP's magazine, *The Crisis*. Addams had proposed a plank supporting racial equality in the Progressive convention. Instead of seeing it adopted, she learned that slates of black delegates from Southern states had been refused accreditation in favor of "lily-white" representation, in the hope of wooing white Southern votes. Political strategy trumped Progressive conviction: "Even in that remarkable convention where, for the moment, individual isolation was dissolved into a larger consciousness and where we caught a hint of the action of 'the collective mind,' so often spoken of and so seldom apprehended, I was assailed by the old familiar discomfort concerning the status of the colored man."[14] In the end Addams swallowed her discomfiture, and backed

Jane Addams as a Bull Moose Progressive, on the campaign trail in 1912. (Jane Addams Collection, Swarthmore College Peace Collection)

the Bull Moose as the best she was likely to get. Some other NAACP members resigned themselves to the same conclusion: "We *had* to think of what more either of the other two parties wo'd give [the Negro] and of the hypocritical attitude of the Republicans for years back—the questions 'What more' and 'What better' faced us squarely," wrote one of Addams's allies.[15] It turned out that even Addams, the most reliably radical supporter of Americans' common interest in democracy, was willing to make a compromise at the expense of American blacks, whose plight went, as was customary, largely unmentioned through the campaign.

This significant exception aside, Roosevelt committed himself, as a progressive campaigning with Addams, to the more democratic conception of Americans' shared interest. That uncertain night in Milwaukee, he put before his audience what might have been his last statement of a progressive credo. The progressive movement was

> a movement for justice now—a movement in which we ask all
> just men of generous hearts to join with the men who feel in
> their souls that lift upward which bids them refuse to be satis-

fied themselves while their countrymen and countrywomen suffer from avoidable misery. Now, friends, what we Progressives are trying to do is to enroll rich or poor, whatever their social or industrial position, to stand together for the most elementary rights of good citizenship, those elementary rights which are the foundation of good citizenship in this great Republic of ours.

Here Davis tried again to get Roosevelt to quit. But the ex-President had no intention of stopping now; he was giving the fullest and broadest statement of his democratic principles—with no time to trim or weasel out of his commitments—and, he said, "I have had an A-1 time in life and I am having it now . . . I never in my life was in any movement in which I was able to serve with such whole-hearted devotion as in this; in which I was able to feel as I do in this that common weal. I have fought for the good of our common country."

Roosevelt wanted his listeners to know that if he was going to die, it would be worth the sacrifice. And he thought the Progressive Party, representing the expansion of American citizenship and its rights to people "without any regard to their creed or to their birthplace," was a cause worth dying for. He invoked the German immigrants who fought for the Union in the Civil War, he cited the example of Jacob Riis, and he mentioned the Jews and Catholics he had supported in his career. He dedicated a paragraph to the support of labor unions. And, true to his combative nature, he took a few jabs at Woodrow Wilson for his coziness with the trusts of New Jersey and his opposition to child-labor legislation. Only then, after nearly an hour of speaking, did he exit the stage.[16]

O. K. Davis helped Roosevelt get out of the Auditorium and into his car, which rushed him at last to the hospital. Once there, even the wounded ex-President had to take a seat in the reception area. Waiting anxiously, Davis made conversation by asking why Roosevelt insisted on giving the speech. Roosevelt replied that in thinking about his political career, he had even planned for just this moment—and he had determined that if he was ever shot, he must go ahead with whatever he was doing at the moment. If he was going to give a speech, he must give the speech: it was the least he could do to defy his would-be assassin.

When Davis and other observers thought back on Roosevelt's shooting, they remembered this resolve, rather than the words their leader spoke. But for Roosevelt, only the words gave purpose to his resolve. With the words he held out a promise for which he was prepared to sacrifice himself—a promise that he knew he had already compromised in the course of a campaign that, this late in the autumn, he knew already was doomed to defeat. If there was any single purpose to progressivism as Roosevelt defined it, it was that Americans must all exercise themselves to the utmost, and sacrifice as need be, to prevent the creation of wounded souls like Leon Czolgosz. As he stared that evening into the eyes of the man who shot him, he knew he had so far failed.

A DREAM OF THE DEMOCRACY

The man who shot Theodore Roosevelt was named John Schrank. He was thirty-six and a New Yorker. He emigrated from Bavaria in 1885, at the age of nine. He lived with his aunt and uncle, who brought him up as their son, and who made their living running a saloon on East Tenth Street. Schrank inherited the business, and lived nearby. When he was arraigned before a Milwaukee judge, he said, "I shot Theodore Roosevelt because he was a menace to the country. He should not have a third term. It is bad that a man should have a third term. I did not want him to have one. I shot him as a warning that men must not try to have more than two terms as President. I shot Theodore Roosevelt to kill him. I think all men trying to keep themselves in office should be killed; they become dangerous."[17] When he saw Roosevelt challenge Taft at the Republican National Convention and heard Taft accused of stealing the nomination, Schrank feared that the same thing might happen in November—Roosevelt, losing the election, would accuse the victor of theft and foment a civil war.

So he set out to stalk the presumptive third-termer, armed with a

.38-caliber pistol he bought from a dealer who was willing to ignore
the licensing laws. He followed Roosevelt for nearly a month, through
eight states. Schrank managed to get close enough to shoot Roosevelt
in Chattanooga, and again in Chicago, but he could not get up the
nerve to act until the third time he came face to face with the candidate, in Milwaukee: then he simply pulled the trigger.

When Schrank appeared before the court, he said much what
Czolgosz had: "I am not a lunatic and never was one. I was called upon
to do a duty and I have done it." But he added one claim that saved
him from prison: he said,

> I had a dream several years ago that Mr. McKinley appeared to
> me, and he told me that Mr. Roosevelt was practically his real
> murderer, and not this Czolgosz, or whatever his name was. Mr.
> Roosevelt is practically the man that has been the real mur-
> derer of President McKinley, in order to get the Presidency of
> the United States, because the way things were at that time he
> was not supposed to be a President; all the leaders did not want
> him; that's the reason they gave him the Vice Presidency,
> which is political suicide; that's what I am sore about, to think
> that Mr. McKinley appeared to me in a dream and said, "This is
> my murderer, and nobody else."[18]

This revelation made him certain to be declared legally insane. Under
the legal doctrine of "deific decree," a person who received a command from God—or a reasonable equivalent—to commit murder was
presumed irresponsible for his conduct. And, although it led to peculiar theological thickets, the ghost of William McKinley qualified as
the equivalent of God as far as American law could determine.[19]

Roosevelt and his supporters despaired at this performance. As far
as they could tell, Schrank was not insane at all, merely motivated by
politics. As Roosevelt's doctor said, "Schrank is not crazy . . . Take
that statement of his in Milwaukee. It is a perfectly clear and reasonable argument against a third term, and shows no mark against insanity. The only reasons for charging Schrank with insanity are that he
believes in dreams . . . One of the members of this very party tells me

that his wife, who is a college graduate, believes in them and she is as sane a woman as I ever knew."[20] Roosevelt himself agreed:

> He was not a madman at all . . . I very gravely question if he has a more unsound brain than Senator La Follette or Eugene Debs. He simply represents a different stratum of life and of tempera-ment . . . He had quite enough sense to avoid shooting me in any Southern State, where he would have been lynched, and he waited until he got into a State where there was no death penalty. I have not the slightest feeling against him; I have a very strong feeling against the people who, by their ceaseless and intemperate abuse, excited him to the action, and against the mushy people who would excuse him and all the other criminals once the crime has been committed."[21]

But that vision of McKinley's ghost overrode all arguments as to the assassin's rationality, and robbed Roosevelt of a crucial political point.

As Roosevelt's remark indicated, Schrank's insanity had nothing to do with saving his life; his decision to commit the crime in Wis-consin rather than Illinois, which imposed the death penalty, had kept him from state execution. His legal madness meant only that he would spend the rest of his days in an asylum, rather than in prison. But the would-be assassin's official insanity angered Roosevelt for strategic rea-sons. He needed to treat Schrank as the representative of a political problem. If the man was merely mad, he had no such significance.

Roosevelt's performance on that grim night in Milwaukee repre-sented a calculated personal risk for political gain. Consulting his own long experience as a killer of men and beasts and his practical under-standing of anatomy derived from years at amateur taxidermy, he ob-served the bullet hole, felt its trajectory, and made an educated guess as to the damage it could have caused. He coughed into his hand and, seeing no blood, figured he had suffered only a flesh wound. Allowing doctors to examine him at the Auditorium, he corroborated his initial opinion. A chance remained that he, and they, were wrong—perhaps the bullet lay perilously close to a major blood vessel. But he decided to run that risk so that he could present Progressive voters with the picture of a leader ready to die for their cause—a cause he could now sanctify with his blood, and give to it the fullest, most inclusive expression. It amounted to an impressive and even profoundly moving performance, but it was no less a performance for that. As he told O. K. Davis, he "thought it an exceptional opportunity to drive home . . . the lessons he had been preaching throughout the campaign."[22] It was also a desperate gesture, made by a man losing an election in which he had defined the debates, but in which the critical mass of voters would stay with their traditional party rather than heed his call.

What made Roosevelt's progressive preaching unique was not its embrace of immigrants or women. Immigrants had been well served by the Democratic Party since the 1850s, when the Republican Party had more than a tinge of anti-immigrant and anti-Catholic sentiment that it never quite shook, notwithstanding its shifting economic views of immigrant labor. Nor was the Progressive effort to include white ethnics while excluding American blacks particularly innovative. The Democrats had already made a policy of this tactic, and reliably carried the South and many Northern cities with it. And the Progressive inclusion of women at the highest levels of party management simply followed the lead of local law: by 1912 thirty-one state and territorial governments had legislated some kind of women's suffrage. Moreover, the Socialist Party had strong records on both issues.

But Roosevelt's progressivism did offer one novelty: in extending a welcoming hand to immigrants and women, it brought them together with powerful men of finance and politics in the name of an American national interest that only the Republican Party had previously claimed to represent. The Democrats were the party of sections, of localism, of particular interests—it did not matter whether the interests were incompatible with one another, as long as each respected the others' rights to be let alone. The Socialists made broader claims, but they staked their sense of justice on the rights of humanity, not of Americans in particular. Since the Civil War, only the Republicans had title to the ability to speak on behalf of the nation, that mystical Union given a bloody rebirth by Abraham Lincoln.

Sensing that with the passing decades and the rising tariffs on manufactures the Grand Old Party had lost some of its luster, Roosevelt's Progressives sought to rehabilitate its sense of purpose by expanding it to encompass the new Americans. Unable to get their man the nomination, they left Taft in control of a conservative rump representing narrowly defined business interests, and took their moderate middle in the hope of marrying it to Socialist and Democratic constituencies.

But it was far easier for the Democrats to steal the Progressives' language than for the Progressives to steal the Democrats' voters: and this is what happened. Woodrow Wilson emerged from his states' rights cocoon as a gradually more vocal and inspiring national progressive. Buoying him onward in his effort to speak for the new nation, the traditionally Democratic constituencies of urban immigrant voters and rural native-born farmers turned out in force to elect him President and supply him with a Congress of his own party. As Schrank gloated during his appearance before the court at Milwaukee, the election returned the government to its pre–Civil War status, dominated by the Democratic Party: "The North, South, East, and West are once more and more solidly united, and proudly can we prove to the nations of the world that the spirit of 1776 is still alive and shall never die."[23]

Taking office in 1913, Wilson stood at the head of a united party and a newly powerful, and democratized, federal government: two new constitutional amendments provided a Senate responsive to ordinary voters, and the ability to levy an income tax. The latter measure was perhaps the most precious progressive victory of all. The Populists advocated it in the 1890s and Roosevelt took it up during his presidency because only an alternative form of taxation would allow serious tariff revision. The Supreme Court had struck down an income tax in 1895 as unconstitutional, making an amendment necessary. The Sixteenth Amendment took effect a week before Wilson took office, and his Administration's first revenue bill—the Underwood Tariff of 1913—lowered tariff rates and, by way of some compensation, raised an income tax. The federal government was on its way to a more progressive structure and policy program.

What one assassin gave Roosevelt, another took away. Drawing strength and purpose from the murder of McKinley, Roosevelt used the politically motivated attack on his predecessor as a twofold moral weapon to wield throughout his presidency. On the one hand, he struck at the perpetrators of violence and those who encouraged it. By reserving to himself the right to label as un-American the anarchists and other enemies of the social order, he threatened to ostracize, imprison, or deport those who challenged his vision of America. Though like all his violent talk it remained mainly talk, the possibility of ruthless action loomed over and behind his grinning face, lending it menace and force. On the other hand, he steadily expanded the definition of national interest to cover the improvement of social welfare, trying to prevent the creation of a class of oppressed and excluded Americans. The story of Leon Czolgosz lent poignancy and urgency to this progressive project, and brought Roosevelt together with Addams, Riis, and other social reformers.

But the failure of Schrank's assault to provide a similarly meaningful set of moral lessons robbed Roosevelt of a chance to restate his progressivism persuasively. Czolgosz's insistence that he only did his anarchistic duty rang a troubling bell with many Americans who privately thought there was something to the theory that McKinley stood for an oppressive system. The assassination that launched Roosevelt into the presidency presented him with the opportunity to spin a story of his own duty and gave purpose to his term: he must prevent the emergence of men with such awful conceptions of their political obligations. By contrast, Schrank's attack on Roosevelt cast the old reformer in the role of an ambitious office-seeker. It highlighted his personal determination to occupy the presidency without giving him a political creed to oppose or a social disorder to cure.

The Milwaukee shooting did not kill Roosevelt, but it emphatically punctuated his loss of significance. As he wrote dismally to Jane Addams after the 1912 election, "We have fought a good fight; we have kept the faith; we have gone down in disaster."[24] Addams wrote back, encouraging him to take heart at "the tremendous impulse the campaign has given to social reform measures in which I have been interested for many years, but which have never before seemed to become so possible of fulfillment as at the present moment. I had never

dared hope that within my life-time thousands of people would so ea-
gerly participate in their discussion. I am sure you have been in a large
measure responsible for this outcome."[25] It was some comfort, and it
was moreover true: the years after 1912 saw an outpouring of progressive debate and legislation that fueled the creation of powerful new
progressive institutions.

But without Roosevelt as spokesman, the continuing energy and
interest could not keep the Progressive Party together. It fractured on
predictable lines, with social reformers going one way and business-
minded men like Perkins going another. Roosevelt himself slunk back
to the Republican Party, where he was graciously welcomed—and ac-
corded the neutered status of honored elder statesman, a post nearly as
useless as the vice presidency from which Czolgosz had unexpectedly
sprung him.

Woodrow Wilson could not hold the progressive coalition together,
either. In part it was because he lacked Roosevelt's brio; as one anony-
mous foreign visitor undiplomatically observed, "It may be that Mr.
Wilson possesses all the virtues in the calendar; but for my part I
would rather go to hell with Theodore Roosevelt."[26] But more important, Wilson faced the impossible task of keeping Protestant Bryanite
farmers and laborers in the same party with immigrant Catholics and
Jews. The fragile alliance lasted during his first Administration and
held through the enactment of a spate of progressive reforms, including the creation of the Federal Trade Commission and the Federal Reserve Board, and the passage of the Clayton Antitrust Act. But it
fractured on the issue of immigration. The election of 1916 portended
disaster: congressional Democrats campaigning in rural Western districts pledged themselves to support immigration restriction, while
their urban counterparts pledged to oppose it. Wilson himself promised to oppose it—and did, vetoing a bill to restrict immigration by
applying a literacy test. But Congress passed the law over his veto in
1917. Immigrants would not vote the same ticket as Western progressives in decisive numbers again until 1932, when they propelled Roosevelt's fourth cousin once removed and nephew-by-marriage Franklin
into the White House.[27]

Along with the fight over immigration restriction in 1917, the

First World War came to the United States after three years of plaguing Europe. War fever replaced progressivism on the public stage, and continued through the end of the war into the Red Scare of 1919. Wilson carried the high-mindedness of progressivism into his unsuccessful and self-destructive campaign for the United States to support the League of Nations. Conservative Republicans, led by Henry Cabot Lodge in the Senate, rose to triumph over a broken Wilson and his fragmented progressive coalition.

Although the Progressive Party could not survive Roosevelt's absence, progressivism—as a widespread impulse to political and social reform—certainly could, and did. The example of political maneuvering in Chicago just after the shooting of President McKinley suggested what many reformers well knew: local progressives did not need myths of national community to help them do their jobs. Someone like police chief O'Neill could root business-sponsored corruption out of his party and his department without trying to connect his cause to the plight of Western farmers preyed upon by railroads. Indeed, the national progressivism that Roosevelt was fostering briefly hindered Chief O'Neill in his campaign against Luke Colleran, just as it momentarily inconvenienced Jane Addams on the morrow of McKinley's assassination. Without Roosevelt, progressivism would have had no national champion in the Republican Party—but it might not have needed one. Indeed, Americans in the North and West might have done sooner what they were doing in great numbers by 1910 anyway—joining the Socialist Party, which appealed to citizens tired of corporations controlling their lives and attracted hundreds of thousands of voters who had no particular interest in Marxism. The resulting American socialism would have been progressivism under another, more internationally familiar name, and with a stronger institutional support independent of any particularly magnetic personality.

When journalists bored of Wilson's piety asked Roosevelt if he would run again in 1920, the Bull Moose sadly shook his head, saying, "No, not I. I don't want it, and I don't think I am the man to be nominated . . . the people are tired of my candidacy."[28] He was, as usual, an acute judge of his political fortunes: but it did not matter this time. He died of a heart attack in his sleep on January 6, 1919. When progressive newspaperman Finley Peter Dunne imagined Roosevelt taking his ease in heaven, he pictured the old man at his favorite pastime—spinning a story to "minor journalists who see nothing sacrilegious in laughter."[29]

Even if the success of local reform efforts did not hinge on a Roosevelt Administration, these efforts drew encouragement and clarity of purpose from Roosevelt the man and the murder that had made him President. They learned through him to believe in a national idea of progress that rested upon a trust in Americans' responsibility to one another—even if that responsibility appeared more clearly in Roosevelt's rhetoric than in his everyday life.

Likewise, the psychologists' concern with the character of mankind under American industrialism made great use of the Briggs investigation into the Czolgosz case. The investigation and its conclusions fueled Briggs's rise within Massachusetts politics to his own local progressive career, despite his increasing difference of opinion with his sponsor, Walter Channing.

THEORIES OF MIND AND
POLITICAL MATTERS

On the evening of January 28, 1902, with the McKinley assassination fresh in the public mind and the Roosevelt presidency just dawning, Walter Channing and Lloyd Vernon Briggs headed a panel meeting in Boston's Natatorium Hall. The great hall was full of citizens who came to hear the alienists discuss the sanity of Leon Czolgosz. Briggs, still fresh from his trips to New York, Michigan, and Ohio, summed up the evidence he had accumulated. He had, he said, conducted somewhere between fifty and sixty interviews of various length with people who knew the assassin. He had worked hard to try "as far as possible to exclude unauthentic newspaper reports" from an analysis of Czolgosz's state of mind. And, he said, the evidence pointed in the direction of the assassin's insanity.

First of all, he said, "there was no proof of Czolgosz being an Anarchist beyond his own statements"—he had not attended many meetings or held membership in any organizations. Second, he believed, there was "no proof that anarchy was the source of his delusions"— these delusions being his perceived need to kill the President. Third, there was "nothing in the post-mortem examination to negative a diagnosis of insanity." He was therefore prepared, on the basis of diagnosing a delusion of duty, to declare Czolgosz insane.[30]

Channing's argument covered much the same ground. Seizing on MacDonald's description of Czolgosz as suffering a "political delusion," he argued that delusion was a false belief and holders of false beliefs were ipso facto insane. Moreover, he suggested, Czolgosz fit the pattern of a lunatic regicide—a solitary man fixated on religious or political dogmas, harmless enough until the right opportunity presented itself. Which it usually did; in Czolgosz's case, it came wrapped in the poisonous rhetoric of anarchy.

Although they came to the same conclusion, they arrived by different routes. Channing said simply that "it is to me very difficult to believe that any American citizen of sound mind could plan and execute such a deed as the assasination [sic] of the President, and remain impervious to all influences after his arrest, and up to the time of the execution. Human nature, as I look at it, is not constituted to bear the strain of such a situation."[31] One of his colleagues on the panel, G. Alder Blumer, concurred. "To my mind, the assault on President McKinley is prima facie evidence of insanity. I can't conceive how anyone of sound mind can do the crime which Czolgosz did."[32]

Channing's insistence on the inherent madness of Czolgosz's political delusion resulted only partly from his own political conviction that it was madness to believe that "the President was the enemy of the good working people, and things were getting worse and worse." Speaking "from the standpoint of the medical expert," it was also his professional opinion.[33] He meant this suggestion seriously, for as one of an older generation of psychologists he reached his opinions about human nature by introspection. And it was simply not in him to begin to conceive of the President as inimical to ordinary Americans.

As an editorial in the *Philadelphia Medical Journal* noted in 1901, the older, introspective techniques of psychology were giving ground every day to a new psychology based on laboratory science. The editorial insisted that measurable phenomena "are but superficial and mostly irrelevant manifestations of the 'psyche' within," and wondered whether "we have not swung too far away from the old psychology with its introspective method of study by means of self-consciousness."[34] But the younger generation seemed intent on measuring the operations of the mind.

As befit a younger alienist, Briggs analyzed Czolgosz's case in terms of the newer psychology. Instead of looking into his own soul and asking himself whether a sane man could do what Czolgosz had done, he looked over his notes, reconstructed the environment that operated on Czolgosz, and arrived at this conclusion: "I should say that Leon's secondary ego by which he should have recognized the rights of others, seemed wanting or undeveloped. He never seemed to have the secondary ego from any history that I could obtain. This I consider one of the most important facts developed in the investigation, that is, his inability to recognize the rights of others."[35]

Briggs, in talking of the secondary ego, was using the language developed by the Austrian neurologist Theodor Meynert, whose 1884 handbook *Psychiatrie* (translated into English in 1885) helped develop the new psychology. In Meynert's model of mental development, stimuli to the brain produced the contours of mind. The mind was only ever the product of its environment, and no more. Meynert wanted to get rid of even the notion of instinct—there were no inborn behaviors, only stimulus and response. He ran into trouble with the theory because he found that he needed to account for the individual's sense of individuality. He hypothesized the existence of a secondary ego, which controlled felt urges and supplied the sense of self whose existence he could not actually test.[36]

When Briggs used Meynert's model, he was analyzing Czolgosz's mind solely as the product of its environment. Unlike Channing he offered no opinion as to the truth or falsity of Czolgosz's political belief "that McKinley was not only a ruler but in league with those who ruled the working people, like trusts, corporations, and so on."[37] Briggs reasoned that the stimuli that acted on Czolgosz's brain throughout his life led him to these beliefs, and moreover to the despairing conclusion that only a dramatic and deadly act could begin to set things right. A better environment might have saved him; otherwise, he could not possibly have helped himself.

After the Czolgosz symposium at the Natatorium, Channing thanked Briggs for his help. He praised him for his "great ability and perseverance in following of clues." Late in June he even sent Briggs a check to reimburse him for his expenses on the trip.[38] He wished Briggs well in his private practice, in which the young man did indeed thrive: as Channing wrote him later that summer, "Your practice in Boston . . . seems to me in its financial results to be remarkably good, certainly better than any other young man I have known. When you feel a little discouraged you had better look at your ledger account."[39] Then suddenly, in 1904, Channing began to refuse Briggs's invitations. He let it be known he never wanted to see Briggs again.

Hurt and puzzled, Briggs went his way without Channing's help. In 1905, he married Mary Tileston Cabot, an heir to one of the most respected and financially comfortable families in Boston.[40] Buoyed by her income and family reputation, he continued to succeed not only as a practicing doctor, but as a public figure. He lobbied actively for the passage of legislation devoted to reforming the treatment of the mentally ill, and in 1911 had the satisfaction of seeing three such laws passed by the Massachusetts State Legislature. The laws kept the presumed mentally ill from jail or prison while awaiting examination and commitment; prevented the use of seclusion and restraint in the treatment of the insane; and required state hospitals to offer occupational therapy to the mentally ill, to improve their environment and encourage healthy habits of behavior. These laws were, Briggs believed, "progressive measures," as they addressed the environmental effects that led to vicious behavior. And they were opposed by a variety of doctors, including Walter Channing.[41]

The next year, Briggs's name was put forward by Governor Eugene Foss (an independent politician who had been both a Democrat and a Republican) for the State Board of Insanity. Channing opposed this action as well, backing a resolution of the Boston Society of Psychiatry and Neurology to block Briggs, "regarding him as unfit for the position on account of his sensational criticism of the state institutions without foundation in fact, his efforts to promote unnecessary impractical and ill-advised legislation, and his lack of judgment, experience and professional standing as an alienist."[42]

Briggs tried repeatedly through intermediaries to determine the cause of Channing's opposition to him, but to no avail. Channing simply noted that "a man was not obliged to have friends if he did not want to, and no one had a right to go to such a man if he gave up a friend, and demand the reasons."[43]

Briggs won his appointment to the state board over Channing's opposition, and continued on to a successful career as a progressive. In 1912, he began putting together his own analysis of the Czolgosz case, together with that of two other murderers, to make an argument for reformed legislation dealing with the criminal responsibility of the insane. In 1921, he saw this work come to fruition. The Massachusetts legislature passed a law that became known simply as "the Briggs law," mandating that anyone indicted by a grand jury of a capital offense be examined by the state's Department of Mental Diseases, and "that the report of the examination should be filed with the clerk and be accessible to the court and the attorneys on both sides."[44] The measure would prevent the controversy that dogged the Guiteau and Czolgosz cases by creating a state agency given responsibility for making a determination in the public interest. It cemented Briggs's progressive reputation.

Briggs had made a success of himself in just the way he always wished. By will and work he had overcome his origins, rising from obscurity and modest means to respectability and influence. He could afford to print privately his memoirs and family history, indulge in philanthropy, and continue his political lobbying for reform. But the skirmish with Channing troubled him, and it irked Mary Cabot Briggs, too. Channing's opposition had persuaded Mrs. Briggs's father that Briggs was not to be trusted, and he altered his will to cut her inheritance significantly. The Briggses began to mount a lawsuit against Channing.[45]

While Briggs had become more progressive, Channing grew more conservative. He had always seen the mentally ill chiefly as a class of persons who required sensitive treatment and confinement, but who were unlikely ever truly to heal. Their defects were defects of character, innate and inaccessible to the logic of a sane person. This belief paralleled his general opinion of the poorer classes of people, including blacks and immigrants. He believed they were inherently different, could not be expected to change, and should therefore be kept separate from better society. In consequence he continued his generous support of private, segregated schools for African-Americans, and also began actively opposing immigration. Along with a variety of other old-guard anticorruptionists like his personal lawyer Moorfield Storey, he had come to regard the influx of foreigners as a problem that no program of assimilation could solve. He joined the Immigration Restriction League, from which he launched missives supporting restrictionist senator Henry Cabot Lodge and attacking President Wilson, who had supported restrictionism in his political science books, "but while the campaign was on he talked a good deal the other way."[46] In all these issues, Channing's measure of men presumed an innate, consistent, and unchangeable character that dictated behavior, and it was his evaluation of character that underwrote his opposition to Briggs. As Storey wrote Channing during their campaign against Briggs's appointment to the state board, "I have a low opinion of him as a man, and of course I have no opinion of him as a doctor, but if you were to ask why I think him a poor doctor, it would have to be on the ground that I think he is a poor man."[47]

The charge against Briggs, put about privately and addressed by Briggs in his published account of the story, was that "he had had immoral relations with women." At Mrs. Briggs's indignant request, Dean John Chipman Gray of the Harvard Law School investigated these rumors in 1913 and in a public letter declared himself "of the opinion that these charges are without foundation and that they are false."[48] With this vindication, the Briggses dropped their threat of a lawsuit against Channing—but friends had also pressed them to drop it for other reasons.

While the possibility of a suit loomed, Channing asked a former patient to write him a letter "to explain, if possible," her experience of Briggs's treatment. In the summer of 1901, while under Dr. Briggs's treatment for her nervous condition, she alleged he had made unwanted and immoral overtures: "Had I been a weak woman, had I not been good, and loved my husband, and told him so, over and over again, he would have ruined me. It seems impossible to believe . . . You can't believe, naturally, that he is not moral, but he tried to take advantage of me." Pressed to consider why Briggs might have done such a thing, she said simply, "He has no self control": or as Briggs might have said of himself, he had an underdeveloped secondary ego.[49] When he looked at Leon Czolgosz, he saw someone not altogether unlike himself, and as his later career suggests, it shocked him to action.

If progressivism began as a political creation, it became a conviction. A politician in the Roosevelt years might espouse progressive politics to rope disparate constituencies together in a national coalition, seeking to bind the dissenters of the populist years with the immigrants of the early twentieth century, enticing Southern whites by stigmatizing Southern blacks, and so forth. But along the way progressivism became a way of thinking and speaking about social problems that could be addressed through any political party or none. In the end, what made a progressive was not social class, occupation, or economic interest, but rather a belief about human nature and modern environment, as revealed in one's own experience. And it was not introspective experience that accomplished this, but contact with others vastly different from oneself—and even, sometimes, dangerously so. Contact with people of other classes revealed to Americans of the late nineteenth century the failings in their own character.

Asked what made him a progressive, Theodore Roosevelt replied that it was contact with the working people, thrust upon him by the rough-and-tumble of life in industrial America.

> Well, after a little while I got thrown into close relations with the farmers, and it did not take long before I . . . made up my mind that they really formed the backbone of the land. Then, because of certain circumstances, I was thrown into intimate contact with railroad men; and I gradually came to the conclu-

sion that these railroad men were about the finest citizens there
were anywhere around. Then, in the course of some official
work, I was thrown into close contact with a number of the car-
penters, blacksmiths, and men in the building trades, that is,
skilled mechanics of a high order, and it was not long before I
had them on the same pedestal with the others. By then it was
beginning to dawn on me that the difference was not in the
men but in my own point of view . . . Our prime need as a nation is that every American should understand and work with
his fellow-citizens, getting into touch with them, so that by actual contact he may learn that fundamentally he and they have
the same interests, needs, and aspirations.[50]

This contact inspired not only a sense of commonality, Roosevelt believed, but of guilt at not recognizing the commonality sooner. The
chief experience of becoming a convinced progressive was of recognizing that one had in the past unthinkingly acted in such a way as to
hurt the vulnerable elements of society, doing "something or other
which we should shudder to contemplate now."[51]

Briggs emerged from his close contact with the Czolgosz family
convinced that he had spent that January week immersed in conditions that could create a person entirely unable to respect the rights of
others, someone bent on rising above the working class into which he
had been born by any means necessary, even by murderous and suicidal action. He came away conscience-stricken, sure that in his own
life he had not done enough to alleviate conditions for such people—
but for luck, he might have become one himself. He came away
ashamed of himself and his society. As he later wrote of Czolgosz and
similar cases, "Society here punished the person it created. The original fault was the fault of society. Society, upon whom rests the responsibility, should be arraigned at the bar of Justice and put on trial and
convicted instead of its product."[52] In his later career he did his best to
exercise his stricken social conscience and make good on this belief—
and by willfully changing himself, he disproved the theory of mind he
had borrowed from Theodor Meynert.

Meynert's scheme of human nature was all external stimulus and no inner mechanism. There was no self, except the one developed by environment. Meynert's extreme environmentalism was designed to overcome the influence of religion, idealistic philosophy, or other theories of innate character based on the science of the mind. But as William James noted, Meynert's brain scheme ultimately broke down when it tried to account for human development. First of all, the brain did not undergo a "virgin" birth—it came into the world rich in instinctual reflexes.[53] Second, neither God nor an all-powerful environment ever produced an "ego" or any other inner organ of self: in all its uses the theory of an autonomous inner self was "a 'cheap and nasty' edition of the soul . . . as ineffectual and windy an abortion as Philosophy can show."[54]

James argued that the self was determined neither by God nor by environment, but that it was simply a name we impose on the continuous process of interaction between inborn instinct and external stimuli. Prodded by a mother's nipple, the baby's head reflexively turns toward the proffered breast: and through this sensation the conscious brain learns voluntarily to control the muscles that move the head. Subsequent conscious movements generate new stimuli, and so do we begin to catalogue our experience, which in turn shapes our perceptions of our abilities. "We learn all our possibilities by way of experience," he wrote.[55]

Following this psychology, social philosophers like Jane Addams could argue there was in truth no division between ourselves and our environment, or indeed between any two of us: we are all part of a continuity of social experience. This was also the essence of Roosevelt's plainer revelation: thrown repeatedly into contact with others, we learn that they are but editions of ourselves.

And it was what Briggs discovered, too. Bleak and peculiar as Leon Czolgosz's life was, it did not result from inherent defect or produce an indecipherable social monster. He was the product of strains in a web of circumstance, a complex trap that resulted from the compounding effects of innumerable human decisions. Its strands connected William McKinley and John W. Gates to Emma Goldman and Abe Isaak, and linked Jane Addams and Jacob Riis to Booker T.

Washington and James Parker. For an instant, by an effort of will, Czolgosz thrust himself into the center of that web; then, swallowed up by events he set in motion, he yielded his focal place to Theodore Roosevelt. By an exercise of his own will and words, Roosevelt spent his years in the presidency spinning stories of a world that worked as he would want it. Then, tired of talking, he let go.

NOTE ON CONTROVERSIES, SOURCES,

AND CONTROVERSIAL SOURCES

In the interest of clarity in the text, I have given my interpretation of events without getting into discussions of how my version differs from earlier ones, and why. But as some unpleasant episodes in recent years have shown, there is good cause for historians to explain how, and on what basis, they make their narrative choices. For readers interested in questions of why I should have chosen one interpretation over another, and on what I base this choice, I offer the following explanations and observations, point by point.

1. Historians routinely note that *Czolgosz's trial was rushed*, and that Czolgosz's defense counsel did not try very hard in his behalf. The former is indisputable, and I attribute it here to concern on the part of district attorney Thomas Penney and the Buffalo professional community in general that they get rid of the mess as soon as possible without drawing suspicion to themselves for their speed. The latter proposition I dispute: I believe that, given the limitations Penney imposed, court-appointed counsel Loran Lewis and Robert Titus did a good job, and almost cornered Penney with a feat of courtroom rhetoric.

I base both judgments here on my reading of *the trial transcript*. Historians have not often relied on it. The Buffalo and Erie County Historical Society has two typescript transcriptions of the trial: one, catalogued as manuscript number A64-33, stayed in the possession of the court stenographer, Robert C. Chapin, until the BECHS acquired it from his family. The other, on microfilm no. M65-7, was in the personal collection of Exposition planner Louis Babcock. I cite the Babcock below. The two differ in that the Chapin is double-spaced and includes the impaneling of the jury.[1] The BAEC's director of communications, Roger Parris, scanned the Babcock transcript and translated it into portable document format, and it is now available in this medium on the BAEC website—

http://www.eriebar.org—accompanied by a wealth of other material relating to the assassination and trial.[2] The transcript is useful, because it presents the trial in an unvarnished format. Even so, there were extensive accounts in the newspapers of the period. Where a quotation appears in both the transcript and the newspapers I have preferred the transcript version with one exception ("sane mind," on p. 48, for reasons explained in the endnote).

Although (in the opinion of BAEC lawyers and other lawyers who were kind enough to advise me) the Czolgosz trial was indeed procedurally flawed on a number of grounds—the jury admitted prejudice on being sworn in; the chain of custody of the prisoner and of evidence was shocking—the sincere effort put forth by Lewis and Titus, particularly by Lewis, is worth comment, and I have explained my opinion on this in the text. The trial account in John Lawson's American State Trials (14 Am. St. Tr. 159) is abridged.

2. The opinions of doctors as to McKinley's medical treatment tend to agree with Jack Fisher's judgment in Stolen Glory.[3] Fisher says a man similarly shot today should survive. Dr. Peter Ostrow, Associate Professor of Pathology at the University of Buffalo, who studied the case for the BAEC reenactment, says it is common lore among Buffalo area residents that McKinley's stomach has been preserved, and that one may see a hole in the posterior side that was never repaired—but there is, it appears, no stomach behind the story.[4]

3. Historians rarely note the presence, let alone the role of Jim Parker, though he has begun to feature in public history accounts of the shooting. He does not appear at all, except by implication, in the trial transcript, though he is omnipresent in newspaper accounts in the week after the shooting and before the President's death. As I made clear in the text, I believe Parker was there and did indeed accost Czolgosz before anyone else; I believe the Secret Service covered up his role out of embarrassment; and, as I argued at some length in chapter 3, I believe the way Parker was replaced by O'Brien in the official narrative suggests the way Americans in general and Republicans in particular were learning to set aside the "race problem" in the South in favor of the "race problem" posed by immigration. I have based this judgment on the contemporary accounts published in the Washington Evening Star, the Washington Bee, and the Savannah Tribune. The Star, the capital's premier paper in those days, had especially detailed coverage. Jack Fisher suggests that Secret Service director John Wilkie "was not interested in having his men share credit."[5]

4. Historians routinely refer to Czolgosz's illiteracy, which was after the trial speedily enough proven not to exist through Briggs's digging in January 1902. Czolgosz's handwriting and signature are reproduced in Briggs's book The Manner of Man That Kills, and Waldeck's testimony seems reliably to point to Leon's wide reading. Anarchists claimed annoyance that he did not read their assigned

texts—not that he could not read. District attorneys note that it remains commonplace for capital defendants or prisoners to feign illiteracy.[6]

5. The question of *whether Czolgosz was tortured* often comes up. I expect, as I say in the text, that he was tortured, on either or both of the two occasions when his whereabouts in custody cannot be accounted for. I base this judgment on the remarks of Briggs's informant at Auburn State Prison, and on the general keenness of some law enforcement officers to discover conspiracies (and to exact revenge). The rumor that he was tortured by using light to burn his eyes has the greatest plausibility because he appeared rather swiftly at trial and seemed physically unharmed when he did. Emma Goldman afterward claimed that she knew Czolgosz had been tortured because it took so long bringing him to trial, but this is obviously evidence of a faulty memory on her part.

6. *The role of Jane Addams* in the anarchists' detention in Chicago has often featured in accounts of the case, usually including the story that Addams or her ally Raymond Robins got legal representation for the prisoners. Addams does not say in her memoir that Robins or she did this, and she is quoted to the opposite effect—that is, that Isaak refused representation—in the *Chicago Tribune*. Isaak's granddaughter Grace Umrath also said her grandfather refused representation, though she said the offer came from Clarence Darrow.[7] Darrow did indeed offer, in a letter to Addams after her visit to the jail, to represent the Isaaks.[8] Given that Addams seemed (as mentioned in chapter 5) to know that no representation was going to be necessary, and that she is quoted as saying Isaak did not want any, and that newspapers did not report representation for the anarchists, I incline to the view that Addams did not secure representation for Isaak. Victoria Brown of Grinnell College, whose biography of Addams is forthcoming, was especially kind and helpful in pointing out that this was just the sort of incident Addams liked to use to advance her standing in the public eye. If Addams could have used it more to her advantage, she probably would have.

7. My chief source of information on Czolgosz and his family is *Lloyd Vernon Briggs's cache of notes preserved in the Walter Channing Papers at the Massachusetts Historical Society*, as well as Briggs's correspondence with Channing, and Channing's correspondence with various other subjects of investigation, including Isaak and Goldman. Robert Donovan's *Assassins* pointed me toward these sources. Channing and Briggs went at the case with the clear intention of finding evidence that Czolgosz was insane. But as they entertained no definite theory of the cause of insanity, they collected evidence of all kinds—including familial, environmental, phrenological, and pathological—on Czolgosz's case. Moreover, Briggs copied out his notes as he went along in the investigation. They therefore have excellent standing as a source of evidence. *Briggs's clipping scrapbook, preserved as Crerar Manuscript no. 80 in the University of Chicago Library*, was also a

useful source. *The L. Vernon Briggs Papers at Countway Library of Harvard University* remain uncatalogued—decades after their accession—and, according to Countway staff, are therefore absolutely unavailable to researchers on the possibility that they may contain materials that violate the privacy of patients, even a century later. Given the reasons for the falling-out between Briggs and Channing, it is entirely possible that I might have come across such materials, though I believe I have dealt responsibly with the sensitive material I have already seen. It seems unfortunate that the Countway Library should have remained adamant in this respect. But *Briggs's published memoirs* are so copious, and his correspondence and notes in the Channing papers so considerable, that I believe I have nevertheless well represented his point of view here. Even so, it would have been informative to examine his correspondence with public figures (he was friendly with W. R. Grace, among others) to see how his view of progressivism evolved over the years. Perhaps one day Countway will make this possible.

8. In the matter of *Czolgosz's physical health*, I have taken the guidance of today's physicians that it was probably generally good. They have noted with interest the appearance of the scars in the autopsy notes. *Doctors MacDonald and Spitzka's examination of the body* certainly rules out effects of tertiary syphilis, although the course of advanced syphilis is not absolutely regular or predictable. *Czolgosz's self-medication* could account for what acquaintances called his "dreaminess," but it could not have easily continued during his imprisonment at Auburn. The ultimate conclusion drawn as to Czolgosz's psychological state and his self-diagnosis is mine, and only I can be blamed for its credibility.

9. The persistent tale of *Czolgosz's time in Pennsylvania and/or West Virginia and his marriage there* does not, ultimately, persuade me. Richard Andre, a West Virginia historian, kindly confirmed to me the continuing prevalence of the story there, mentioning that he remembered a local paper running a photograph of the workers at the wire mill with a circle around one and a caption claiming it was Czolgosz. Andre did some research into the story and found a marriage certificate at the local Catholic church. But the marriage record he saw is for a Frank Nauman—not Fred Nieman, let alone Leon Czolgosz.[9] So I am skeptical of the marriage. It seems slightly more plausible that Czolgosz may have spent some time in West Virginia or Pennsylvania in 1901, during periods when his whereabouts are mainly unaccounted for. That he should have been there for upward of five years would contradict the evidence that puts him in Cleveland through the 1890s.

NOTES

ABBREVIATIONS OF MAJOR SOURCES

Channing papers   Papers of Walter Channing, Channing Family Papers. Massachusetts Historical Society, Boston, Mass.

Briggs notes, sets 1 and 2   Notes typed by Lloyd Vernon Briggs during his interviews, in two sets, contained in box 15 of the Channing Papers (above). Briggs's first set of notes covers his interviews of prison guards, physicians, and law enforcement officers in Auburn, West Seneca, and Buffalo, New York. He typed them and sent them to Channing on 1/8/02, before going on to Detroit and Cleveland, where his interviews with Czolgosz's family and childhood acquaintances appear in his second set of typed notes.

Trial transcript   Supreme Court, Erie County [New York]. *The People of the State of New York,* against *Leon F. Czolgosz.* Manuscript no. A64-33, Buffalo and Erie County Historical Society, photocopy held by the Bar Association of Erie County.

Briggs scrapbook   Scrapbook of Lloyd Vernon Briggs, Crerar Manuscript no. 80, University of Chicago Special Collections.

LCMP   Library of Congress Motion Picture, Broadcasting, and Recorded Sound Division, Washington, D.C.

National edition   *Works of Theodore Roosevelt,* ed. Hermann Hagedorn. National edition. 20 vols. New York: Charles Scribner's Sons, 1927.

Letters   *The Letters of Theodore Roosevelt*, ed. Elting E. Mori-
                           son, John M. Blum, and John J. Buckley. 8 vols.
                           Cambridge, Mass.: Harvard University Press, 1951.
Personal abbreviations   WC = Walter Channing; LVB = Lloyd Vernon
                           Briggs; TR = Theodore Roosevelt

PREFACE

1. William Roscoe Thayer, *The Life and Letters of John Hay*, 2 vols. (Boston: Houghton Mifflin, 1915), 2:333. Thayer writes that he got the story from Kipling.
2. Booker T. Washington, *My Larger Education: Being Chapters from My Experience* (Garden City, N.Y.: Doubleday, Page, 1911), 169; TR to Bellamy and Maria Storer, April 17, 1901, *Letters*, 3:57.

1: A WEEK AT THE FAIR

1. Robert J. Donovan, *The Assassins* (London: Elek Books, 1956), 104.
2. William Jennings Bryan, *The First Battle: A Story of the Campaign of 1896*, 2 vols. (1896; reprint Port Washington, N.Y.: Kennikat Press, 1971), 1:206.
3. Charles Austin Beard and Mary Ritter Beard, *The Rise of American Civilization*, 2 vols. (New York: Macmillan, 1927), 2:375–76.
4. "President McKinley's Speech at the Pan-American Exposition" (Thomas A. Edison, Inc., 1901), Film no. LC 1811, LCMP.
5. "The Mob Outside the Temple of Music" (Thomas A. Edison, Inc., 1901), Film no. LC 1350, LCMP.
6. H. H. Kohlsaat, *From McKinley to Harding: Personal Reminiscences of Our Presidents* (New York: Charles Scribner's Sons, 1923), 88–89.
7. Theodore Roosevelt, *American Ideals, The Strenuous Life, Realizable Ideals*, National edition, 13:138, 142.
8. Silas Bent, *Ballyhoo: The Voice of the Press* (New York: Boni & Liveright, 1927), 76.
9. H. W. Brands, *T.R.: The Last Romantic* (New York: Basic Books, 1997), 406.
10. TR to Edward Bellamy and Maria Storer, April 17, 1901, *Letters*, 3:57.
11. Foster testimony, Trial transcript, p. 77.
12. Lloyd Vernon Briggs, *The Manner of Man That Kills* (Boston: Richard G. Badger, 1921), 239.
13. Jack Fisher, "McKinley's Assassination in Buffalo: Time to Put the Medical Controversy to Rest?" *Buffalo Physician*, Spring 2001, 12–19.
14. TR to Henry Cabot Lodge, September 9, 1901, *Letters*, 3:142.
15. Fisher, "McKinley's Assassination," 15.
16. TR to Alice Roosevelt Cowles, September 7, 1901, and TR to Paul Morton, September 7, 1901, *Letters*, 3:139, 141.

17. TR to Henry Cabot Lodge, September 9, 1901, *Letters*, 3:141.
18. Kohlsaat, *From McKinley to Harding*, 12.
19. TR to Alice Roosevelt Cowles, November 13, 1896, and TR to Brooks Adams, March 21, 1898, *Letters*, 1:566, 798.
20. TR to Henry Cabot Lodge, September 9, 1901, *Letters*, 3:142.
21. TR to Alice Roosevelt Cowles, April 26, 1896, *Letters*, 1:650.
22. Richard Hofstadter, *The American Political Tradition and the Men Who Made It* (New York: Alfred A. Knopf, 1948), 284.
23. *Guiteau's Case*, District Court, S.D. New York, January 25, 1882, 10 F. 161, p. 162.
24. Anthony Platt and Bernard L. Diamond, "The Origins of the 'Right and Wrong' Test of Criminal Responsibility and Its Subsequent Development in the United States: An Historical Survey," *California Law Review* 54:3 (August 1966), 1227–60, esp. 1236–37.
25. Foster's testimony, Trial transcript, p. 76.
26. Ibid., pp. 76–77.
27. Consider Vallely's behavior in *Anderson v. Abeel*, Supreme Court of New York, Appellate Division, First Department, July 1904, 96 A.D. 370, p. 534.
28. Vallely's testimony, Trial transcript, pp. 102–3.
29. Johann Most, *Revolutionäre Kriegswissenschaft: Ein Handbüchlein zur Anleitung betreffend Gebrauches und Herstellung von Nitro-Glycerin, Dynamit, Schiessbaumwolle, Knallquecksilber, Bomben, Brandsätzen, Giften, u.s.w., u.s.w.* (New York: 1885).
30. *People v. Most*, Court of Appeals of New York, June 16, 1891, 128 N.Y. 108.
31. Cited in James Joll, *The Anarchists* (Cambridge, Mass.: Harvard University Press, 1980), 118.
32. Briggs notes, set 1, p. 19.
33. Ibid.
34. Roger Parris, ed., *Excerpt from the Buffalo Police Department Annual Report for the Year 1901*, Bar Association of Erie County, http://www.eriebar.org/about/pb.html.
35. Quackenbush testimony, Trial transcript, p. 63.
36. Ibid.; and also in the official record of Czolgosz's statement of September 6, 1901, which appears in Joseph Fowler, Floyd S. Crego, and James M. Putnam, "Official Report of the Experts for the People in the Case of the People v. Leon F. Czolgosz," pamphlet, Briggs scrapbook, p. 81.
37. Sidney Fine, "Anarchism and the Assassination of McKinley," *American Historical Review* 60:4 (July 1955), 777–99; esp. 781–82.
38. Briggs scrapbook, p. 81.
39. Quackenbush testimony, Trial transcript, p. 65.
40. Ibid.
41. F. L. Oswald, "The Assassination Mania," *North American Review* 171:526 (September 1900), 314.

42. Briggs notes, set 1, p. 27.
43. John Henry Wigmore, A Treatise on Evidence, 4 vols. (Boston: Little, Brown, 1904), 1:770 n. 2.
44. In re Klock, Supreme Court of New York, General Term, Fourth Department, October 1888, 3 N.Y.S. 478.
45. In re Lyddy's Will, Surrogate's Court of New York, New York County, May 10, 1888, 4 N.Y.S. 468, p. 469. The expert here was Allen McLane Hamilton.
46. In re Klock. Owing in part to long tradition, the ability of laypersons to witness the sanity of testators remained an exception to the rise of expert opinion. See Wigmore, A Treatise, 1:778.
47. People v. Rice, Court of Appeals of New York, June 6, 1899, 159 N.Y. 400. The courts had previously dealt with an "insanity expert" in People v. Nino, April 28, 1896, 149 N.Y. 317.
48. Wigmore, A Treatise, 1:762.
49. Cited in Samuel R. Gross, "Expert Evidence," Wisconsin Law Review 1991 Wis. L. Rev. 1113, p. 1114.
50. Charles E. Rosenberg, The Trial of the Assassin Guiteau: Psychiatry and Law in the Gilded Age (Chicago: University of Chicago Press, 1968).
51. William James, The Principles of Psychology, 2 vols. (New York: Henry Holt, 1890). See especially the beginning of James's discussion "Will," beginning on 2:486. The idea of a mind as instinct dependent on environment for its development, and the consequent blurring of cause and effect, were refined into mechanical precision in John Dewey, "The Reflex-Arc Concept in Psychology," Psychological Review 3 (1896), 357–70.
52. Walter Channing, "The Connection Between Insanity and Crime," American Journal of Insanity 42:4 (April 1886), 452–72.
53. A. W. Hurd to WC, December 16, 1901, Channing papers, box 4.
54. Cited in G. Alder Blumer to WC, Channing papers, box 4.
55. Bull testimony, Trial transcript, p. 110.
56. Ibid., p. 111.
57. Briggs notes, set 1, p. 27.
58. Briggs scrapbook, p. 81.
59. Ibid.
60. Cited in Fisher, "McKinley's Assassination," 15.
61. Briggs, Manner of Man, 241 n.

2: THE LETTER OF THE LAW

1. LVB to WC, January 8, 1902, Channing papers, box 4.
2. Allen McLane Hamilton, Recollections of an Alienist, Personal and Professional (New York: George H. Doran Company, 1916), 362.
3. Briggs notes, set 1, p. 25.
4. LVB to WC, January 8, 1902, Channing papers, box 4.

5. Briggs notes, set 1, p. 25.
6. Ibid., p. 26.
7. LVB to WC, January 8, 1902, Channing papers, box 4.
8. *Excerpt from the Buffalo Police Report.*
9. Kohlsaat, *From McKinley to Harding*, 96. The account of McKinley's deathbed draws on this source.
10. Ibid., 8–9.
11. Hofstadter, *American Political Tradition*, 282–83.
12. TR to Albion W. Tourgee, November 8, 1901, *Letters*, 3:190.
13. Kohlsaat, *From McKinley to Harding*, 98.
14. Ibid., 101.
15. AWH to WC, December 9, 1901, Channing papers, box 4.
16. "Carlos Frederick MacDonald," *National Encyclopedia of American Biography* (New York: White, 1924).
17. Details of Kemmler's electrocution in Carlos F. MacDonald, "The Infliction of the Death Penalty by Means of Electricity," *New York Medical Journal* 55 (May 7, 1892), 505–9, and Arnold Beichman, "The First Electrocution," *Commentary* 35:5 (May 1963), 410–19.
18. Carlos F. MacDonald, "The Legal Versus the Scientific Test of Insanity in Criminal Cases," *American Journal of Insanity* 56:1 (July 1899), 21–30; esp. 22, 27.
19. AWH to WC, December 9, 1901, Channing papers, box 4.
20. Carlos F. MacDonald, with Edward Anthony Spitzka, "The Trial, Execution, Autopsy and Mental Status of Leon F. Czolgosz, alias Fred Nieman, the Assassin of President McKinley," *American Journal of Insanity* 58:3 (January 1902), 369–404, esp. 384–85.
21. AWH to WC, December 9, 1901, Channing papers, box 4.
22. Trial transcript, p. 5.
23. Ibid., p. 6.
24. Dr. Herman Mynter testimony, Trial transcript, p. 38.
25. Gaylord testimony, Trial transcript, p. 28.
26. Ibid., pp. 29–30.
27. Quackenbush testimony, Trial transcript, p. 63.
28. Ibid., p. 69.
29. Trial transcript, p. 112.
30. AWH to WC, December 9, 1901, Channing papers, box 4.
31. Trial transcript, p. 117. The transcription says "some mind," but I believe this to be an error for "sane mind"; the accounts in the papers feature much the same quotation but say "sane mind": see, e.g., "Orderly Trial," *New York Herald*, September 25, 1901, p. 5.
32. Trial transcript, pp. 117–18.
33. Ibid., p. 121.
34. *People v. Nino*, 43 N.E. 853, April 28, 1896, p. 853.

35. Trial transcript, p. 129.
36. MacDonald and Spitzka, "Trial," 373.
37. Trial transcript, p. 135.
38. "President Roosevelt at the Canton Station" (Thomas A. Edison Company, September 26, 1901), Film no. LC 1814, LCMP.
39. Briggs notes, set 1, p. 11.
40. Charles Hamilton Hughes, "Medical Aspects of the Czolgosz Case," *Alienist and Neurologist* 23 (January 1903), 40-52, esp. 42.

3 : DESCENT

1. Channing, "The Connection Between Insanity and Crime," 452-72, esp. 468.
2. MacDonald and Spitzka, "Trial," 188.
3. James Freeman Clarke, *Memorial and Biographical Sketches* (Boston: Houghton, Osgood and Company, 1878), 181.
4. Lloyd Vernon Briggs, *Arizona and New Mexico, 1882; California, 1886; Mexico, 1891* (Boston: Privately printed, 1932), 9.
5. Ibid., 189. On Hawaiian experiences, Lloyd Vernon Briggs, *Experiences of a Medical Student in Honolulu, and on the Island of Oahu, 1881* (Boston: David D. Nickerson Company, 1926).
6. Briggs, *Arizona*, 59.
7. "Not an American," *Buffalo Evening News*, September 9, 1901, p. 7.
8. "The Attempted Murder of the President," *Journal of the American Medical Association* 37:11 (September 14, 1901), 702.
9. Donovan, *The Assassins*, 81 n.
10. "M'Kinley's Colored Defender," *Savannah Tribune*, September 14, 1901, pp. 1-2.
11. "Acted as a Hero," *Washington Star*, September 7, 1901, p. 1.
12. "How Czolgosz Shot President M'Kinley," *Buffalo Evening News*, September 7, 1901, p. 7.
13. "James Parker's Experience," *Washington Evening Star*, September 10, 1901, p. 1.
14. Ibid.
15. "Fair Play to the Negro," *Washington Bee*, September 14, 1901, p. 1.
16. Editorial column, *Savannah Tribune*, September 14, 1901, p. 2. Also Robert E. Perdue, *The Negro in Savannah, 1865-1900* (New York: Exposition Press, 1973).
17. "James B. Parker," *Washington Evening Star*, September 11, 1901, p. 6.
18. TR to Booker T. Washington, September 14, 1901, *Letters*, 3:149. On migration, see Bureau of the Census, *Historical Statistics of the United States, Colonial Times to 1970* (Washington, D.C.: Government Printing Office, 1975), 1:95.

19. Kohlsaat, *From McKinley to Harding*, 23.
20. Herbert Croly, *Marcus Alonzo Hanna: His Life and Work* (New York: Macmillan, 1912), 175.
21. Booker T. Washington, *Up from Slavery* (Garden City, N.Y.: Doubleday, Page, 1900), 213, 221–22. On black voting, see Alexander Keyssar, *The Right to Vote: The Contested History of Democracy in the United States* (New York: Basic Books, 2000), 115.
22. Ibid., 221.
23. Cited in Clarence A. Bacote, "Negro Officeholders in Georgia Under President McKinley," *Journal of Negro History* 44:3 (July 1959), 217–39, esp. 218–19.
24. Ibid.
25. Ibid., 233.
26. Ibid., 235; also H. Wayne Morgan, *William McKinley and His America* (Syracuse: Syracuse University Press, 1963), 415ff.
27. Bacote, "Negro Officeholders," 233.
28. Booker T. Washington, *My Larger Education: Being Chapters from My Experience* (Garden City, N.Y.: Doubleday, Page, 1911), 169.
29. "American Civilization?" *Washington Bee*, October 26, 1901, p. 4.
30. Ibid.
31. "To Break the Solid South," *Washington Bee*, October 12, 1901, p. 1.
32. Theodore Roosevelt, *Winning of the West*, National edition, 8:156.
33. Theodore Roosevelt, *American Problems*, National edition, 16:40; Theodore Roosevelt, *Winning of the West*, National edition, 8:84.
34. Theodore Roosevelt, *New York*, National edition, 10:435–36.
35. Theodore Roosevelt, *Winning of the West*, National edition, 8:44.
36. See David Blight, *Race and Reunion: The Civil War in American Memory* (Cambridge, Mass.: 2001), 341ff.
37. Theodore Roosevelt, *Gouverneur Morris*, 7:248.
38. "Did Jim Parker Do It?" *Washington Evening Star*, September 13, 1901, p. 6.
39. "M'Kinley's Colored Defender," p. 1.
40. Ibid.
41. "Negroes Lynch Negroes," *Washington Evening Star*, September 12, 1901, p. 7.
42. "President Shot Down," *Washington Evening Star*, September 6, 1901, third extra, 6:30 p.m., p. 1.
43. Ibid., fourth extra, 8:10 p.m., p. 1.
44. "Acted as a Hero," *Washington Evening Star*, September 7, 1901, p. 1.
45. Booker T. Washington to the Editor of the Montgomery *Advertiser*, September 23, 1901, *The Booker T. Washington Papers*, 14 vols., ed. Louis R. Harlan and Raymond W. Smock with Barbara S. Kraft (Urbana, Ill.: 1972–1989), 6:217.
46. "Wipe Out Anarchy and Lynch Law," *Washington Bee*, September 21, 1901, p. 1; "Two Crimes Compared," *Chicago Broad-ax*, September 28, 1901, p. 1.

47. Trial transcript, p. 114.
48. Leon F. Litwack, *Trouble in Mind: Black Southerners in the Age of Jim Crow* (New York: Alfred A. Knopf, 1998), 284.
49. "Acids Destroy Body," *Savannah Tribune*, November 2, 1901, p. 1.
50. See, e.g., Nettie F. Trowbridge to WC, May 2, 1915 ("you have been a supporter of the work at Calhoun for a number of years"), Channing papers, box 9; and Henry Cabot Lodge to WC, February 8, 1913, Channing Papers, box 8.
51. Briggs, *Arizona*, 137. Ellipsis in the original.
52. Lloyd Vernon Briggs, *Capital Punishment: Not a Deterrent, It Should Be Abolished* (Boston: Wright and Potter Printing Company, 1940), 75.

4: KILLER ANARCHISM

1. LVB to WC, January 8, 1902, Channing papers, box 4.
2. Thomas Mott Osborne, *Within Prison Walls* (New York: D. Appleton and Company, 1914), 5.
3. Briggs notes, set 1, p. 2, and LVB to WC, January 8, 1902, box 4.
4. Ibid., p. 3.
5. Ibid., p. 5.
6. LVB to WC, January 8, 1902, Channing papers, box 4.
7. Briggs notes, set 1, p. 14.
8. John N. Ross to LVB, March 3, 1902, Briggs scrapbook, p. 90.
9. Briggs notes, set 1, p. 12.
10. Ibid., p. 15.
11. Ibid., p. 3.
12. Ibid., p. 9.
13. Ibid., p. 25.
14. Ibid., pp. 19–20.
15. LVB to WC, January 10, 1902, Channing papers, box 4.
16. Albert Beveridge, "The Statesmanship of Theodore Roosevelt," in National edition, 7:xxi.
17. Timothy J. Hatton and Jeffrey G. Williamson, *The Age of Mass Migration: Causes and Economic Impact* (New York: Oxford University Press, 1998).
18. Timothy J. Hatton and Jeffrey G. Williamson, "Unemployment, Employment Contracts, and Compensating Differentials: Michigan in the 1890s," *Journal of Economic History* 51:3 (September 1991), 605–32.
19. Peter Glassgold, ed., *Anarchy!: An Anthology of Emma Goldman's Mother Earth* (Washington, D.C.: Counterpoint, 2001), 5–6.
20. Theodore Roosevelt, "Social Evolution," *American Ideals*, National edition, 13:223.
21. Theodore Roosevelt, "The Menace of the Demagogue," *Campaigns and Controversies*, National edition, 14:237.

22. Theodore Roosevelt, First Annual Message as President, *State Papers*, National edition, 15:84–85.

23. Ibid., 15:88.

24. Ibid., 15:92.

25. Ibid., 15:95.

26. Ibid., 15:100.

27. Ibid., 15:101.

28. Ibid., 15:84.

29. Briggs also trusted Corner because he had some experience working with psychologists and the mentally ill; despite Corner's express effort to correct his impressions, he regarded Corner's earlier career in psychology as rather grand. See G. E. Corner to LVB, January 23, 1902, Channing papers, box 4; also Briggs, *Manner of Man*, 284, where he repeats what Corner told him not to, that he was once superintendent of a hospital for the insane.

30. WC to LVB, December 21, 1901, Briggs scrapbook, p. 81.

31. "New York Anarchists Safe," *Chicago Tribune*, September 8, 1901, p. 5.

32. "Seek Proof of Conspiracy," *Chicago Tribune*, September 8, 1901, p. 3.

33. Paul Avrich, *The Haymarket Tragedy* (Princeton: Princeton University Press, 1984), 203.

34. Ibid., 208–10.

35. TR to Anna Roosevelt, May 15, 1896, *Letters*, 2:100.

36. Avrich, *Haymarket*, 163.

37. Ibid., 205.

38. Eric Rauchway, *The Refuge of Affections: Family and American Reform Politics, 1900–1920* (New York: Columbia University Press, 2001), 99.

39. "Seek Proof of Conspiracy," *Chicago Tribune*, September 8, 1901, p. 3.

40. "Anarchists Deplore Crime," *Chicago Tribune*, September 7, 1901, p. 2.

41. "Captain Schuettler at Work," *Chicago Tribune*, September 8, 1901, p. 5.

42. *Washington Star*, fourth extra, 8:10 p.m., September 6, 1901, p. 1.

43. See the recollection of Grace Umrath, Isaak's granddaughter, in Paul Avrich, *Anarchist Voices: An Oral History of Anarchism in America* (Princeton: Princeton University Press, 1995), 23–28.

44. "Assassin Gets Inspiration Here," *Chicago Tribune*, September 8, 1901, p. 2.

45. A. Isaak to WC, September 6, 1902, Channing papers, box 4.

46. Briggs notes, Briggs scrapbook, p. 106.

47. Insert, A. Isaak to WC, September 6, 1902, Channing papers, box 4; also "Assassin Gets Inspiration Here," p. 2.

48. Briggs, *Manner of Man*, 317.

49. "Assassin Gets Inspiration Here," p. 2.

50. Glassgold, *Anarchy!*, 17. From *Mother Earth*, October 1906.

51. Briggs, *Manner of Man*, 320–21.

52. A. Isaak to WC, September 6, 1902, Channing papers, box 4.

53. Glassgold, *Anarchy!*, 18.

54. "Assassin Gets Inspiration Here," p. 2.
55. Avrich, Anarchist Voices, 46.
56. "E. Colton" [Emma Goldman] to Charles A. Beard, January 26, 1928, Emma Goldman Papers.
57. Ibid.; Martha Sanger, Henry Clay Frick: An Intimate Portrait (New York: Abbeville, 1998), 194–95.
58. Recollection of Jeanne Levey, in Avrich, Anarchist Voices, 57.
59. Emma Goldman, Red Emma Speaks, rev. ed., ed. Alix Kates Shulman (New York: Schocken, 1983), 311.
60. Emma Goldman to WC, October 18, 1902, Channing papers, box 4.
61. Ibid.
62. Goldman, Red Emma Speaks, 311.
63. Emma Goldman to WC, October 18, 1902, Channing papers, box 4.
64. On corruption, see Peter H. Argersinger, "New Perspectives on Election Fraud in the Gilded Age," Political Science Quarterly 100:4 (Winter 1985–86), 669–87. On ethnic populations and progressivism, see James J. Connolly, The Triumph of Ethnic Progressivism: Urban Political Culture in Boston, 1900–1915 (Cambridge, Mass.: Harvard University Press, 1998).
65. Matthew Frye Jacobson, Barbarian Virtues: The United States Encounters Foreign Peoples at Home and Abroad, 1876–1917 (New York: Hill & Wang, 2000), 183.
66. Paul Michael Green, "Irish Chicago," in Ethnic Chicago, ed. Peter d'A. Jones and Melvin G. Holli (Grand Rapids, Mich.: William B. Eerdmans Publishing, 1981), 213–59, esp. 220ff.
67. See, e.g., Francis O'Neill, ed., O'Neill's Music of Ireland: Eighteen Hundred and Fifty Melodies (Chicago: Lyon and Healy, 1903); Francis O'Neill, ed., The Dance Music of Ireland: 1001 Gems (Chicago: Lyon and Healy, 1907); also Nicholas Carolan, A Harvest Saved: Francis O'Neill and Irish Music in Chicago (Cork: Ossian Publications, 1997).
68. "Colleran Tries to Dodge Again," Chicago Tribune, September 7, 1901, p. 1.
69. "Six Anarchists in Custody Here," Chicago Tribune, September 7, 1901, p. 5.
70. "Refuse Bail to the Anarchists," Chicago Journal, September 10, 1901, clipping on frame 55-590 of the Jane Addams Papers Microfilm Edition.
71. "Emma Goldman in Law's Grasp," Chicago Tribune, September 11, 1901, p. 1; Goldman, Red Emma Speaks, 301.
72. "Anarchists," Chicago Tribune, September 12, 1901, p. 1.
73. Goldman, Red Emma Speaks, 302–3.
74. "Police Unable to Prove a Plot," Chicago Tribune, September 15, 1901, p. 4.
75. "Local," Chicago Tribune, September 25, 1901, p. 1.
76. "Says Colleran Aided 'Con' Men," Chicago Tribune, September 28, 1901, pp. 1–2.
77. "Robert E. Burke Is Indicted," Chicago Tribune, October 6, 1901, pp. 1–2;

"Oust Colleran from Police Force," *Chicago Tribune*, November 21, 1901, p. 1.

78. Illustrations in the *Chicago Tribune*, September 8, 11, and 14, 1901.

79. Briggs, *Manner of Man*, 331.

80. Emma Goldman to Charles Henry Mitchell, January 22, 1938, in Briggs scrapbook, p. 80.

5: ALL-AMERICAN

1. Briggs notes, set 2, p. 1.

2. Carl Frederick Wittke, *The German-Language Press in America* (Lexington: University of Kentucky Press, 1957), 206ff.

3. Briggs notes, set 2, p. 1.

4. Ibid. Summary descriptions of the family history come from these notes unless otherwise indicated.

5. Ibid., p. 3.

6. Ibid., pp. 3-5.

7. LVB to WC, January 8, 1902, Channing papers, box 4.

8. Agaton Giller, quoted in Matthew Frye Jacobson, *Special Sorrows: The Diasporic Imagination of Irish, Polish, and Jewish Immigrants in the United States* (Cambridge, Mass.: Harvard University Press, 1995), 1-2.

9. Ida M. Tarbell, *The Life of Elbert H. Gary: A Story of Steel* (New York: D. Appleton, 1925), 82ff.; Kenneth Warren, *Big Steel: The First Hundred Years of the United States Steel Corporation, 1901-2001* (Pittsburgh: University of Pittsburgh Press, 2001), 7-21; Thomas F. Campbell and Edward M. Miggins, eds., *The Birth of Modern Cleveland, 1865-1930* (Cleveland: Western Reserve Historical Society, 1988), 22, 58.

10. John Bodnar, *The Transplanted: A History of Immigrants in Urban America* (Bloomington: Indiana University Press, 1985), 170-71.

11. Thomas Archdeacon, *Becoming American: An Ethnic History* (New York: Free Press, 1983), 113.

12. Hatton and Williamson, *Mass Migration*, 11-12.

13. Stephan Thernstrom et al., eds., *Harvard Encyclopedia of American Ethnic Groups* (Cambridge, Mass.: Belknap Press of Harvard University Press, 1980), 793.

14. Roger Daniels, *Not Like Us: Immigrants and Minorities in America, 1890-1924* (Chicago: Ivan R. Dee, 1997), esp. 17ff.

15. Otto Pflanze, *Bismarck and the Development of Germany*, 3 vols. (Princeton: Princeton University Press, 1990), 2:106; see also 2:179-206.

16. Hatton and Williamson, *Mass Migration*, 11ff.

17. Heather Cox Richardson, *The Greatest Nation of the Earth: Republican Economic Policies During the Civil War* (Cambridge, Mass: Harvard University

Press, 1997), 162–67; Emily Greene Balch, *Our Slavic Fellow Citizens* (New York: Charities Publication Committee, 1910), 220.

18. Howard P. Chudacoff, "Success and Security: The Meaning of Social Mobility in America," *Reviews in American History* 10:4 (December 1982), 101–12; James A. Dunlevy and William K. Hutchinson, "The Impact of Immigration on American Import Trade in the Late Nineteenth and Early Twentieth Centuries," *Journal of Economic History* 59:4 (December 1999), 1043–62.

19. For data on the size and cost of farms see Balch, *Our Slavic Fellow Citizens*, 324–25. On the patterns of agriculture in the late nineteenth century, see Steven Stoll, *Larding the Lean Earth: Soil and Society in Nineteenth-Century America* (New York: Hill & Wang, 2002).

20. John S. Garner, *The Model Company Town: Urban Design Through Private Enterprise in Nineteenth-Century New England* (Amherst: University of Massachusetts Press, 1984), 1.

21. *People ex rel. Moloney v. Pullman's Palace-Car Co.*, Supreme Court of Illinois, October 24, 1898, 175 Ill. 125.

22. Rogers City Centennial Committee, *Centennial History and Photo Album* (Rogers City, Mich.: 1871), 19–21.

23. Samuel H. Williamson, "What Is the Relative Value?" Economic History Services, April 2002, http://www.eh.net/hmit/compare/.

24. Alexander Keyssar, *Out to Work: The First Century of Unemployment in Massachusetts* (Cambridge, U.K.: Cambridge University Press, 1986), 45; also Frank Hatch Streightoff, *The Standard of Living Among the Industrial People of America* (Boston: Houghton Mifflin, 1911), 159ff.

25. Hatton and Williamson, "Unemployment," 610–11.

26. William F. Ogburn, *Progress and Uniformity in Child Labor Legislation: A Study in Statistical Measurement* (New York: Columbia University Press, 1912), 71–78.

27. Viviana Zelizer, *Pricing the Priceless Child: The Changing Social Value of Children* (New York: Basic Books, 1985), 58.

28. Ibid., 59–60.

29. Balch, *Our Slavic Fellow Citizens*, 324.

30. Ogburn, *Progress and Uniformity*, 79–81.

31. On Posen, see Konrad Bercovici, *On New Shores* (New York: The Century Company, 1925), 123–27.

32. Tamara K. Hareven and Maris A. Vinovskis, "Patterns of Childbearing in Late Nineteenth-Century America: The Determinants of Marital Fertility in Five Massachusetts Towns in 1880," in idem, eds., *Family and Population in Nineteenth-Century America* (Princeton: Princeton University Press, 1978), 96.

33. Doris Weatherford, *Foreign and Female: Immigrant Women in America: 1840–1930* (New York: Schocken Books, 1986), 20.

34. Balch, *Our Slavic Fellow Citizens*, 376.
35. Ibid., 377.
36. Bureau of the Census, *Eleventh Census of the United States* (1890), v. 4, pt. 1 (Vital and Social Statistics), 444.
37. Using the Bohemian death rate as a Slavic death rate for people ages 15–45. *Eleventh Census*, v. 4, pt. 1, 35.
38. Ogburn, *Progress and Uniformity*, 132.
39. Briggs notes, set 2, p. 18.
40. Geoffrey D. Austrian, *Herman Hollerith: Forgotten Giant of Information Processing* (New York: Columbia University Press, 1982), 15.
41. The experiment is impossible: the punch cards from the 1890 census were destroyed, partially by fire and firemen, and then entirely by Congress. Kellee Blake, " 'First in the Path of the Firemen': The Fate of the 1890 Population Census," *Prologue* 28:1 (Spring 1996), 64–81.
42. Lee C. Soltow, "Evidence on Income Inequality in the United States, 1866–1965," *Journal of Economic History* 29:2 (June 1969), 279–86, esp. 283.
43. For the discussion of Jane Addams, I have relied on the interpretations in Rosalind Rosenberg, *Divided Lives: American Women in the Twentieth Century* (New York: Hill & Wang, 1992), 25–35; Louis Menand, *The Metaphysical Club: A Story of Ideas in America* (New York: Farrar, Straus & Giroux, 2001), 313–15; Christopher Lasch, *The New Radicalism in America, 1889–1963: The Intellectual as a Social Type* (New York: Alfred A. Knopf, 1965), 3–37; and the generous assistance of Victoria Brown.
44. Grace Abbott quoted in Barbara Sicherman, "Colleges and Careers: Historical Perspectives on the Lives and Work Patterns of Women College Graduates," *Women and Higher Education in American History*, ed. John Mack Faragher and Florence Howe (New York: W. W. Norton, 1988), 130–64, on 151.
45. Lasch, *New Radicalism*, 24–27.
46. Allen F. Davis, *Spearheads for Reform: The Social Settlements and the Progressive Movement* (New York: Oxford University Press, 1967), 12.
47. Jane Addams (quoting from her own "Subjective Necessity of Social Settlements"), *Twenty Years at Hull-House* (New York: Macmillan, 1910), 120.
48. Ross Firestone, *Swing, Swing, Swing: The Life and Times of Benny Goodman* (New York: W. W. Norton, 1993), 24.
49. "Jane Addams Visits Station," *Chicago Tribune*, September 9, 1901, p. 4.
50. Carter H. Harrison, *Stormy Years* (Indianapolis: Bobbs-Merrill, 1935), 49.
51. Jane Addams to Lillian D. Wald, September 17, 1901, Lillian D. Wald Papers, Columbia University Libraries Special Collections; Jane Addams Papers Microfilm Edition, Frame 4-210.
52. "Jane Addams Visits Station," *Chicago Tribune*, September 9, 1901, p. 4; Addams, *Twenty Years at Hull-House*, 278–81; Allen F. Davis, *American Heroine: The Life and Legend of Jane Addams* (New York: Oxford University Press, 1973), 117.

53. Jane Addams, *Democracy and Social Ethics*, ed. Anne Firor Scott (Cambridge, Mass.: Harvard University Press, 1964), 14.

54. Cited in Lasch, *New Radicalism*, 12.

55. Residents of Hull House, *Hull House Maps and Papers* (New York: Thomas Y. Crowell, 1895), 4, 5, 22, 23; emphasis added.

56. Thomas L. Haskell, *The Emergence of Social Science in America: The American Social Science Association and the Nineteenth-Century Crisis of Authority* (Urbana: University of Illinois Press, 1977), 203; Rosalind Rosenberg, *Beyond Separate Spheres: Intellectual Roots of Modern Feminism* (New Haven: Yale University Press, 1982), 32ff.

57. *Hull House Maps and Papers*, 14, 193.

58. Jacob Riis, *How the Other Half Lives: Studies Among the Tenements of New York* (New York: Charles Scribner's Sons, 1890), 3, 5.

59. TR to Jacob Riis, January 23, 1899, *Letters*, 2:921.

60. Jacob Riis, *Theodore Roosevelt the Citizen* (New York: The Outlook Company, 1904), 105–6.

61. Edith Patterson Meyer, *"Not Charity but Justice": The Story of Jacob A. Riis* (New York: Vanguard, 1974), 80.

62. Theodore Roosevelt, *Autobiography*, National edition, 20:205.

63. Theodore Roosevelt, "How I Became a Progressive," in *Social Justice*, National edition, 17:316–17.

64. Riis, *Theodore Roosevelt the Citizen*, 65.

65. Ibid., 64.

66. Theodore Roosevelt, "Birth Reform," *The Foes of Our Own Household*, National edition, 19:156.

67. See Matthew Frye Jacobson, *Whiteness of a Different Color: European Immigrants and the Alchemy of Race* (Cambridge, Mass.: Harvard University Press, 1997), esp. 39–90.

68. Cited in Peter Novick, *That Noble Dream: The "Objectivity Question" and the American Historical Profession* (Cambridge, U.K.: Cambridge, 1988), 81.

69. Riis, *Theodore Roosevelt the Citizen*, 65.

70. Jacob Riis, *The Making of an American* (New York: Macmillan, 1922), 329.

71. "The Uncle of His Country" [cartoon], *Life*, August 25, 1904, p. 604.

72. Thomas L. Masson, "Hooray!" *Harper's Weekly*, December 28, 1907, p. 1904.

73. Riis, *Theodore Roosevelt the Citizen*, 353.

74. TR to Cecil Spring Rice, August 11, 1899, *Letters*, 2:1053.

75. Gary Gerstle, *American Crucible: Race and Nation in the Twentieth Century* (Princeton: Princeton University Press, 2001), 49.

76. Roosevelt, "How I Became a Progressive," 317.

77. Theodore Roosevelt, First Annual Message as President, *State Papers*, National edition, 15:84–95; Fine, "Anarchism," 788–89, 799.

78. James, *Principles of Psychology*, 1:196–87.

79. Theodore Roosevelt, *Hunting Trips of a Ranchman*, National edition, 1:329.

David McCullough made the first part of this sentence the epigraph and interpretive touchstone of his Roosevelt biography, *Mornings on Horseback* (New York: Simon and Schuster, 1981).

80. James Weber Linn, *Jane Addams: A Biography* (New York: D. Appleton, 1935), 272.
81. Jane Addams, "A Modern Lear," in *The Jane Addams Reader*, ed. Jean Bethke Elshtain (New York: Basic Books, 2002), 163–75; esp. 175.
82. Linn, *Jane Addams*, 273.
83. Addams, *Twenty Years at Hull-House*, 282.

6: THE INTERPRETATION OF DREAMS

1. Briggs notes, set 2, p. 17.
2. Ibid., p. 19.
3. Morgan, *William McKinley*, 125, 27.
4. Henry Cabot Lodge, *The Democracy of the Constitution and Other Addresses and Essays* (1915; reprint New York: Books for Libraries, 1966), 191 and 200.
5. Morgan, *William McKinley*, 124.
6. TR to Anna Roosevelt Cowles, June 14, 1896, *Letters*, 1:543.
7. Morgan, *William McKinley*, 128–31.
8. See W. Jett Lauck, *The Causes of the Panic of 1893* (Boston: Houghton, Mifflin, 1907), 1–34; and Milton Friedman and Anna Jacobson Schwartz, *A Monetary History of the United States, 1867–1960* (Princeton: Princeton University Press, 1963), 106ff.
9. Morgan, *William McKinley*, 148.
10. Stephen L. Goodale, *Chronology of Iron and Steel* (Pittsburgh: Pittsburgh Iron & Steel Foundries, 1920), 175, 198, 201; also Croly, *Marcus Alonzo Hanna*, 66.
11. Briggs, *Arizona and New Mexico, 1882; California, 1886; Mexico, 1891*, 14, 161.
12. Lauck, *Causes*, 4–5, 10.
13. Naomi R. Lamoreaux, *The Great Merger Movement and American Business, 1895–1904* (Cambridge, U.K.: Cambridge University Press, 1985), 63.
14. On the nature of speculative bubbles, see Robert Shiller, *Irrational Exuberance* (Princeton: Princeton University Press, 2000), 60–67. See also Charles P. Kindleberger, *Manias, Panics, and Crashes: A History of Financial Crises*, 3rd ed. (New York: John Wiley, 1996).
15. Lloyd Wendt and Herman Kogan, *Bet a Million! The Story of John W. Gates* (Indianapolis: Bobbs-Merrill, 1948), 66, 96.
16. Cited in Lamoreaux, *Great Merger Movement*, 66.
17. Lauck, *Causes*, 93.
18. Ibid., 99, 107; Charles Hoffmann, "The Depression of the Nineties," *Journal of Economic History* 16:2 (June 1956), 137–64, esp. 138.

19. Croly, *Marcus Alonzo Hanna*, 170.
20. Lamoreaux, *Great Merger Movement*, 63–67; Hoffman, "Depression," 138.
21. Henry B. Leonard, "Ethnic Cleavage and Industrial Conflict in Late Nineteenth-Century America: The Cleveland Rolling Mill Company Strikes of 1882 and 1885," *Labor History* 20:4 (Fall 1979), 524–48.
22. David Brody, *Steelworkers in America: The Nonunion Era*, new ed. (Urbana: University of Illinois Press, 1998), 81.
23. Cited in Leonard, "Ethnic Cleavage," 539.
24. Brody, *Steelworkers*, 99.
25. Briggs notes, set 2, p. 20; "Pushed," *Cleveland Plain Dealer*, June 14, 1893, p. 8; "With Short Hands," *Cleveland Plain Dealer*, July 15, 1893, p. 8; American Iron and Steel Association, *Directory to the Iron and Steel Works of the United States* 15th ed. (Philadelphia: American Iron and Steel Association, 1900), 33.
26. Ibid., p. 21; also Walter Channing, "The Mental Status of Czolgosz, the Assassin of President McKinley," *American Journal of Insanity* 54 (1902), 233–78, esp. 239.
27. Edward Bellamy, *Looking Backward, 2000–1887*, ed. John L. Thomas (Cambridge, Mass.: Belknap Press of Harvard University Press, 1967), 140–41; also John L. Thomas, *Alternative America: Henry George, Edward Bellamy, Henry Demarest Lloyd and the Adversary Tradition* (Cambridge, Mass.: Belknap Press of Harvard University Press, 1983), 239ff.
28. Thomas, *Alternative America*, 355, 233–36.
29. Briggs notes, set 2, p. 21.
30. *The Origins, Objects, and Principles of the Knights of the Golden Eagle* (Youngstown, Ohio: The Commercial Printing Company, 1900); in Channing papers, box 4.
31. Briggs notes, set 2, p. 12.
32. Statement from the Broadway Bank, enclosure in Ludwig Darmstadter to LVB, January 24, 1902, Channing papers, box 4.
33. Briggs notes, set 2, p. 28.
34. Ibid., p. 12.
35. Ibid., p. 14.
36. Henry Adams to Elizabeth Cameron, September 28, 1901, *Letters of Henry Adams*, 6 vols., ed. J. C. Levenson et al. (Cambridge, Mass.: Belknap Press of Harvard University Press), 5:297.
37. William James to Henry James, September 10, 1901, and September 21, 1901, *The Correspondence of William James*, 7 vols., ed. Ignas K. Skrupskelis and Elizabeth M. Berkeley (Charlottesville: University of Virginia Press, 1992–99), 3:178, 3:180.
38. "Mob Makes Man Retract," *Chicago Tribune*, September 16, 1901, p. 2.
39. "Nearly Mob Mrs. Nation," *New York Herald*, September 9, 1901, p. 7; "Resent Expressions of Joy," *Chicago Tribune*, September 7, 1901, p. 2.

40. Cited in Oliver Carlson and Ernest Sutherland Bates, *Hearst, Lord of San Simeon* (New York: Viking, 1936), 112.
41. David Nasaw, *The Chief: The Life of William Randolph Hearst* (Boston: Houghton Mifflin, 2000), 118, 156; cited in Donovan, *Assassins*, 101.
42. "Czolgosz in Mining Region," *Washington Star*, September 13, 1901, p. 6.
43. "Past Suspicious Incidents," *New York Times*, October 15, 1912, p. 3.
44. Robert C. Allen, "The Peculiar Productivity History of American Blast Furnaces, 1840–1913," *Journal of Economic History* 37:3 (September 1977), 605–33.
45. Robert H. Wiebe, "The Anthracite Strike of 1902: A Record of Confusion," *Mississippi Valley Historical Review* 48:2 (September 1961), 229–51; esp. 239–40.
46. Cited in Iris Harvey, review of *The Great Pierpont Morgan* by Lewis Allen, *The Economic Journal* 60:237 (March 1950), 152–55, esp. 153.
47. George E. Mowry, *The Era of Theodore Roosevelt and the Birth of Modern America, 1900–1912* (New York: Harper Torchbooks, 1962), 137.
48. Cited in Jean Strouse, *Morgan: American Financier* (New York: Random House, 1999), 449.
49. First annual message, *State Papers*, 91.
50. Mowry, *Era*, 134ff.
51. Elliott J. Gorn, *Mother Jones: The Most Dangerous Woman in America* (New York: Hill & Wang, 2001).
52. "Assassin Czolgosz Said to Have Been Married in Charleston," *Parkersburg* (W. Va.) *Gazette*, September 12, 1901, cited in Richard A. Andre and Stan B. Cohen, *Kanawha County Images*, 2 vols. (Charleston, W. Va.: Pictorial Histories Publishing, 1987–2001), 2:210.
53. Ibid.
54. Briggs notes, set 2, p. 19.
55. Ibid., p. 9.
56. Ibid., p. 28.
57. Ibid., p. 11.
58. Ibid., p. 29.
59. Ibid., p. 8.
60. Ibid., p. 12.
61. Ibid., p. 16.
62. A. B. Spurney to H. C. Eyman, copy to WC, February 16, 1902, Channing papers, box 4.
63. Briggs notes, set 2, p. 9.
64. Ibid., p. 13.
65. Ibid., p. 13.
66. Ibid., p. 22.
67. Ibid., p. 24.
68. Ibid., pp. 8–9.

69. Leon Czolgosz to Waldeck Czolgosz, July 14, 1901, Briggs scrapbook, p. 111.
70. Briggs notes, set 2, p. 26.
71. Ibid., p. 28.
72. MacDonald and Spitzka, "Trial," 379.
73. Cited in Allan M. Brandt, No Magic Bullet: A Social History of Venereal Disease in the United States Since 1880 (New York: Oxford University Press, 1985), 34; also 40ff.
74. MacDonald and Spitzka, "Trial," 397.
75. Ibid., 403.
76. A. Ravogli, Syphilis in Its Medical, Medico-Legal, and Sociological Aspects (New York: Grafton, 1907), 176.
77. Claude Quétel, History of Syphilis, trans. Judith Braddock and Brian Pike (Baltimore: Johns Hopkins University Press, 1990), 131.
78. Ibid., 174.
79. Cited in LVB to WC, September 19, 1902, Channing papers, box 4.
80. Ravogli, Syphilis, 183.
81. Ibid., 214.
82. A. B. Spurney to H. C. Eyman, copy to WC, February 16, 1902; also LVB to WC, September 19, 1902, Channing papers, box 4.
83. Ravogli, Syphilis, 215.
84. LVB to WC, September 19, 1902, Channing papers, box 4.
85. MacDonald, "Trial," 380.
86. Briggs notes, set 2, p. 7.
87. Ibid., p. 11.
88. George Chauncey, Gay New York: Gender, Urban Culture, and the Making of a Gay Male World, 1890–1940 (New York: Basic Books, 1994), esp. 66–86.

7: AN IRRESISTIBLE IMPULSE

1. Oscar King Davis, Released for Publication: Some Inside Political History of Theodore Roosevelt and His Times, 1898–1918 (Boston: Houghton Mifflin Company, 1925), 375–78.
2. Stuart Pratt Sherman, Americans (New York: Charles Scribner's Sons, 1922), 264.
3. Lochner v. New York (1905), 198 U.S. 45; Adair v. United States (1908), 208 U.S. 161.
4. John M. Blum, The Progressive Presidents (New York: W. W. Norton, 1980), 48.
5. Theodore Roosevelt, Autobiography, National edition, 20:397.
6. George Haven Putnam, introduction to The Winning of the West, National edition, 11:ix.
7. Charles A. Beard, Contemporary American History, 1877–1913 (New York: Macmillan, 1914), 273, 258.

8. Sherman, *Americans*, 285, 274.

9. Kohlsaat, *From McKinley to Harding*, 161–62.

10. Beard, *Contemporary American History*, 357.

11. Ibid., 299.

12. Robert F. Hoxie, "The Socialist Party in the November Elections," *Journal of Political Economy* 20:3 (March 1912), 205–23, esp. 215n.

13. Nick Salvatore, *Eugene V. Debs: Citizen and Socialist* (Urbana: University of Illinois Press, 1982), 198.

14. Jane Addams, "The Progressive Party and the Negro," in *The Social Thought of Jane Addams*, ed. Christopher Lasch (Indianapolis: Bobbs-Merrill, 1965), 173.

15. Celia Parker Woolley to Jane Addams, October 8, 1912, Jane Addams Microfilm, 7-203.

16. The transcription of Roosevelt's comments appears as "The Leader and the Cause," in National edition, 17:319–30.

17. "Sanity Board Named to Examine Schrank," *New York Times*, November 13, 1902, p. 9.

18. "Full Text of Assassin's Confession," *New York Times*, October 16, 1912, p. 2.

19. Under *Guiteau's Case*, "deific decree" qualified as an insane delusion: p. 171.

20. "Do Not Believe Schrank Is Insane," *New York Times*, October 20, 1912, p. 2.

21. TR to John St. Loe Strachey, December 6, 1912, *Letters*, 7:676–77.

22. O. K. Davis, *Released for Publication*, 387.

23. "Schrank to Asylum, Declares He Is Sane," *New York Times*, November 23, 1912, p. 11.

24. TR to Jane Addams, November 5, 1912, Swarthmore College Peace Collection, Jane Addams Papers, Series 1; Jane Addams Papers, Microfilm Edition, Frame 7-374.

25. JA to TR, Swarthmore College Peace Collection, Jane Addams Papers, Series 1; Jane Addams Papers, Microfilm Edition, Frame 7-441.

26. Sherman, *Americans*, 257.

27. David Sarasohn, *The Party of Reform: Democrats in the Progressive Era* (Jackson: University Press of Mississippi, 1989); Elizabeth Sanders, *Roots of Reform: Farmers, Workers, and the American State, 1877–1917* (Chicago: University of Chicago Press, 1999).

28. Sherman, *Americans*, 260.

29. Cited in William M. Gibson, *Theodore Roosevelt Among the Humorists: William Dean Howells, Mark Twain, and Mr. Dooley* (Knoxville, Tenn.: University of Tennessee, 1980), 62. According to the *New York Times*, Dunne campaigned for the Progressives in 1912. "Mr. Dooley Makes Roosevelt Laugh," *New York Times*, October 25, 1912, p. 5.

30. "Czolgosz Not Sane," *Boston Herald*, January 29, 1902, p. 3.

31. Walter Channing, "Mental Status," 271.

32. "Czolgosz Not Sane."

33. Channing, "Mental Status," 271.
34. "The New Psychology," *Philadelphia Medical Journal*, October 12, 1901, p. 579.
35. Briggs notes, set 2, p. 30.
36. Otto M. Marx, "Nineteenth-Century Medical Psychology: Theoretical Problems in the Work of Griesinger, Meynert, and Wernicke," *Isis* 61:3 (Autumn 1970), 355–70.
37. Briggs notes, set 2, p. 31.
38. WC to LVB, June 5, 1902, and June 27, 1902, Briggs scrapbook, p. 93.
39. WC to LVB, August 15, 1902, Briggs scrapbook, p. 94.
40. Lloyd Vernon Briggs, *History and Genealogy of the Briggs Family, 1254–1937*, 3 vols. (Boston: Charles E. Goodspeed and Company, 1938), 2:813.
41. Lloyd Vernon Briggs, A *Victory for Progress in Mental Medicine: Defeat of Reactionaries: the History of an Intrigue* (Boston: Wright & Potter, 1924), 1–2.
42. Typed resolution in Channing papers, box 7.
43. WC notes on an interview with Vincent Bowditch, July 21, 1908, Channing papers, box 16.
44. Briggs, *History*, 3:1034.
45. Briggs, *Victory*, ix.
46. Prescott F. Hall to WC, February 24, 1913, Channing papers, box 8.
47. Moorfield Storey to WC, November 23, 1912, Channing papers, box 7.
48. Briggs, *Victory*, 294.
49. Letter to WC, no date, Channing papers, box 16.
50. Theodore Roosevelt, *The Strenuous Life*, National edition, 13:483.
51. "Roosevelt Reveals How He Progressed," *New York Times*, October 20, 1912.
52. Briggs, *Manner of Man*, 7.
53. James, *Principles of Psychology*, 1:76.
54. Ibid., 1:365.
55. Ibid., 2:487.

NOTE ON CONTROVERSIES, SOURCES, AND CONTROVERSIAL SOURCES

1. Telephone conversation with Jeannine Lee, New York Supreme Court, July 26, 2002; telephone conversation with Linda Kennedy, BECHS, September 12, 2002.
2. Conversation with Roger Parris, July 30, 2002.
3. Jack C. Fisher, *Stolen Glory: The McKinley Assassination* (La Jolla: Alamar Books, 2001).
4. Conversation with Peter Ostrow, July 30, 2002.
5. Fisher, *Stolen Glory*, 213n. 10.
6. Conversation with Frank Housh, Assistant District Attorney of Erie County, July 30, 2002.

7. Avrich, *Anarchist Voices*, 25.
8. Clarence Darrow to Jane Addams, September 11, 1901, Swarthmore College Peace Collection, Jane Addams Papers, Series 1; Jane Addams Papers, Microfilm Edition, Frame 4-207.
9. Telephone conversation with Richard Andre, July 21, 2002; see Andre and Cohen, *Kanawha County Images*, 2:210.

ACKNOWLEDGMENTS

As the foregoing note on controversies, sources, and controversial sources indicates, I have relied freely on the opinions of experts, most of whom had only a professional interest in my work. In almost all cases, they responded with enthusiasm and generosity, and I benefited tremendously from their insights and assistance. My work on this project gave me ample and heartening evidence that the community spirit of intellectual inquiry in America remains alive and well, both inside and outside the academy.

My colleagues in the History Department at the University of California, Davis, have provided invaluable encouragement, and David Biale, Karen Halttunen, Sally McKee, Lisa Materson, Kathy Olmsted, Alan Taylor, and Clarence Walker read and offered insightful comments and criticism on the manuscript. Professional colleagues outside the department, including Glenn Altschuler, Alan Brinkley, Scott Casper, Scott James, and John McWhorter, were kind enough to do the same. So were my family. Jim McGowan supplied me with a helpful Emma Goldman item. Henry Korn generously gave practical and scholarly legal insight into Czolgosz's custody and trial.

As this book draws together many disparate strands of Progressive Era historiography, I benefited from discussions with scholars of wide-ranging expertise, including Glenn Altschuler, Richard Bensel, David Brody, Victoria Brown, Howell Harris, Scott James, Mara Keire, Peter Lindert, Elizabeth Sanders, and William Summerhill.

The staff of the Massachusetts Historical Society provided a model of archival service, interest, and professional help. Nicholas Graham, Kate DuBose, Carrie Foley, and Jean Powers showed unfailing patience and hospitality during my visit there and helped tremendously in correspondence afterward.

At the University of Chicago's Crerar Library Special Collections, Debra

Levine and Jay Satterfield offered prompt and kind assistance, and Debs Cane of Northwestern University (who came to me through the good offices of Tim Breen) did a fine and sympathetic job of surveying L. Vernon Briggs's scrapbook.

Roger Parris, communications director of the Bar Association of Erie County, was thoughtfulness itself, arranging a lunch for me with some of the BAEC's members who participated in a reenactment of the Czolgosz trial, providing me with a copy of the trial transcript, and in general sharing notes. Jeannine Lee, senior librarian of the New York Supreme Court, and Linda Kennedy of the Buffalo and Erie County Historical Society generously spared the time to talk over the origins of the various trial transcripts with me.

Closest to home, the interlibrary loan division of the Peter J. Shields Library at UC Davis provided an indispensable and always reliable service in getting everything from everywhere. Dr. Bill Ellis gave an expert reading of the autopsy. Dr. Tom Sands clarified the effects of strychnine and potassium iodide. Dean Steve Sheffrin and the University of California gave material assistance.

This book went through a number of changes before arriving at its final form, and it could never have done so had not Farrar, Straus and Giroux/Hill and Wang showed an unmatched confidence in the work and its merit. I am especially grateful to my editor, Thomas LeBien, for his hard work and faith in my ability.

The book is dedicated to the most recent male migrants on both sides of my family. My great-grandfather I know only through his written commentary on Ecclesiastes; my grandfather I knew from my birth till his death. Both came to an America shaped by Theodore Roosevelt, and both shaped me.

INDEX

Adams, Henry, 171
Addams, Jane: on Czolgosz, 149–50;
and Isaak case, 131, 135–36; settle-
ment work and progressivism of,
131–39, 144, 147–49, 192–94,
201, 203, 212
Addams, John, 132
African-Americans, see American
South; Great Migration; Parker,
James B.; race and racism; Recon-
struction; Washington, Booker T.
Alexander II (tsar of Russia), x
alienists, 20–25; see also insanity
Altgeld, John P., 13, 99
American Federation of Labor, 165
American frontier, 23, 58, 73, 79–80,
89; see also American West
Americanization, see education; mi-
grants and migration
American South, 58, 66–74, 159, 200;
see also Hanson, J. F.; Ivory,
Thomas; lynching; McKinley,
William; Parker, James B.; race and
racism; Roosevelt, Theodore; Wash-
ington, Booker T.
American Steel and Wire Company,

purchase of Cleveland Rolling Mill
wireworks by, 117, 170
American West, 58–60, 73–74,
91–92, 121–30, 157, 200, 202; see
also American frontier
anarchism and anarchists: in Chicago,
98–103, 131, 135–36; Czolgosz
and, 16–18, 86–89, 100–5; 1881
meeting of, x; insanity and, 20,
48–49; lynching and, 77–78;
progressivism and, 89–96;
Roosevelt on, 94, 146; see also
Berkman, Alexander; Goldman,
Emma; Haymarket episode;
Isaak, Abraham; Most, Johann;
terrorism
anthracite strike of 1902, 172–74; see
also miners and mining
Auburn State Prison (New York), 40,
53, 83–89

Babcock, Louis, 171
Baer, George, 173
Bakunin, Mikhail, 135
Balch, Emily Greene, 128